Violence, Values, and Justice in the Schools

RODGER W. BYBEE

Carleton College

E. GORDON GEE

West Virginia University

Allyn and Bacon, Inc.

BOSTON   LONDON   SYDNEY   TORONTO

Library of Congress Cataloging in Publication Data

Bybee, Roger W.
  Violence, values, and justice in the schools.

  Includes index.
  1. School discipline—United States.   2. School
violence—United States.   3. School discipline—Law
and legislation—United States.   I. Gee, E. Gordon,
1944-   . II. Title.
LB3012.B9   371.5   81-12710
ISBN 0-205-07387-5   AACR2

Printed in the United States of America.

Printing number and year (last digits):
10 9 8 7 6 5 4 3 2 1   86 85 84 83 82 81

This book is dedicated to
our parents

Wayne and Genevieve Bybee

Elwood A. and Vera S. Gee

Contents

SPECIAL NOTE ABOUT REFERENCES

This book, as an interdisciplinary endeavor, has created some peculiar problems for the authors. One of the major difficulties involved the most appropriate way to footnote the material. It was decided to follow generally the social science format for end-of-chapter references, except for Chapters Two and Three. These chapters are mainly legal or legal/historical in nature and, therefore, ease of further research by the reader dictated that the authors use the legal citation format as contained in *A Uniform System of Citation* (Harvard Law Review, 1976). We hope that the shift in formats is helpful rather than distracting.

Preface

Violence, Values, and Justice in the Schools is intended as a practical reference for administrators, teachers, counselors, school boards, and those who must deal with the problem of violence in the schools. It is an exploration of disruptive behavior, students' rights, and the resolution of conflicts in the educational setting. With this exploration we hope the reader will gain a greater insight into the problems and prospects of these most difficult issues confronting educational institutions. As valuable as such insights may be, all of us as educators also face the problem of having to deal with these issues *today*. We have therefore attempted to offer a practical agenda for immediate adoption to help reduce alienation, educate for democratic values, encourage appropriate behaviors, and resolve school-related conflicts.

Discipline problems are perennial topics in discussions of education. In recent years, however, attention has shifted to more intense disruptions, assaults, vandalism, and violence in American schools. The rise of violence in schools is a unique phenomenon in the history of American education. Concerns about this problem are widespread: the public, along with school personnel, are seeking remedies. Clearly a problem as serious as violence in the schools needs more than casual analysis and suggestions for change. Although there have already been several excellent surveys on the problem, still there is need for further analysis accompanied with practical suggestions. School personnel complain of highly abstract, academic approaches to a concrete problem such as violence in the schools. Understandably educators want to resolve the problem more than they want to be informed about its theoretical causes. However, school personnel are also becoming weary of simple remedies that do not resolve complex problems and practical recommendations that worked for one person but not others. So what does one do? This book represents our attempt to answer this question, to meet the need for recommendations based on a rationale.

Why the title *Violence, Values, and Justice?* The fact of violence in schools troubles many citizens because Americans have a long history of trust and confidence in education. This important institution is now the locus of severe civil disorder perpetrated by students, those very persons who are to reap the benefits of schools. This statement may sound abstract, but it does represent the perceptions of many citizens who are not in schools on a daily basis and who form their ideas from the media. For many school personnel the threat of violence and disruption is a very real issue and one that detracts from the goals of teaching; in this way the problems of violence and vandalism influence larger numbers than the reported statistics indicate.

Though we have used violence in the title, our discussions and recommendations are applicable to less intense conflicts between students and teachers. These are the everyday "discipline problems" confronting all teachers, counselors, and administrators. Extreme forms of disruptive behavior in schools have helped to clarify how we are, and how we ought to be, resolving minor disciplinary situations.

Use of the word "values" seemed appropriate on many different levels: the values of students relative to schools and teachers; the values underlying the approaches school personnel use to resolve conflicts; the values of the community as they are represented in schools; and the change in the values of youth who progress from obedient to disobedient behaviors. Educators can no longer escape discussions of values for they are represented in rules, policies, practices and, most importantly, behaviors. Thus we think it is important that educators clarify their values, especially regarding issues as crucial and ever-present as ways to resolve conflicts with students.

Justice is the principle we have used as the foundation for our rationale and subsequent recommendations. Equally sound recommendations could no doubt result if other principles, such as honesty, were used. Justice is a concept embedded in the American heritage and represents a value to which all subscribe. This does, however, present a problem. A theory of justice is so complex that school personnel have difficulty applying its principles in practice. Overcoming that inability in application is an aim of the book. In early chapters we review the concept and then later discuss justice in the specific context of school and classroom conflicts. It is impossible to give specific recommendations for all school boards, administrators, counselors, teachers, aides, and other school staff. We have, however, presented recommendations upon which school personnel can act, and in so doing can apply general concepts of justice to their unique situations.

Acknowledging all the contributions that persons have made to the book would be impossible. Many students, colleagues, and friends deserve our recognition and gratitude. We especially wish to recognize the following for their various contributions to the project: Mary Becker, Helen Berwald, Patricia Bybee, Karin Case, Nancy Gustafson, Neil Lutsky, Susan Marks, Nancy Marsh, Jerry Sturgill, and Richard Teutsch. We wish also to thank the Mellon Foundation and Carleton College for financial assistance in the final typing of the manuscript.

RWB

EGG

CHAPTER ONE

Violence, Values, and Justice: Problems and Perspectives

INTRODUCTION

We begin our third century as one of the most technologically advanced societies in human history. Our progress has brought medical advances that prolong life and manufactured products that promote leisure. These life-saving, comfort-giving advances have, however, given rise to a series of problems including a polluted environment, depleted energy resources, a wavering economy, and social and political institutions that strain under demands for reform.

It is time to reexamine personal and social values, for many of these problems are the result of the values that guide our decisions. Our values, the standards we assign to ideas, policies, or behaviors, naturally differ among individuals and thus give rise to many conflicts and problems. But, while differences in values may create social and political conflicts in the short run, over the long run it is precisely these differences that create the tensions necessary for change and progress to occur.

Education has not been overlooked in the current reexamination of contemporary values. In particular, the alarming rate of school violence, vandalism, and classroom disruption has stimulated many questions concerning policies and practices in American schools. As usual the questions and recommendations represent a continuum of views from liberal to conservative. This is yet another demonstration that the American public takes very seriously the education of its youth. It appears that "lack of discipline" is a major problem in the eyes of the American public, as this issue has been ranked as the highest concern every year, except one, since 1969 in Gallup polls of public attitudes about education.

It is the premise of this book that there are important relationships not yet explored among violence in the schools, individual and social values, and the specific value of justice as they affect the American educational system. Violence in schools and less extreme forms of classroom disruption have led to a reevaluation of the rights and responsibilities of youth toward

1

school personnel and, conversely, of school personnel toward youth. As a result of this rethinking of the interaction between educators and students, school personnel are beginning to develop new values and attitudes. They are searching for new models and policies to help them deal constructively with the inevitable conflicts between school rules and the behavior of youth in the educational setting.

One of the most significant of these policy questions involves the relationship of the concept of justice to the schools, particularly when discipline problems arise. Justice as it applies to the resolution of school conflicts is becoming increasingly difficult to understand, especially in light of recent United States Supreme Court decisions, while at the same time it is taking on ever greater importance to the educational enterprise.

In order to help educators confront squarely the intersecting issues of violence, values, and justice, we review in this chapter the most recent statistics concerning violence in American schools. A discussion follows of the relationship among values and school rules and moral development. We briefly present the theme of justice in various contexts, such as social, legal, theological, and philosophical, and then discuss it in an educational context with specific reference to certain Supreme Court decisions and what these mean for school personnel. In the final section we present some ideas on moral education and outline some of the issues that will guide the discussions in later chapters. The discussion of each topic is brief, for we return to many of the ideas and explore them in greater detail in later chapters.

VIOLENCE IN SCHOOLS

The Safe School Study

With the publication of *Violent Schools—Safe Schools*[1] we now have a more accurate understanding of the nature and extent of violence and vandalism in American education. The National Institute of Education conducted the survey, which was mandated by Congress in 1974 and finally published in January 1978.

The Safe School Study was conducted in three phases. Phase I was a mail survey of more than 4,000 elementary and secondary school principals. The principals were asked to report illegal or disruptive activities in their schools for a given month. There were nine one-month reporting periods between February 1976 and January 1977. The reporting month was assigned to schools on a random basis. Phase II involved on-site surveys of 642 junior and senior high schools. Students, teachers, and administrators were asked to report experiences they had had with theft, robbery, attacks, and other disruptive activities. Additionally, they were asked about themselves, their schools, and their communities. Phase III was an intensive case study of ten schools. These schools had a history of relatively high rates of violence and vandalism, which over a short time had been substantially reduced.

The Safe School Study helped focus on the question of the extent of school violence. School violence and vandalism increased throughout the 1960s, leveled off in the early 1970s, and appears to be declining slightly in the 1980s. Eight percent of the nation's schools, about 6,700, report that violence is a serious problem. The problem seems to be concentrated in the lower levels of secondary schools, and the percentage of schools affected increases with an increase in community size. That is, the likelihood of serious crime is greater in urban areas. However, the majority of schools with serious problems are in suburban and rural areas.

There is another interesting statistic that relates directly to the justice-and-conflict theme of this book. At least 157,000 incidents of crime and disruption occur in American schools in a typical month. Of these, only 50,000 are reported to police. These statistics, it seems, indicate that each month well over 100,000 serious school conflicts are resolved in some way by school personnel. If the majority of crimes and disruptions in schools are resolved by educators, it appears clear that developing effective and equitable means of resolving conflicts, maintaining school rules, and achieving educational objectives should be a priority of school personnel. The following statistics further illustrate the extent of violence in the schools.

Violence Toward Persons

Personal theft is the offense reported most often by students and teachers. Eleven percent (2.4 million) of secondary students and twelve percent (128,000) of teachers report having had something stolen in a typical month. Most thefts are minor, usually less than one dollar.

Physical attacks affect one and three-tenths percent (282,000) of secondary students each month. One-half of one percent (5,200) of teachers are physically attacked each month. Attacks on teachers tend to be more serious than those on students.

Robberies affect one-half of one percent (112,000) of students and one-half of one percent (6,000) of teachers each month. The amount of money involved is usually small and injury is rare.

Violence Toward Property

The cost of violence against school property is high. There are 11,000 incidents (one out of ten schools) of breaking and entering each month: average cost, $183.00; 13,000 incidents of theft of school property: average cost, $150.00. The most frequent offense against school property is vandalism, which occurs at a rate of 42,000 incidents each month, affecting one of four schools at an average cost of $81.00. Overall, the annual cost of repairing the damage done to school property is more than $200 million.

The statistics cited above obviously indicate that violence in schools is a serious and nationwide problem. But these statistics reflect only reportable violence and vandalism. What of "normal" classroom disruptions, discipline problems, and less serious infractions of school rules and policies? It can only be surmised that the problems in these areas are staggering and warrant the immediate attention of policy makers, administrators, school boards, teachers, and parents as well as persons indirectly concerned with the functioning of schools and the development of youth, such as lawyers, judges, police, and social workers.

School Factors

What are some of the factors associated with schools experiencing high rates of violence and vandalism? First, large size and particularly impersonality seem to contribute to higher rates of violence and vandalism. Second, systematic classroom and school discipline, that is, firm and consistent enforcement of rules by classroom teachers and school administrators and coordination among all school personnel, results in lower levels of student violence and property loss. Third, arbitrary and unnecessarily punitive enforcement of rules appears to be a factor contributing to student crime. Schools where such practices exist are usually characterized as having weak disciplinary policies. Fourth, the school's reward system also is related to student behavior. Schools that emphasize good grades seem to have lower rates of violence but higher rates of vandalism. It is not too surprising to find that schools where grades are important have less crime. Conversely, in violent schools many students do not care about courses, grades, and other evaluative criteria; they simply give up on school since it does not seem to make any difference in their lives. Their feelings of powerlessness and lack of control over the system can result in violent and disruptive behavior. How, then, can the higher rates of vandalism in schools that emphasize good grades be explained? The Safe School Study found three factors that influence the degree of property loss: desire for academic success; desire for success in leadership roles; and the use of grades for disciplinary purposes. If, in a system of high competition, low availability of rewards, and unfair distribution of rewards, a student fails, the student may feel denied and vent anger and aggression against the rewarding system—the school. Finally, two other factors, relevance of the curriculum and student alienation, were discovered to influence the level of violence and vandalism. Student violence is higher in schools where the curriculum and instruction are not aligned with the interests and needs of the students. Violence also is higher in schools where students feel they have little influence over what happens to them. In the students' view, the future depends on others or on luck rather than on their own efforts and plans.

Examination of the factors related to school violence and vandalism inevitably leads to consideration of values. On the one hand there are the values espoused and perpetuated by the school as a social institution. On the other hand there are the values held or challenged by the students. Understanding the interaction between these two value systems, one social, the other personal, is central to understanding the problems being experienced in American education.

THE QUESTION OF VALUES

Student Alienation

One word may well summarize the relationship among values and school factors related to violence and vandalism—alienation. Simply defined, alienation is the condition of being separated, being removed, or being isolated from one's group or society. There also is the implied process of eroding the social bond between the individual and society, or, in the case of the schools, the social institution. For the purpose of understanding this problem we refer to Melvin Seeman's important essay, "On the Meaning of Alienation."[2] Seeman suggests five components that influence alienation. We believe there are significant relationships between these components and the school factors contributing to violence and vandalism. First, *powerlessness* is the individual's belief that he or she is unable to influence his or her world under the present rules. This belief is found in students who are and have been unable to obtain good grades and who therefore believe that they are destined to failure—a prophecy that is then fulfilled. Second, *meaninglessness* is the lack of a clear set of values by which to interpret the world. In this case, the school does not make sense for some students, especially when rules are indefensible and arbitrary and the curriculum irrelevant. Third, *normlessness* is the breakdown in the regulatory power of social values over individual behavior. Combined with this is the expectation that personal needs and goals can only be fulfilled through socially unapproved behavior. Normlessness most probably is one of the problems arising in schools with ineffective and inconsistent discipline policies. The rules are administered arbitrarily or unfairly. In effect, they teach the student there are no rules, or that the rules are not meant to be obeyed. If students learn these lessons in relation to minor school rules, it is not an unreasonable generalization to think they might apply the idea to more serious acts of violence and vandalism. Fourth, *isolation* is the individual's feeling of being apart from the social institution. The clearest example is the large and impersonal school. Finally, *self-estrangement* is an individual's reliance on external rewards such as grades or leadership positions and the subsequent frustration when he or she does not receive the expected grades or positions of leadership.

The relationship between the components of alienation and school violence reveals a great disparity between the differing value systems of the student and the institution. Furthermore, the interaction between the two systems is dominated by processes that exacerbate rather than resolve the differences. This suggests the need for fair and equal treatment in the administration of school rules and policies.

School Governance

Indeed, the conclusion that there is a need for fair and equal treatment in the administration of school rules and policies is supported by findings from the Safe School Study. During the Phase III case studies, effective leadership and governance emerged as vital factors in turning schools from centers of violence and disruption to places of safety and learning. In brief, a firm, fair, and consistent system of school administration was the key to reducing violence. This conclusion could be applied to all schools, not just those experiencing high rates of violence and vandalism.

The school principal also was discovered to play a major role in reducing violence according to the Safe School data. The principal's visibility and availability to students and staff were particularly important. Of equal or greater value was the ability of the administrator to initiate and maintain a structure of order in the school. This discovery probably also applies to classroom teachers, though the Safe School Study did not specifically investigate this point. The Safe School Study concluded that "the structure of order and authority in school comes from a variety of sources including the principal, the faculty, and the community; but eventually it is communicated through rules." (1, p. 170)

How these rules were established and enforced differentiated violent schools from safe schools. Again the pattern of firmness, fairness, and consistency emerged. What this meant in practice was that all members of the school system were aware that rules existed and that there were consequences for breaking them, that exceptions to the rules were very rare, and that rewards and punishments were fairly and equally distributed.

Obviously, factors other than the school, such as home and peers, also influence the behavior of adolescents. Educators can control those contributions the school environment itself might be making to the problems of violence and vandalism that occur within school walls. Others, however, must become involved in changing the causal factors beyond the school doors. It will take the combined efforts of students, schools, communities, colleges, and universities to help reduce the problem of violence in the schools. There is not one place to start, but many, and not one solution, but many, since the American public appears now to be particularly concerned with the values and ethical development of youth.

Today all institutions within our society are being called on to develop higher ethical standards. Much of this burden has fallen upon our educational system, from kindergarten through graduate school and including institutions that are privately endowed as well as publicly supported. The importance of values in education no longer appears to be in question. Rather, the questions now involve how best to educate for moral development, and, for purposes of this book, how to translate that values education into a reduction of violence and classroom disruption. We hypothesize that the answers to these questions can partially be found in considerations of one particular value: justice.

In *Democracy in America* Alexis de Tocqueville stated: "Scarcely any political question arises in the United States which is not resolved, sooner or later, into a judicial question." American justice has been strongly influenced by the spirit of the times. Throughout its history, judicial interpretation of the United States Constitution has varied with the need to meet the nation's crises: civil war, industrial change, economic depression, and response to the cries for equal opportunity and respect for human rights. America's current educational problems also have given rise to the concomitant legal issues of student rights, teacher rights, and administrative responsibilities. For example, the failure of many educators to provide students with certain protections resulted in the courts assuming an educational role and creating certain "student rights." Neglect for the rights of women and the handicapped, as guaranteed under the Equal Protection Clause of the Fourteenth Amendment, led to passage of a variety of federal statutes specifically directed towards ensuring rights for particular groups. The judicial and legislative process has helped to redefine values for educators and to provide protection for the rights of students in schools. No examination of specific judicial decisions pertaining to education, and their impact, would be complete without a prior examination of the idea of justice and its relationship to values and education.

A CONSIDERATION OF JUSTICE

We start with the question—what is justice? After a simple definition, other ideas concerning justice and this concept's relationship to values and the law will be briefly presented. The purpose of this exposition will be to expand and clarify the definition while introducing some of the many implications justice might have for contemporary educational problems such as classroom disruption. Because educators do not, as a rule, deal with the concept of justice qua justice, a broad and interdisciplinary presentation of the concept is appropriate. Philosophers, theologians, and psychologists have long struggled with the concept of justice; it has been discussed widely and not only within the confines of the law and court decisions, though this is the educator's usual association with the concept.

A Definition

What is justice? Justice is the fair and equal treatment of individuals in similar situations. From this simple definition it can be seen that justice is founded on the idea of equality among persons and on the belief that the treatment of individuals concerning, for instance, rewards, punishments, goods, and services, should be for all intents and purposes the same as long as their circumstances are similar. Already one can detect the types of difficult questions that must be resolved. Are individuals equal? Even if they are, can they be treated equally? Are there ever "similar situations"?

Historical Guides

In the United States the administration of social justice has been directly influenced by The Declaration of Independence and the Preamble to the Constitution of the United States. Therefore an examination of these documents appears essential. The Declaration of Independence states:

> We hold these truths to be self-evident, that all men are created equal; that they are endowed by their Creator with certain unalienable rights; that among these are life, liberty, and the pursuit of happiness. That, to secure these rights, governments are instituted among men, deriving their just powers from the consent of the governed.

We do not intend a word-by-word analysis of this theoretically difficult portion of The Declaration of Independence, a task already ably accomplished by others. Rather, we wish only to make a few points that should be considered in light of our specific concerns about education. In the assertion "We hold these truths to be self-evident . . ." are contained the propositions that the following enumerations *are* truths and that we (the people) believe or affirm (hold) them to be so clear as not to require demonstration. But there is question as to whether the statements following this opening clause are "self-evident." While the validity of the propositions of equality, rights, and just powers can be defended, it must be said that they are not logically self-evident. The following clause, "that all men are created equal," must mean that individuals are equals as persons, as human beings. To say this another way, though individuals differ in many ways they do not differ in humanness, and therefore they are politically equal and, especially as related to this study, equal before the law. This means that when general law confers rights or imposes restrictions, those rights and restrictions extend to all persons, or conversely, that the law shall not confer special rights or privileges on particular individuals, no matter their calling or office. We must here ask to what degree do the rules and policies of schools extend equally to all students?

The next section, "that they are endowed by their Creator with certain unalienable rights," means that these rights cannot be nullified, revoked, or changed. And, "that among these are life, liberty and the pursuit of happiness" indicates first, that there are more rights than those listed, and second, that Jefferson and the other framers probably thought that this triad encompassed the basic rights. What does "life, liberty and the pursuit of happiness" mean for students in schools? It should mean that students have freedom from physical harm, that rights will not be arbitrarily denied, and that basic human needs will be fulfilled to the greatest degree possible, given the goals and constraints of the educational system.

Having set forth the individual's rights, the Declaration then moves to the government's role in relation to those rights: "that, to secure these rights, governments are instituted among men, deriving their just power from the consent of the governed." For purposes of this book the important point of this sentence is that authoritative powers of a government are just and legitimate only if they are derived through the consent of the governed. Certainly the implication here is that students and parents, as well as school personnel, should be given the opportunity to participate in the development of rules and policies governing their schools. From this point the Declaration moves to a discussion of the basis for revolution and the situations in which the right to revolution becomes a duty.

The Preamble to the Constitution of the United States also mentions that, in part, the function of the Constitution is to establish justice. We shall not consider all six of the objectives stated in the Preamble nor shall we consider their relation to one another. Rather, our consideration focuses on the second clause of the Preamble and the phrase ". . . in order to . . . establish justice." The second clause relates directly to the first, "in order to form a more perfect union," in that a unified society (or school) must have a semblance of order in the interactions among persons. Order, in schools or governments, is in part contingent on justice. Earlier discussion has already presented examples of how this concept might operate in the schools.

There are three identifiable types of relationships involving order and justice between individuals and societies. These ideas can be applied either to the United States government or to a classroom. First, there are the rights, duties, and obligations any one person has with respect to society. This is contributive justice. Second, there are the rights, duties, and obligations that individuals have with respect to one another. This is commutative justice. Third, there are the rights, duties, and obligations organized society has with respect to its members. This is either retributive or distributive justice.

Contributive justice deals with the obligations of individuals to act for the good of society. Conscription into the armed forces during war is an example. Certain classroom behaviors such as listening, showing respect for class members and the teacher, and taking responsibility for duties might be included in this category. Commutative justice concerns the stated rights of one person and the obligation of others to respect those rights. Examples include the right to free speech, the right to safety and security, and the right of privacy. Also included are certain rights, such as due process, that exist even though an individual has violated a school rule or policy. Distributive justice is the opposite of contributive justice. Distributive justice involves what is due the individual from organized society as a whole. Its goal is that each person should have his or her fair share of the goods and services of society. The distribution of the school's rewards and punishments is an example from the education arena, as is the issue of equality of educational opportunity. When these are fairly apportioned it can be said that distributive justice has been done. A later clause of the Preamble calls for distributive justice as a means of promoting the general welfare. Retribution, the right of society to give punishments for violations of the rights of others or of society, may also be included in this category.

The Law

It is not a large jump from the abstract principles of The Declaration and Preamble to the application of these principles vis-a-vis legal concerns. In *The Morality of Consent*[3] Alexander Bickel has very nicely stated the connection between laws and values.

> To acknowledge no values at all is to deny a difference between ourselves and other particles that tumble in space. The ineducable value, though not the exclusive one, is the idea of law. Law is more than just another opinion; not because it embodies all right values, or because the values it does embody tend from time to time to reflect those of a majority or plurality, but because it is the value of values. Law is the principal institution through which a society can assert its values. (3, p. 5)

So it is that school rules also represent the values that educational institutions hold to be important. When school personnel and students no longer value the institution, the stage is set for problems, such as violence. This conclusion also was drawn by former Supreme Court Justice Arthur J. Goldberg in a paper entitled "The Role of Law in a Free Society."[4]

> An unjust society heeds disrespect for and disobedience of law and promotes acts of civil disobedience. People obey and respect law not solely

out of fear of punishment but also because of what the law does for them; the durability and reliability it gives to institutions; the reciprocity that comes from keeping one's word; and the expectation, grounded in experience, that the just process of law will right their wrongs and grievances. Whenever just expectations go unrealized or legitimate grievances go unredressed, confidence in the law declines; people become alienated from authority and from the law; instability becomes widespread and violence is resorted to. (4, p. 405)

While the context of this quotation is society in general, it is also applicable to the school as a social system. Former Justice Goldberg makes clear what happens when justice is not realized: confidence in law (or school rules) diminishes and disobedience increases. The Safe School Study also supports this finding as one of the contributing factors in violent schools.

Justice Goldberg went on to state:

In affirming my faith in our democratic processes and the rule of law as the ultimate safeguard of our liberties, I am mindful that the most crucial challenge confronting our entire system of justice is the need to make our declared legal principles and our constitutional protections into a workable and working reality for those to whom they must often seem to be the sheerest of illusion and promissory deception. (4, p. 406)

Here Goldberg is referring to "residents of social ghettos," "urban and rural poor" and the "economically and socially deprived." It is true that many youth responsible for school crime are included in these categories and have even been involved in the juvenile justice system, but this is not the primary emphasis to draw from this quotation. The applicability of Goldberg's challenge is less than direct; schools are not courts and youth are not adults. Still, there are fundamental ways of treating persons that are just and that can be applied in the classroom. Justice can and should be a reality in the schools.

Theology

The definition of justice as equal treatment of individuals in similar situations brings to mind the common symbol of blind Justice; she is blind to the person, weighing both sides of the issue. Blind Justice also has a sword, a symbol of power and precision; it represents her ability to cut through the unnecessary and divide the controversy into equal parts, all of which are then to be judged with impartiality. This image of legal justice is mechanical, calculating, and exact.

In theological terms justice is more than a norm, an even division; it is a challenging goal to be pursued even in the face of obstacles. Righteousness, the concept of meeting moral standards, is seen as directly related to the idea of justice.

One theological image of justice stands in sharp contrast to the legal image:

> Let justice roll down like waters,
> And righteousness like a mighty stream.
>
> —Amos 5:24

It is very difficult to determine the exact distinction between the biblical meaning of justice and righteousness.[5] It appears that justice is a mode of action, a process such as has been discussed in this chapter, while righteousness is a personal quality, as suggested by Psalms 37:9: "The righteous shall inherit the land." Some argue that justice is primarily legal, while righteousness is associated with compassion for the oppressed. This view is evident in the earlier quotation from Arthur Goldberg and is defended in his book, *Equal Justice*.[6]

In *Love, Power and Justice*[7] the theologian Paul Tillich describes a special relationship between love and justice. Love, Tillich states, is the compelling factor of life driving toward the reunion of the separated, and justice is the form in which the reunion occurs. This justice transcends proportional justice that gives retribution in reward and punishment. Tillich also speaks of creative justice that transforms by accepting the unacceptable. Creative justice is love. In a sense Paul Tillich's creative justice, forgiveness in order to reunite the separated, is similar to righteousness when this term is used synonymously with benevolence, kindness, and generosity. Within this discussion it can be seen that the theologians are concerned with more than the logic of justice; they have extended the meaning of justice to include compassion for other humans. Their justice is a value actively pursued.

Philosophy

Philosophical views of justice also are prevalent. Many individuals cite as a positive value "the greatest good for the greatest number," a variation on Jeremy Bentham's utilitarianism. Here, pleasure is a chief goal in life, and so the greatest happiness for the greatest number should be the ultimate in social justice. "The greatest good for the greatest number" and "equal treatment of persons in similar situations" may appear to be conflicting statements. Can relevant differences among individuals be demonstrated to justify the inequality of treatment that seems to be suggested by the utilitarian principle? In essence, the first phrase asserts that there may be injustice to some for the good of many, and that the guiding principle should be the maximization of personal welfare. It is also the case that this idea is usually espoused by that majority that by and large is already receiving the "greatest good."

Utilitarians, however, would argue that behind being in the majority lies a "relevant" difference justifying the inclusion of some and exclusion of others. One also could argue, as has Joel Feinberg,[8] that some modes of treatment are deserved. Some individuals deserve to be treated in certain ways because of conditions such as eligibility, entitlement, or worthiness. The concept of justice as desert seems applicable to schools with reference to grades, rewards, and punishments, and even praise and blame. Of course, reparation and liability also would be included. The conflict between justice as a utilitarian ideal and justice as desert is the age-old conflict between "they were all doing it" and "I don't care what they are doing; you should have known differently and deserve to be punished."

A second approach is presented in *A Theory of Justice* by John Rawls[9] who also attacked the utilitarian model so prevalent in our society. Rawls's theory of social justice embodies the following general concepts:

All primary goods—liberty and opportunity, income and wealth, and the basis of self respect—are to be distributed equally unless an unequal distribution of any or all of these goods is to the advantage of the least favored. (9, p. 303)

In this approach equality, not the greatest good, is the guiding principle. Inequalities are only permissible if they are to everybody's advantage. There should be no total sacrifice of welfare; everybody should benefit, though benefits differ depending on the person's status. It is a case of justice and compassion combined as we saw earlier. Here, however, the argument is couched in philosophical, not theological terms.

Rawls has provided, in essence, an updated version of Immanuel Kant's categorical imperative which would require a person to act only as that person would have others act in the same situation. An intuitive idea of Rawls's approach to justice can be gained by considering the design of a theoretical society of which you are to be a member. Goods and services must be distributed in some manner, but you do not know your position in the society. For example, what system of justice would you design for a society that is to be 95 percent slaves and 5 percent slave owners, assuming *you do not know whether you will be a slave or an owner*. Or, more directly applicable to problems in schools: what should be the guiding principles of social justice in a society where one-half of one percent of the people will be attacked each month, only you do not know whether you will be the attacker, the attacked, or an onlooker? Or finally, what should constitute social justice where there is a rule system to handle disruptions but you do not know whether you will be enforcing the rules or violating the rules.

Before turning to psychological aspects of justice, mention should be made of Walter Kaufmann's philosophical critique of justice in *Without Guilt and Justice*.[10] Kaufmann denies that justice can be done because there will always be an essential inequality. Neither retribution nor distribution can be done fairly, so the ideal of justice is unachievable. We now turn to a closer look at values and justice as they relate to the psychology of moral development. It is in this context that justice is most often considered by educators.

Psychology

With the continuing saga of recent social problems the public has once again turned to the school system to assure that the moral development of youth will be better in the future. In response to this social pressure most teachers have become somewhat familiar with various theories of moral development, especially those of Jean Piaget, Lawrence Kohlberg, and June Tapp. Value clarification techniques such as Sidney Simon's also have become popular with educators.[11] This discussion will be very brief as we will return to further consideration of ethical development.

In the 1930s Jean Piaget was actively studying the moral development of children. The results of his studies were published in *The Moral Judgment of the Child*.[12] Piaget identified two broad stages of moral development. Young children, generally preadolescent in age, see rules as sacred and immutable because they have been set by adults. At this stage of moral realism rules are simply not to be transgressed; if they are, it is wrong and the violator must be punished. There can be no exceptions, no procedural considerations, and no consideration of circumstances. At about twelve years of age the stage of moral relativism develops. Rules are seen as guides, as requirements for the smooth functioning of groups. There are exceptions, processes, and circumstances that must be considered in meting out rewards and punishment.

Lawrence Kohlberg has advanced and clarified many of Piaget's original ideas.[13, 14] There are three levels of moral reasoning according to Kohlberg. Each of these levels has two stages. For our purposes we will outline only the major levels of preconventional, conventional, and postconventional moral development.

At the preconventional level the child sees cultural rules as good or bad, right or wrong, and interprets these rules in terms of the consequences for obeying or not obeying.

At the conventional level the individual is concerned with maintaining the expected order vis-a-vis family, school, nation, and so on. Conformity to the existing order is perceived as being valuable in its own right and is actively supported and justified. This is the level of "fitting in," "having good intentions," or "being nice." In its later stages this level has a "law and order" orientation.

The highest level of development is postconventional. Here moral values are defined apart from particular individuals and specific groups. This is the level embodied in our legal system and Constitution. At the highest stage an individual would appeal to universal ethical principles, such as the Golden Rule or Kant's categorical imperative. The values of universal justice or reciprocity between individuals and groups and a concern for the dignity and integrity of all human beings are reflected at this level.

June Tapp and Felice Levine have developed a theory of legal socialization that incorporates many of these concepts. Their essay, "Legal Socialization: Strategies for an Ethical Legality,"[15] is especially important as it applies directly to our theme of violence, values, and justice in American education.

JUSTICE IN EDUCATION

In *Simple Justice*[16] Richard Kluger detailed black Americans' long and persistent struggle for equality under the law. Slaves, it might be recalled, were considered as property rather than as persons and thus were excluded from the injunction "all men are created equal." Many of the issues dealing with blacks' quest for equality dealt with education. A good example of the struggle for justice and equality is found in the significant 1954 Supreme Court decision of *Brown v. The Board of Education of Topeka, Kansas*, 374 U. S. 485 (1954). Essentially the Court held that its 1896 ruling in *Plessy v. Fergusson*, 163 U. S. 537 (1896), which promulgated the so-called "separate but equal" doctrine, was unconstitutional. The Court ruled that separate education for blacks was not, by definition, equal, and that blacks should be admitted to public schools on a nonsegregated basis. In the *Brown* case the underlying judicial rationale was based on concepts of equality of educational opportunity. The issue of what constitutes educational equality of opportunity was, of course, not swept away by *Brown*, but continues as one of the burning policy and legal questions confronting American society.

More recently the judicial system has moved from the broader, and perhaps less complex, questions surrounding equal educational opportunity to deal with the examination of some of our values with regard to student disciplinary procedures. These decisions are directly related to the resolution of contemporary education problems of violence and disruption. In the following paragraphs several of the more important of these Supreme Court decisions are briefly reviewed.

Student Rights

One of the most important statements concerning the rights of students was handed down by the Supreme Court in 1969. The case of *Tinker v.*

Des Moines Independent School District, 393 U. S. 503 (1969) involved the students' freedom of expression concerning the Vietnam War. In upholding the wearing of black armbands as a protest against the war the Court ruled that "the Constitution does not stop at the public school doors," thus putting student and adult rights on equal footing. Relative to our earlier discussion of rights, students are, indeed, "persons" under the Constitution.

Due Process

In *In re Gault,* 387 U. S. 1 (1964), the Supreme Court rejected the closed nature of proceedings against juveniles. This was the first in a series of decisions requiring that juveniles be afforded some form of due process protection. The *Gault* decision can be read as requiring that juveniles be given similar due process protection to that afforded adults. For example, before a youth can be found guilty and penalized, punished, expelled, or suspended from schools there should be 1) a notice of charges, 2) right to counsel, 3) right to question witness, 4) immunity from self-incrimination, and 5) a right to a review of the decision.

Two more decisions also relate directly to due process rights for students and extend the judicial thrust that began in *Gault.* In *Goss v. Lopez,* 419 U. S. 565 (1975), the Supreme Court ruled that a ten-day suspension could cause sufficient damage to a student's educational program to warrant a due process hearing (however informal). The Supreme Court also provided a remedy for the denial of a student's constitutional rights in *Wood v. Strickland,* 420 U. S. 308 (1975). In that case the Court held that school officials cannot claim ignorance of, or ignore, a student's constitutional rights, and that, in fact, school officials and school board members can be held personally liable for civil damages for violation of those rights.

Corporal Punishment

There are two recent decisions addressing issues raised by the corporal punishment of students. While excessive use of physical force is illegal as a general rule, in *Baker v. Owen,* 423 U. S. 907 (1976), the Court upheld a lower court ruling which found that schools can override the parents' wishes concerning forms of punishment and even exercise a "reasonable use of corporal punishment." In *Ingraham v. Wright,* 430 U. S. 651 (1977), the Court decided that, within reason, school officials could paddle students and that corporal punishment does not constitute cruel and unusual punishment under the Eighth Amendment to the Constitution.

Grades

The reduction of grades as a punitive measure has been cited earlier as a factor contributing to student alienation. It is worth noting that several decisions have been handed down concerning this practice. In *Wermuth v. Bernstein and the Board of Education of the Township of Livingston, Essex County* (Decision of the New Jersey Commissioner of Education, 121 (1965)), *Minorics v. Board of Education of Phillipsburg* (Decision of the New Jersey Commissioner of Education, March 24, 1972)) and *Dorsey v. Bale,* 521 S.W. 2d 76 (Ky. Ct. of App. 1975), the rulings were that grades should not be used for disciplinary purposes, thus protecting students from arbitrary practices that may have long-term and unpredictable effects.

These recent Supreme Court decisions and other rulings make clear that youth have certain basic rights as guaranteed by the Constitution, putting them on a nearly equal footing with adults. We know that educators are sometimes fearful and frustrated in their attempts to deal with disruptive youth. In such situations it is not easy to coolly apply due process procedures or other judicially sanctioned rights. Indeed, in some situations, the problem requires immediate attention. Educators are searching for more effective means of applying the legal standards that have been established for their schools. By now it should be clear that the purpose of this book is to advocate neither a laissez faire nor a "get tough" approach to discipline problems. Justice applied to educational problems should provide guidelines for the fair, firm, and consistent enforcement of rules and policies.

MORAL EDUCATION

The specific problem of violence and discipline in schools also raises the general problem of moral education. The issue of moral education has received a great deal of attention in recent years.[17, 18] Often, however, the approach to moral education is largely psychological and ignores significant factors that lie outside of the realm of psychology. We have tried to present the value of justice in a context broader than psychology without excluding important findings from this discipline.

A Just School

One of the most vital yet difficult tasks of any educational system is training students for citizenship and developing appropriate ethics and values for living in a democratic society. School personnel play a key role in this education though it is often not a part of the formal, visible curriculum. Indeed, the results of a national survey indicate that socialization "is the dominating goal of many educators."[19] Our aim is not to suggest a curriculum that will reduce violence by developing a conceptual understanding of justice, though we are not opposed to this and do offer suggestions regarding curriculum and instruction throughout the book. Rather, our aim is broader. If anything, it would approximate what Lawrence Kohlberg has called a "just community" approach to moral education. Our aim is the development of justice as a viable aspect of interactions within the school; in short, a just school.

Active participation in the school's social and political structure by students provides stronger lessons in moral education than formal presentations on topics such as "Law in America" or "Democracy in Action."

To the extent to which it is possible to encourage student involvement in matters pertaining to curriculum, formulation of rules, discipline procedures, and student rights and obligations, two valuable goals of moral education might well be served. First, students are more likely to accept rules and procedures developed through mutual interchange and discussion. A more responsible student body can be produced through involvement in the governing process. Second, mutual discussion and involvement among students and school personnel may well provide a practical means of educating for citizenship values in a concrete and meaningful setting too often ignored by educators.

Problems and Issues

School personnel are confronted with many problems that require practical consideration and resolution. At the same time, these many issues accumulate into a climate of moral education that permeates the school. Here are some of the issues that are important to school discipline and to moral education.

1. What kinds of student conduct should be amenable to the disciplinary process? Should discipline be limited to conduct that would otherwise be criminal, or should it include disruptive conduct in general, or such matters as hair length or dress code violations?

2. What is the range of conflicts appropriate for "discipline"?

3. What are appropriate sanctions, consequences, or other dispositions for various offenses?

4. A variety of alternatives to suspension can be envisioned. Individualized behavior contracts "officially notarized" with a school seal, use of school ombudsmen, and peer group counseling are approaches that do not require extensive community investment. Special education programs or work-study alternatives may be useful in the case of special discipline problems. Consideration of which offenses can best be dealt with through rehabilitative devices is of vital importance.

5. The *Goss* opinion developed minimal due process requirements for suspensions of up to ten days. It left open the possibility that more extensive procedures would be required for more severe sanctions. *Ingraham*, on the other hand, opens up the possibility that less extensive procedures would be required for minor disciplinary problems.

Questions that should be considered in the development of school discipline policies include the following. What due process protections are required in school discipline cases? Beyond minimum constitutional requirements, what procedural protections are desirable for the complainant and the student as a matter of prudence and fair play? The central theoretical issue under consideration is the extent to which school discipline proceedings should resemble criminal adversary processes. The discipline policy should identify appropriate procedures for various situations. "Appropriateness" must include consideration of the interests of students, teachers, and school administrators.

6. In what circumstances will school administrators and teachers be financially liable in school discipline cases? *Wood v. Strickland* makes clear that school administrators are not immune from damage suits under Section 1983 of Title 42 of the United States Code. Damage awards might occur when a school official "knew or reasonably should have known that the action he took within his sphere of official responsibility would violate the constitutional rights of the student." This general language raises questions about the kinds of knowledge that can be imputed to an administrator. The effect of a discipline policy in clarifying a school official's responsibility and liability should be explored. Statutory and state liability questions should be analyzed as well, so that school officials will know where they stand and be protected against harassment and malicious damage suits.

7. What is the proper relationship between school officials and police and district attorneys in connection with school discipline and the enforcement of the criminal law? How should the administrator deal with cases in which both areas overlap? The school's discipline policy should consider these issues and provide appropriate solutions.

8. To what extent is parent and student input into the rule-making process necessary and proper? Would such input into the rule-making process enlarge constituency acceptance of results and reduce the instances of court review of administrative decisions?

9. What procedures might be developed by school boards for internal appeals of disciplinary proceedings? The use of mixed parent–teacher–student review might be explored. Further possibilities of utilizing arbitration devices in this area might be explored as well.

10. Many localities use corporal punishment as a disciplinary technique. Under what conditions and for which offenses should it be allowed, especially in light of the *Ingraham* opinion? Because state law on these and other issues varies considerably, school policies should provide alternative proposals in cases where state and local laws vary. The school system may also exercise its right not to use corporal punishment and implement other consequences for rule violations.

SUMMARY

Violence, vandalism and student disruption are significant factors influencing American education. School-related disruption extends to all corners of the country and includes urban, suburban, and rural school systems. In short, violence and discipline problems in schools are a major concern to educators and the public.

One of the first ways that values come into consideration in schools is in the search for the causes of student disruption. Student alienation, resulting from a change in values orienting an individual toward the school system, is a contributing factor to the problem. Student alienation can be summarized as a combination of powerlessness, meaninglessness, normlessness, isolation, and self-estrangement. In some cases the schools are contributing to student alienation. In gaining a perspective on the problem one must consider the values of students, of school personnel, and of the school system itself as expressed in the form of rules.

One value school personnel should consider is justice, the fair and equal treatment of individuals in similar situations. Our position vis-a-vis justice in the schools is supported by The Declaration of Independence and the Preamble to the Constitution of the United States. In addition, there are legal, theological, philosophical, and psychological foundations for the use of justice as a guide for educational policy making.

In recent years the Supreme Court has ruled that public school students have the same rights guaranteed other persons. Students should be afforded due process before they are denied education. The authors suggest that this view represents a broader theory of moral education.

REFERENCES

1. National Institute of Education, *Violent Schools—Safe Schools* (Washington, D. C.: U. S. Government Printing Office, 1978).
2. Melvin Seeman, "On the Meaning of Alienation," *American Sociological Review* 24 (December 1959): 783–91.
3. Alexander Bickel, *The Morality of Consent* (New Haven: Yale University Press, 1975).
4. Arthur J. Goldberg, "The Role of Law in a Free Society," *Georgia Law Review* 7, no. 3 (1973): 403–9.
5. Abraham Heschel, *The Prophets* (New York: Harper & Row, 1971).
6. Arthur J. Goldberg, *Equal Justice* (New York: Farrar, Straus and Giroux, 1971).
7. Paul Tillich, *Love, Power and Justice* (New York: Oxford University Press, 1954).
8. Joel Feinberg, "Justice and Personal Desert," in Carl J. Friedrich and John Chapman (Eds.), *Justice: NOMOS VI* (New York: Atherton Press, 1963).
9. John Rawls, *A Theory of Justice* (Cambridge: Harvard University Press, 1971).
10. Walter Kaufmann, *Without Guilt and Justice* (New York: Dell Publishing, 1973).
11. Sidney Simon et al., *Values Clarification* (New York: Hart Publishing Co., 1972).
12. Jean Piaget, *The Moral Judgement of the Child* (New York: The Free Press, 1965).

13. Lawrence Kohlberg, "Moral Development," *International Encyclopedia of Social Science* (New York: Macmillan Free Press, 1968).
14. Lawrence Kohlberg, "The Cognitive-Developmental Approach to Moral Education," *Phi Delta Kappan* (June 1975): 670–77.
15. June L. Tapp and Felice J. Levine, "Legal Socialization: Strategies for an Ethical Legality," *Stanford Law Review* 27, no. 1 (1974): 1–72.
16. Richard Kluger, *Simple Justice* (New York: Alfred A. Knopf, 1976).
17. Barry I. Chazan and Jonas F. Soltis (Eds.), *Moral Education* (New York: Teachers College Press, 1975).
18. Richard Hersh, Diana Paolitto, and Joseph Reimer, *Promoting Moral Growth: From Piaget to Kohlberg* (New York: Longman, 1979).
19. Robert Stake and Jack Easley, *Case Studies in Science Education* (Washington, D. C.: U. S. Government Printing Office, 1978).

CHAPTER TWO

School Discipline and the Rights of Youth: An Historical Perspective

INTRODUCTION

The Supreme Court of the United States has declared that students in the public schools today enjoy constitutional rights tantamount to those that have long been recognized for their parents. A public school student comes to school clothed with constitutional rights, and these rights are not left at "the school house gate."[1] Only with the threat of material and substantial disruption of the educational process will these rights yield. This constitutional concern for public school students, however, is a fairly recent development. The greatest part of the republic's history has been a judicial hesitation about intrusion into the area of education, and about interference with the judgment of educators in disciplinary matters.

The historical judicial response to school disciplinary methods can be viewed in three periods.[2] The first period, which began with colonization and continued until about 1850, may be characterized as a time of "judicial laissez faire." During this period courts were generally inclined to ignore education: federal courts considered it a state and local matter beyond their expertise, and state courts were loath to interfere in an area that was commanded by specialists. The second and longest period, lasting roughly the century from 1850 to about 1950, saw growing state judicial attention to educational matters. During this period state courts began to exercise jurisdiction over the schools and developed a substantial case law that interpreted state legislative enactment and common law doctrine in a way that permitted educational practices that would defy contemporary constitutional principles. The third period, which began in the 1950s with the seating of the Warren Court and continues until today, may be called a "reformation." During this period two secondary stages have occurred. One stage occurred with the desegregation decisions of the 1950s and '60s; the other stage represents the current posture of the judiciary. The desegregation decisions brought the schools under the direct supervision of the courts, the courts retaining a watchdog jurisdiction over them until their mandates were carried into effect. Thus the courts intervened in matters affecting not only discipline, but administration, organization, and pedagogy. The current stage has brought somewhat of an easing of judicial innovation in educational matters. This began in 1973 with the landmark case of *San Antonio Independent School District v. Rodriguez,*[3] in which the United States Supreme Court declared that education, or the opportunity for education provided by the state, is not a fundamental right, one arising explicitly or implicitly from the Constitution. This "strict constructionism" represents the contemporary attitude of the Burger Court, a Court that in the aftermath of the Warren Court's social activism and far-reaching constitutional doctrine has been called a Court of "consolidation"— one willing to enhance the doctrines inherited from the Warren Court, but unwilling to break new doctrinal ground.[4]

This chapter explores these judicial developments as well as the influences that may have had some causal effect upon them. Bound by the principle of *stare decisis*—or precedent—the judicial response to student disciplinary methods has historically been slow. Nonetheless, judicial doctrine in this area has not developed in a vacuum. Historical events and social attitudes have had some effect. It will be noted that the school disciplinary methods that have come to judicial scrutiny have not changed much: suspension, expulsion, and corporal punishment have remained in consistent use throughout our history. What has varied is judicial tolerance of their severity. For example, judicial attitudes about corporal punishment in the schools have derived from adult perceptions of children— whether they are demons or angels—and from the social indulgence of this kind of sanction. Attitudes about suspension and expulsion have been affected by the changing assumptions about the role of education in society. At the beginning of this country's history, education was considered as a sort of recreational luxury superfluous to the more important occupations of planting and harvesting the crop. Later, education was thought of as a socializing instrument to harmonize a pluralistic nation. Today it is seen as the primary avenue to material success and individual autonomy. Provided by the government, education has been elevated to the status of property, the revocation of which cannot constitutionally occur without certain measures of fairness. These attitudes, as well as changing ideas about the judiciary's role in regulating governmental activity, have affected the judicial response to school disciplinary methods.

THE FIRST PERIOD: JUDICIAL LAISSEZ FAIRE

The early educational history of this country reveals little legal involvement with education. Educational opportunities mainly occurred at the private level—in private schools, in dame schools, or in the classic one-room school with its single teacher whose services were contracted for by the parents of attending children. The exception to this rule was in the New England states, where the Puritans established public education at the outset of colonization. Teachers who abused the authority given them to act *in loco parentis,* or in the place of the students' parents, were privately reprimanded—either dismissed by contracting parents or retaliated against by the students themselves. Not until late in this period, and then only in extreme cases, did the state courts take jurisdiction over civil and criminal cases against abusive teachers.

The Colonial Period

The antecedents of today's disciplinary practices and problems may be traced as far back as colonization.[5] Colonization began in 1630 with the "Great Migration" to the New World of those dissatisfied with conditions in Europe. In the American wilderness lay the promise of relieving those problems, at least economically, by exploiting the natural resources of this new land. The culture and institutions of the Old World were transplanted to help compensate for the dislocation of the new environment. In addition, the migrants brought a certain utopianism that altered those old institutions for a new and different purpose. Since 90 percent of the migrants to the colonies were English it was natural that English language, custom, and tradition predominated. Even though the English colonists' environment, religious motivation, and sense of destiny differed from that of the country from which other colonists came, every aspect of colonial culture had a distinctly English flair. In the Puritan and Quaker communities, the educational institutions replicated those the colonists had been familiar with in England. In the southern colonies, the plantation system was distinctly reminiscent of the old English manorial system.[6]

It was in New England that the English educational antecedents were most successfully transplanted. Because of the poor topography and soil, the New Englanders were forced to use subsistence farming and gather together in towns. Fishing and, later, manufacturing would compensate for this lack of agrarian opportunity, but the formation of towns meanwhile provided the necessary setting for the establishment of schools.[7] Professor Lawrence Cremin points to the fact that the Puritans emigrated as families as another important factor in the development of educational opportunity in New England.[8] And Puritanism itself was an important factor because knowledge, in its scheme, was a fundamental part of obtaining saving faith by the individual predestined elect. To the Puritans, ignorance was perceived as the chief obstacle in the way of salvation.[9] Of course this ignorance was perceived to be spiritual rather than intellectual, and education consequently has a strong religious flavor that derived from an unwavering reliance on holy writ.[10]

The other colonies had a more commercial orientation. All but Pennsylvania of the middle colonies were economically motivated. The Quakers had come to the New World with religious imperatives similar to those of the Puritans, education being likewise a part of their system for salvation. Eventually Philadelphia became one of the important intellectual centers of the New World, a center of colonial writing and publishing, as well as the home of the guiding intellectual spirit of Benjamin Franklin. But the middle colonies in general were inhabited by a great diversity of people, with a variety of language, tradition, religion and political orientations. Consensus in educational matters was thus difficult.[11]

While the middle colonies were divided by an ideological separation, the southern colonies also suffered a separation that hindered the development of education: geographical separation. The agrarian economy of the South discouraged the development of towns such as those found in New England. The population was instead widely distributed on plantations and farms. Thus the proximity necessary for the inception of centralized schools was lacking, and schooling was generally unavailable for all but the upper-class families who could afford to maintain tutors on the plantation. Therefore, as opposed to the democratic town schools that early developed in New England, southern education was class-oriented and individualistic. Though the dominant faith of the South was Anglicanism, religion failed to inspire educational opportunity as it did in the North, Anglicanism being more passive about ignorance than Puritanism. The South also lacked the familial structure of the New England colonies: it was the place to which the indentured servants migrated, along with indigent and orphaned children. Yet the most persistent obstacle to the development of southern educational opportunity was the existence of a system of chattel slavery. That education would make the slaves conscious of their lot and incite rebellion was a perennial fear.[12]

Thus it was only in the New England Puritan community that there was early established an almost universal system of popular education. This would later be the model for the rest of the country in the development of public education. The Massachusetts Bay School Laws of 1642 and 1647 laid the basis for this system by requiring the compulsory maintenance of town schools, as well as the compulsory education of all children. The Puritan orientation toward education provided the town school with strong predecessors and established the groundwork for the Education Laws. Almost as soon as the colonists of New England set foot on American soil, or at least as soon as the first roofs were raised over their heads, dame schools began. A dame school was the gathering of neighborhood children to the home of one woman in the neighborhood who taught the alphabet and other rudimentary skills. Sometimes the teacher was hired as a servant who taught the children of the household and those of others. In that case the school was called a petty school. In some towns "free" schools were founded in order that all children of the community might attend.[13]

The Education Law of 1642 ordered the town selectmen to determine periodically whether parents and masters were complying with the obligation to educate their children, or the children under their authority, "for the calling and employment" that they must someday assume. Those found not in compliance with this command were to be fined. Enforcement was difficult though, so in 1648 an amendment to the statute required that children be taught an orthodox catechism, something more measureable than "calling and appointment."[14]

In 1647, the requirement for compulsory schools was established with The "Old Deluder Law," a statute meant to preserve religious orthodoxy and otherwise to encourage the education of the young.[15] The statute's language illustrates the religious sentiment that governed the educational environment it helped create, an environment that presumed the inclination of the child to sin:

> It being one chief project of that old deluder, Satan, to keep men from the knowledge of the Scripture, as in former times by keeping them in an unknown tongue, so in these latter times by persuading from the use of tongues, that so at least the true sense and meaning of the original might be clouded by false glosses of saint-seeming deceivers, that learning may not be buried in the grave of our fathers in the church and commonwealth, the Lord assisting our endeavors.
>
> It is there for ordered that every township in this jurisdiction after the Lord hath increased them (in) number to fifty householders, shall then forthwith appoint one within their town to teach all such children as shall resort to him to write and read, whose wages shall be paid either by the parents or masters of such children, or by the inhabitants in general. . . .[16]

Primary education was of greatest concern, but there were other forms as well. The "Old Deluder Law" also required the setting up of grammar schools. These were the initial forms of secondary education that developed alongside the elementary schools. These schools corresponded closely with the English Latin Grammar Schools and prepared young men of the colonies for the university.[17]

Informal educational opportunities always preceded and accompanied the development of more formal institutions.[18] It is likely that the majority of New England youth went the route of apprenticeship rather than attend the local version of the English Latin Grammar School and then the university. This was so not necessarily by choice, but because the grammar schools existed only in a minority of larger Puritan settlements.[19] The apprenticeship laws of the mother country were eventually reproduced in New England, with the added requirement that masters go beyond the training of the child for a vocation to the provision of a basic education in religion and the civil law.[20] Also, families in general responded to the educational inclinations of the society and taught children vocational skills as well as the reading ability necessary for religious activity.[21]

Within all these educational situations, whether formal or informal, adults commanded the respect and attention of children in some kind of domestic relationship. In a parent–child relationship the authority of the parent over the child was nearly absolute. All but death or maiming were within the parental prerogative to correct rebellious children. This measure of parental authority was backed by governmental willingness, following biblical tradition, to put to death children over sixteen who cursed or smote their natural father or mother.[22] Commensurate with this parental authority was the authority given those who stood in the place of parents, or *in loco parentis*: teachers in the dame, petty, or free schools, and masters who entered the master–servant relation of apprenticeship. Within the bounds of those relationships adults—whether parents, masters, or teachers—could be quite severe in their punishment of children.

Colonial severity in the punishment of children derived from the seventeenth-century perception of the child and from the scriptures. The adult perception of the child in the New England colonies corresponded to the theology that reigned there. To the Puritans the child was born in ignorance and filled with the tendency to sin. Children were seen as the objects of possible salvation if taught the doctrines and principles of Christianity. Otherwise they would remain demons incarnate, totally depraved, as evidenced by their fractiousness with each other, their disinclination to obey, and their general vulgarity.[23] Also, without the psychological understandings that came later, children were considered as miniature adults and judged according to adult expectations. Portraits of children of the time show them dressed in adult apparel, assuming adult postures. And it was not unusual to find fifteen- and sixteen-year-olds entering an adult's world of labor.[24] As depraved little adults, children were considered lower members of the social hierarchy, subject to their father or their master. The leading Puritan divine of the time, William Perkins, wrote:

> In the good man or master of the familie resteth the private and proper government of the whole household, and he comes not unto it by election, as it falleth out in other states, but by the ordinance of God settled even in the order of nature. The husband indeed naturally bears rule over the wife, parents over their children, masters over their servants.[25]

In the colonial period, and persisting even today in certain pockets of evangelism, adults believed their responsibility to correct children to be established by biblical injunctions such as:

> Withhold not correction from the child, for if thou beatest him with the rod he shall not die. Thou shalt beat him with the rod, and shalt deliver his soul from hell.[26]

The confidence that this was the will of God encouraged the use of the birch whip in maintaining order in the colonial classroom. Cotton Mather's epigram, "Better Whipped than Damned," most succinctly illustrates the tone of the period.[27]

Documents from the period do not show any examples of litigation involving the discipline of a colonial student. This does not mean that there was not at least some tacit definition of students' rights in the colonial classroom. For example, the very nature of educational institutions in New England provided methods other than the law for the delimitation of teachers' authority and the resolution of conflicts between parent and teacher when the teacher appeared to have stepped beyond proper bounds. Though teachers were considered to stand *in loco parentis* in the course of their activities with children during the school day, a number of informal or indirect limitations on their prerogatives existed: 1) especially with the dame and petty schools, the teacher was a personal acquaintance of the parents and therefore conscious of the effect disciplinary actions might have upon the teacher's relationship with the parents; 2) the teacher's employment in a community school was always subject to the unique governmental authority of New England, the town meeting; 3) since payment for teaching was often made in kind, in the form of food and lodging, teachers whose practices were not approved of could literally find themselves out in the cold; and 4) since classes were comprised of students of a wide age group, a teacher could be restrained by the potential retaliation of older, and larger, students.

Cases most likely to come before a colonial tribunal, and to the attention of the public, involved the abuse of apprentices by their masters. Here the rights of the child and the liability of the master were more clearly defined by statutes and indenture agreements.[28] For disrespect or physical retaliation, an apprentice could be whipped publicly and imprisoned. This was done on the master's complaint, the master generally being the sole witness. For example, in 1669 Daniel Rumball, master of apprentice Charles Hill, complained to the Quarterly Court of Essex County, Massachusetts, that his apprentice was disrupting his family. Hill had grown in the four or five years of his apprenticeship to an "unruly frame of spirit and carriage." Twice he had thrown his master down, one time drawing blood. Once he had run at his master with a chair, threatening to break his neck. All this, with a host of other indiscretions such as swearing, lying, and speaking contemptuously of the mayor, had become intolerable to the family. Upon Rumball's complaint, the court ordered that Hill be "whipped and sent to the house of correction to remain during the court's pleasure."[29]

Though presumptions favored the master, there were certain responsibilities whose breach was reckoned against him in damages or other punishment. In the case of *Smith v. Carrington*,[30] apprentice Mathias Smith was allowed to bring an action on the case for his master's having not taught him fully in the trade of a turner. Since Smith was "damnified" for not having been "perfected in the trade of a turner," Carrington, his master, was liable to him for a total of about twenty pounds plus costs.

Beyond the responsibility of the master to teach a trade, his behavior toward his apprentice, not easily monitored, was constrained by little more than Christian piety. Punishment could be harsh, but there was certain limits to brutality. In the *Case of Fowler*, around 1680, Phillip Fowler was brought before the court to answer for the abuse of his apprentice, Richard Parker.[31] After hearing Fowler's rendition of the justification for punishment—that the boy was "unruly"—the court agreed that the boy was deserving of punishment, "yet they did not approve of the manner of punishment given, in hanging him up by the heels as butchers do beasts for slaughter, and cautioned said Fowler against such kind of punishment. He was ordered to pay costs."

The Early Republic

Benjamin Rush sensed the historical watershed of the Revolution when he wrote that it was "a new opening in human affairs which may prove an introduction to times of more light and liberty and virtue than have yet been known."[32] Certainly the Revolution, and the later writing of a constitutional charter, had a significant impact upon the development of educational opportunity and method. Education took on new importance in the republic as a means to accomplish the cohesion of a diverse populace.[33] The Puritan objectives of education became increasingly secondary as commercialism and nationalism grew—as commercial and national salvation became primary to individual salvation. As the country rolled from the eighteenth century into the nineteenth, the necessity for achieving a national identity was more and more seen as a task to be accomplished through the popularization of education. Through education would the national culture be developed and transmitted. Through education would the millenial purpose of America be achieved.

That education would be a source of the country's connective tissue only became evident as the tremendous changes of the nineteenth century unfolded. One obvious change was in population. Where there had been only three million members of the thirteen colonies in prerevolutionary America, by 1790 there were four million. By 1830 the population of the country numbered thirteen million.[34] These millions arrived as immigrants whose backgrounds represented different cultures and familial systems. Most plowed the ground and helped push the country westward, but others stood at looms and assembly lines as the Industrial Age began. American industrialism made the factory a new educational institution, as manufacture—its learning and doing—moved out from the household. Thus arose a clearer definition of the boundary between the household and the community. Also, educational objectives came to be defined in terms of economic necessity instead of religious obligation. Yet the great economic boom of postrevolutionary America gave rise to a spirit of reform and the invocation of the public—increasingly in the form of government—to serve individual needs. Eventually this reforming spirit resulted in public education, but it revealed itself in a number of other institutions as well: the almshouse, the asylum, the reformatory, and the penitentiary.[35]

In the early days of the republic—before 1830—the American landscape remained for the most part agrarian. The greatest change of the American mind towards children would occur as the country shifted its attention from the land to the city, but meanwhile the child remained a part of the familial economy of the farm. Engaged with their parents in the enterprise of survival, children were early expected to share the duties and responsibilities of their elders. Childhood and adolescence were barely recognized as stages through which the children passed on their way to adulthood. So it was not uncommon for a child to be seen carrying on the physical labor of an adult.[36]

The religious orientations of the prerevolutionary years remained strong, but at the turn of the century, the ideas of the European Enlightenment were beginning to appear in forms other than declarations of independence and constitutional government. New England Calvinists persisted in their search for God's will in the scriptures, amongst themselves, and in the manifestations of God's power in nature. For the Calvinists the primary struggle in life was still against sin, and the most significant part of that struggle was against the depravity of children. But Calvinism gradually began to give way to Unitarianism in New England. The Unitarians rejected the harsh scrupulousness of Calvinism, and, relying on the more enlightened ideas that had been unleashed in the American and French Revolutions, perceived life through more hopeful eyes.[37] Locke's idea of the *tabula rasa* countered the Puritan notions of original sin, and Rousseau's *Emile* spoke of greater tolerance and understanding in the nurture of children.[38] Children were increasingly perceived as distinct from adults, as passing through stages in their development towards adulthood. Childish truculence and disobedience were not manifestations of sin, but evidence of innocence—of the lack of understanding of sin. Though this change of views was hardly abrupt, by the early years of the nineteenth century it had developed enough among a few vocal numbers to challenge New England Calvinism.

During this period education came to be seen as the medium through which the principles of the new republicanism would be transmitted. Education was thus to be given the difficult assignment of generating a free and virtuous society, of forming a national character, and making homogeneity out of diversity. But these were the ideas of a few savants; their popularization would take time.

Thus, like the economy, the sociology, and the weather, American education was in a state of constant change in the postrevolutionary years, for the populace at large was uncertain of what role it would play in whatever the future of the country would be. In the northern states, particularly in New England, education was more and more perceived as a vehicle of nationalism. But in New England the idea of public education had long been popular, and as the New England economy became more commercial, the schools were assigned the universally popular role of preparation for commercial opportunity. But in every other region of the country there was some uncertainty about education. Popular education in the Middle States remained only an ideal, as cultural and religious factions failed to cooperate. Southerners, troubled by the prospect of educating a slave to rebel, maintained their elitist institutions and continued to remain isolated socially and geographically. Formal education on the frontier was occasional at best. When the settlers came from eastern states that actively supported education—principally the New England states—the founding of schools accompanied the clearing of the forest and the breaking of the virgin soil. But matters of survival were paramount on the frontier, and survival generally did not include education. Thus education was assigned to a second order of priority and only occurred if prosperity liberated sufficient time and energy for study.[39]

Educational opportunity thus depended upon locality. Though plans existed for national education, educational endeavor was usually private. There was a great deal of hesitation in the republic with regard to the assignment of educational programs to the government. Not only were the taxes required to support such an endeavor an unpopular prospect, but so was the notion of encouraging government to be the broker of ideas. According to the reformers, the proposed schools would be nonsectarian, but in the popular mind the divorce of education from the church was not yet complete.[40]

By 1830 the movement for public education would be recognizable and potent. Its beginning, however, lay in idealistic educational plans drafted with an eye to the achievement of utopia, and in the initial attempts to formulate systems of finance. The Land Ordinance of 1787 allocated the sixteenth section of each township to the maintenance of public schools. State constitutions regularly made provisions for education. Yet the public remained recalcitrant. All of these plans met with popular distaste for the central government's entering an area that had before been a prerogative of the people and generally associated with matters of conscience. The notion that education was the role of the church, of charity, or of parents themselves, persisted. Beyond that, there was a certain dubiousness about the importance of education—especially secondary education—as it was apparent that fortunes could be made without it. Besides, education was thought to have the tendency to implant "obnoxious" ideas in the minds of the young.[41]

Thus the development of educational opportunities was uneven in the early national period. In some regions, state and city support of education increased, but private educational endeavors were more common. Most common were the town schools. These were of unpredictable quality, as much depended upon the particular teacher or succession of teachers.

A succession of town school teachers was remembered for their abilities and their disciplinary methods in a memoir by Reverend Warren Burton.[42] Though Burton recalled at least one teacher with fondness, most were remembered for their severe, and even bizarre, disciplinary practices. After the kind and beautiful instructress, Mary Smith, went off to be married, Mehitabel Holt, whose visage and demeanor were as intimidating as her name, arrived at the school. At the slightest sign of youthful restlessness, Mehitabel would twist an ear or crack a head with her thimbled finger; for a whisper a student would be imprisoned in the darkness of a closet or tied to a chair post for an hour. But Mehitabel Holt was followed by an even more severe schoolmaster. At the first of the school year this schoolmaster announced a long list of rules to govern the students' behavior. The students speculated that if the schoolmaster attempted to enforce them all, there would be little time for anything else.

This schoolmaster's disciplinary measures to enforce his innumerable regulations bordered on the inhumane. Of course there was the traditional slap on the hand with a ferule or the whipping with a rod on the back. But another method was the forced holding of a heavy book or lead inkstand at arm's length "till muscle and nerve, bone and marrow were tortured with the continued exertion." If the arm bent at all the schoolmaster would give the student's elbow a whack to return it to a horizontal level. "I well recollect," wrote Burton, "that one poor fellow forgot his suffering by fainting quite away." Another method was the forced standing in a stooped posture with a finger on the head of a nail in the floor. "It was a position not particularly favorable to health of body, or soundness of mind; the head being brought about as low as the knees, the blood rushing to it and pressing unnaturally on the veins, causing a dull pain, and a staggering dizziness." The pain of this experience was compounded by its taking place directly in front of the schoolroom stove. Yet another method was called the "anti-whispering process." This procedure involved pulling the student's mouth open to the point of pain and then inserting a chip of wood between the teeth to hold it open. "I would not have it understood," Burton explained, "that this master was singular in his punishments; for such methods of correcting offenders have been in use time out of mind. He was distinguished only for resorting to them more frequently than any other instructor within my own observation."

Another schoolmaster not fondly remembered was Augustus Starr, who took up teaching after a turn fighting the French at sea. After being sought out by an acquaintance looking to secure another teacher for the town school, Starr came to the classroom like an officer to the bridge. He soon proved as abusive with his hand as with his tongue. Once he knocked a student down with his fist; at another time he threw a stick of wood from the woodpile, making a dent in the wall at the back of the room that indicated the damage that would have occurred to the skull of the student he had aimed for but missed. Finally the larger members of the class began to conspire to mutiny. When one afternoon late in the schoolyear a smaller student was struck with a ruler for some minor infraction, causing a cut in his head that drew blood and screams, the older brother of the injured child and three others were upon the privateer in an instant. The ruler was pulled from his hand and he was carried kicking and cursing from the schoolhouse and pitched headlong down a steep ice-and-snow-covered incline that sloped away from the school ground. He did not return.[43]

THE SECOND PERIOD: GROWING STATE INVOLVEMENT

The Age of the Common School

The thirty-some years before the Civil War witnessed increased expansion of the country. In the period between 1830 and 1860 the territory of the United States expanded 1,234,566 square miles. In the same amount of time the population of the country increased by almost twenty million, an increase that occurred largely in the cities. In 1820 a little more than 7 percent of the population lived in urban areas of 2,500 people or more. By 1860 urban areas of 2,500 or more people held 20 percent of the population. And there were more than 100 cities with populations of more than 10,000. With this growth of territory and population came a growth in national spirit and identity as progressivism declared a more optismistic outlook on human nature and Jacksonianism seemed to vindicate it.[44]

By 1830 Calvinism was definitely on the decline. Reports of conditions in the streets and in the best of homes that appeared to corrupt children and enlarge the effects of their innate depravity defied the traditional Calvinist injunction that parents apply themselves to the conversion of their children. Also conflicting with traditional Calvinism was a growing American individualism. As Bernard Wishy states: "The course of the nurture expert was clear. He had to suggest a way to develop the child's will that would do justice to American ideals of individualism while at the same time saving that freed and expanded will from indulging in the corruption so plaguing American society."[45] To accomplish a new theory of child development, the reformers imported the ideas of Jean Jacques Rosseau and of Swiss educator Johann Heinrich Pestalozzi. Their ideas inspired the metaphor that a child is a delicate young plant whose successful nurture is attained by slow, patient, and tender care. In fact, the compromise Wishy suggests between these enlightened ideas and the Calvinist traditions was initially spoken of by Horace Bushnell, who suggested that sin be "weeded out" instead of beaten. Rather than attempting to break the will with the rod, gentler means of changing behavior were to be used, and the rod resorted to only when these failed. The catch word of the reformers was persuasion, or "moral suasion." However, the art of rational persuasion was probably accomplished only by a few.[46]

Nonetheless, Calvinist attitudes were easing. Nationally read writers were publicly rejecting the orthodoxy of their fathers, and natural and worldly joys were achieving a legitimate place in the life of the pious child. Influenced by Rousseau, Americans were writing of the "waxen state of children's minds," and of the child's body as a "miniature temple." Instead of the methodical conquering of the child's "innate depravity," writers referred to the child's environment, to pure example, and to loving nurture as the ultimate determinants of the child's destiny. But traditionalists vehemently answered these heresies, and the literature of the period retained solid roots in Calvinist orthodoxy. For example, Bushnell's *Views of Christian Nurture*[47] could not escape the notion of depravity, but it did counteract the traditional Calvinist notion of flailing at evil, setting the stage for what would be far-reaching reform. By the end of the Civil War, the complete rejection of the notions of depravity and of innate tendencies to wickedness would begin to appear in the popular literature.[48]

The Common School Movement that began in the 1830s was the genesis of the public education that we know today. The movement was a result of the rise of egalitarianism. Men who were dissatisfied with the educational opportunities of their states initiated a drive for the improvement of existing public education and its extension to every locale and child. One of the announced objectives was to establish an environment in which social order and mutual respect among classes would be fostered. But such a program was not without opposition: the resistance to public financing persisted, as did the pragmatism that distrusted abstract education in favor of the development of manual skills.[49]

The establishment of common schools was not without precedent, nor was the plan without powerful advocates. Unitarian Horace Mann became its most powerful spokesman. Robert Dale Owen was influential among the working classes. All relied upon the European philosphers and practitioners in their arguments for democratic education and more systematic nurture of the child's mind.

Horace Mann had attended town schools in Massachusetts. Experiencing ignorant and cruel teachers, and never able to attend school for more than eight to ten weeks of the year, he early swore that he would correct what he perceived to be serious faults in the educational system of his day. Though he forsook Calvinism for Unitarianism, he believed that society should be governed by a strict Puritanistic moral code. At the same time he advocated the Pestolozzian abandonment of harsh punishment and drills. Preaching the merits of centralization of educational functions on the state level, Mann urged that the common school promote social harmony, develop a moral and intelligent citizenry, and provide for the full development of each individual. Destructive forces he saw to be overcome by popular and uniform education were the widening gap between the classes, political and sectional devisiveness, and the schismatic tendencies of sectarianism.[50]

Therefore, two important tenets of the Common School Movement were that education be nonsectarian, though Christian, in character, and that no harsh punishment be used. Both were vehemently opposed by the Calvinists in New England and by other factions elsewhere. In New England the opposition of conservative churchmen was that the movement would completely sever the ties between the church and the state—that it was therefore "nonreligious." The disinclination of reformers to use corporal punishment was also called nonreligious, for it was contrary to God's word in the scriptures. Other areas of disagreement existed between religious groups. In New York fears similar to those of the Calvinists—that the public school would rob children of religious or sectarian inclinations— were voiced by the Irish Catholic population. And in Philadelphia the Catholics and the Protestants battled over which version of the Bible the new schools would use.[51]

But notwithstanding these disagreements, the Common School Movement struggled forward. During Mann's tenure in Massachusetts as director of the state's schools, state appropriations and local school taxes more than doubled. New buildings were constructed, the school year was lengthened, and teachers' salaries were increased by more than fifty percent. In 1852 the Massachusetts legislature passed compulsory attendance laws. Twelve weeks per year were required by law, six of them continuous, setting the precedent for the passage of compulsory attendance laws in other states. As the initial requirements of the movement were met, the quality of the teacher became an important issue. Pestalozzi had set an example of training teachers for the specialized vocation of teaching children. The American response to this practice was the normal school, a school dedicated to the improvement of teacher knowledge and technique. In 1860 there were only twelve normal schools in the nation, but by 1865 there were twenty-two. While only a fraction of the country's teachers trained in a normal school, the rapid increase in the number of these institutions indicates that new attention was being directed to the quality of teachers in the public school.[52]

Opposition persisted. Residents of several states objected to the property tax levied to support public schooling. Sectarians continued to resist the evil of the state's usurping a responsibility that was meant for the churches. On the frontier, the Common School Movement initially was resisted mostly through inattentiveness. Other things were simply more important than education to most people who were engaged in opening the West. Only with the New England influence was education provided there. As before, where New Englanders settled, the movement for common schools, teachers' associations, and school journals was commenced. Otherwise the frontier outposts of the country relied upon envoys of the eastern reformers. For example, the National Board of Education, founded by Catherine Beecher, sent hundreds of young women to the new states.[33]

While the years following 1830 in the nothern states saw important advancements in educational theory and in continued popularization, the southern states continued to lag. The South of 1830 actually saw the passage of antiliteracy laws to keep blacks from becoming educated. The South had avoided the new nationalism and had continued to pursue its own path of economic, political, and social development. A rigid class system persisted, and property ownership was required for voting. There were also strong regionalistic sentiments in the South. The 1850s brought even greater devisiveness as southerners talked of cultural independence and separatism. School books with a southern orientation were published and used in southern schools. It was a situation that resisted change. The class structure would simply not allow for education of the poor and laboring classes, since knowledge would only arouse dissatisfaction. Popular education was therefore neglected, while education for the upper class flourished. In 1850 the southern states had an illiteracy rate of 20.3 percent in the native white population over twenty years of age. In the Middle Atlantic states the rate was only 3 percent, and in New England, it was .42 percent. In 1861 the number of days of school attendance per person of school age in the North was between fifty and sixty-five. In the South the average was only ten.[54]

Though reformers preached against it, corporal punishment persisted. In 1840, one teacher boasted of having whipped a dozen boys consecutively for not being able to discern the difference between "immorality and immortality." A coeducational school in Boston reported in 1844 an average of 130 floggings per day upon a total school population of 250. The practice had many supporters whose arguments were based on chapter and verse of holy writ. But in some areas the reformers were more compelling in their arguments. For example, through the influence of Horace Mann, who expressed the policy that beating was to be used after all efforts at "moral suasion" had failed, beatings in Boston's schools numbered only seventy-four in 1851.[55]

There were other influences that brought about the change. One of them was the fact that the Common School Movement placed greater emphasis on women teachers, as the sex thought to be particularly suited to the nurturing of children. In 1840 the percentage of male teachers in Massachusetts public schools was 60; by 1860 it had declined to 14, indicating a dramatic shift in teaching personnel.[56] Another influence was the change in ethical theories that was occurring among educators.

The dominant psychology of the day was Scottish natural realism. This school of psychology posited three great divisions of the human mind: intellect, sensibilities, and the will. As part of "sensibilities," moral nature was in turn seen as having two elements: moral emotions, and feelings of obligation. Because sensibility was concerned with feelings, emotions, and desire, a purely academic education was perceived as insufficient. The moral sentiments had also to be trained. Francis Wayland's *Elements of Moral Science* emphasized the susceptibility of the moral faculty to improvement by exercise. Thus definite programs of character training were urged for the schools. And because one's moral character was a product of feelings, it was urged that the whole atmosphere of the classroom create the proper feelings in a child's heart.[57]

Thus the inner life of the child was becoming a concern of educators. Because of its dramatic nature, the effects of corporal punishment were carefully scrutinized. That harsh punishment actually had a damaging effect upon the moral capacity of the child became a frequent argument. J. Orville Taylor wrote: "I believe that much of the malignity of men had its origin in the injudicious punishment of children."[58] But those who vehemently insisted that corporal punishment should never be used probably hurt their cause by alienating their opponents. When Horace Mann spoke publicly of the German schools' not relying on physical coercion, a group of principals in Boston rose up in arms. They called Mann inexperienced and idealistic, and, crying realism, argued for the necessity of corporal punishment. Clergymen joined the battle saying that the opponents of corporal punishment were seeking to undermine a practice that had been established by the commands of God.[59]

So the issues were again religious. What was human nature—to be born depraved and naturally prone to sin (if so, it would be necessary to turn people from sin to the ways of righteousness); or were people born naturally good, endowed with the sentiments and powers necessary for salvation (if so, it was likely that the fear of physical pain would cause harm)?[60] The ranks of the reformers swelled, and by the 1850s their antipathy toward corporal punishment achieved widespread expression in educational literature. However, even with this new emphasis in educational theory, the effect on practice was less immediate. School officials increasingly objected to physical punishment as the first recourse where other methods might work. In 1841 the Boston School Committee ordered its teachers "to practice such discipline in the schools as would be exercised by a kind, firm, judicious parent in his family, [and to] avoid corporal punishment when good order can be preserved by milder measures."[61] School reports of the period show, in complaints by parents of the severity of some teachers, a growing distaste for the customary methods of discipline. This distaste is apparent in the parent's objections as well as in the school board's inclination to report the incidents and to take some action against the teacher.[62] Hardly any cases were reported in the courts before 1850, but as education became more of a public affair—part of the growing role of government—the courts were compelled to define more clearly the powers of public school teachers in respect to the legal rights of their students.

Early Development of State Judicial Doctrine

The earliest state court case to deal with the scope of authority to be given teachers to discipline their students was State v. Pendergrass in 1837.[63] This case affirmed the common-law understanding that the teacher enjoyed a nearly absolute authority that corresponded to the authority traditionally presumed for parents. The court stated that the duty of parents was to "train up and qualify children for becoming useful and virtuous members of society." In order to accomplish this task, parents had to be able to command obedience, control stubborness, quicken diligence, and reform bad habits. Therefore, the law allowed parents the power to administer moderate punishment when they believed it just and necessary. The legal limit to this power, however, had to be in "malicious" punishment that seriously endangered life, limbs, or health; disfigured children; or caused them other permanent injury. Such punishment was considered "immoderate."[64]

In *Pendergrass* a teacher was prosecuted for criminal assault and battery of a six-year-old girl. After "mild treatment" of the girl "had failed," the teacher had resorted to whipping her with a switch. This whipping caused marks on the girl's body that disappeared in a few days, but there was also evidence that two other marks were made with a larger instrument, one on the child's arm and another on her neck. At trial the judge had instructed the jury that the right of the teacher was coextensive with that of the parent and that the jury should be cautious in finding the teacher's punishment excessive. Nonetheless, the jury found for the punished child and convicted the teacher of assault and battery. In reversing this conviction, the North Carolina Supreme Court held that a teacher exceeded the limits of authority only when the teacher punished maliciously or caused "lasting mischief." Thus a teacher could punish to any extent that did not result in permanent injury, so long as this was done in good faith and not with "malice."[65]

In coming to this conclusion, the court found that the power granted to teachers and schoolmasters to correct students was a power analogous to that of parents and in fact delegated to teachers by them. Therefore, the teacher enjoyed the same power of moderate correction granted parents, and the severity of the punishment, within the bounds of permanent injury and malice, were specifically left by the law to the discretion of the teacher. In fact the teacher's methods were to be presumed correct, for the teacher was "the judge." Only if it could be clearly proven that a teacher had used authority as a cover for malice could it be said that the teacher had abused this authority. A correct charge to the jury would have been that if it could not infer clearly from the evidence that the punishment inflicted had produced, or in its nature was calculated to produce, lasting injury, then the jury had to conclude that the teacher had not exceeded his authority. Otherwise, the jury could only convict the teacher if it was convinced that he had not acted honestly in the performance of his duties and was only gratifying his malice.[66]

Clearly this permanent injury/veiled malice holding favored the teacher and presumed the necessity for corporal punishment. In fact the court explained that the "welfare of the child [was] the main purpose for which pain [was] permitted to be inflicted."[67] The court also explained that any other circumscription of teacher authority must occur by the informal mechanisms that had historically corrected teacher abuses:

> We think that rules less liberal towards teachers cannot be laid down without breaking in upon the authority necessary for preserving discipline and commanding respect; and that although these rules leave room for indiscrete severity, with legal impunity, these indiscretions will probably find their check and correction in parental affection, and in public opinion; and if they should not, that they must be tolerated as a part of those imperfections and inconveniences, which no human laws can wholly remove or redress.[68]

The *Pendergrass* rule remained the sole articulation of the common-law authority of teachers for at least a decade, and was followed unquestioningly by other state courts.[69] Eventually, however, some state courts became persuaded by the arguments of the Common School Movement reformers against corporal punishment and moved to limit, but not eliminate, the *in loco parentis* authority of the teacher to apply corporal punishment. In *Cooper v. McJunkins*[70] the Indiana Supreme Court wrote in 1853 that:

> The very act of resorting to the rod demonstrates the incapacity of the teacher for one of the most important parts of his vocation, namely, school government. For such a teacher the nurseries of the republic are not the proper element. . . . It can hardly be doubted that public opinion will, in time, strike the ferule from the hands of the teacher, leaving him as the true basis of government only the resources of his intellect and heart. Such is the only policy worthy of the state and of her otherwise enlightened institutions. It is the policy of progress. The husband can no longer moderately chastise his wife, nor according to the more recent authorities, the master his servant or apprentice. Even the degrading cruelties of the naval service have been arrested. Why the person of the schoolboy with his shining morning face should be less sacred in the eye of the law than that of the apprentice or sailor, is not easily explained. It is regretted that such are the authorities, but courts are still bound by them. All that can be done without the aid of legislation is to hold every case strictly within the rule, and if the correction be in anger or in any other respect immoderately or improperly administered, to hold the unworthy perpetrator guilty of assault and battery.[71]

In response to this antipathy towards corporal punishment abuses, the Massachusetts Supreme Court rejected the *Pendergrass* rule in favor of a narrower articulation of teacher authority in the case of *Commonwealth v. Randall*.[72] In that case the Massachusetts court upheld a lower court jury instruction that had allowed the jury to convict a teacher of assault and battery if it found his punishment of the student to be "excessive." This instruction had been given instead of a *Pendergrass* malice instruction.

Though *Randall* was considered the leading case for this turnabout, the Vermont case of *Lander v. Seaver*[73] contained a more explicit statement of the *Randall* rule. This statement became the standard of later cases.

Lander was a quaint case that involved the punishment of a vocal eleven-year-old boy, who after returning home from school and while driving his father's cow past his teacher's house, said something about "Old Jack Seaver." Having said this in the hearing of some of his classmates and Old Jack Seaver himself, Lander was whipped the next morning with a small rawhide. The explanation for Lander's punishment was that he had degraded his teacher before his classmates by his disrespectful language, thereby undermining his teacher's authority. After a trial of the teacher upon a plea in tort for assault and battery, the jury found, after receiving *Pendergrass* instruction, that the teacher had not exceeded the bounds of the authority given him to act *in loco parentis*.[74]

The Vermont Supreme Court overturned his decision upon the ground that the malice instruction had been improper. To reject the malice test, the court rejected the historical assumption that the teacher's *in loco parentis* power was coequal with that of the parent for the purposes of education. To support this reasoning the court relied upon an often quoted passage from *Blackstone's Commentaries:*[75]

> The master is *in loco parentis,* and has such a portion of the powers of the parent committed to his charge, as may be necessary to answer the purposes for which he is employed.

An English annotator, in a note to the passage, very properly adds,

> This power must be temperately exercised, and no schoolmaster should feel himself at liberty to administer chastisement coextensive with the parent.[76]

The court also relied upon the logic that the parent–child relationship was clearly distinct from the teacher–student relationship. The reason the parent was allowed nearly unbridled control over his child and the authority to punish with severity short of "malice or wicked motives or an evil heart," was because of the intimacy of the family relationship. According to the court the law respected the privacy of the familial relationship because it was historically presumed that parents have a natural affection for their children, and that this affection acts as a restraint upon cruelty and abuse. The teacher, on the other hand, ". . . has no such natural restraint. Hence he may not safely be trusted with all a parent's authority, for he does not act from the instinct of parental affection."[77]

Therefore, the court declared, the teacher is to be ruled by reasonableness. The reasonableness of a teacher's punishment of a student would be determined from all the surrounding circumstances, only one of them being motive:

A schoolmaster has the right to inflict reasonable corporal [*sic*] punishment. He must exercise reasonable judgment and discretion in determining when to punish and to what extent. In determining upon what is a reasonable punishment various considerations must be regarded, the nature of the offence, the apparent motive and disposition of the offender, the influence of his example and conduct upon others, and the sex, age, size and strength of the pupil to be punished.[78]

Of course, the court warned, the teacher must be allowed some measure of discretion, especially since reasonable persons may disagree on what circumstances make punishment reasonable. Thus a teacher should be given the benefit of the doubt in close cases, particularly if his motives are pure. Only if the punishment applied is "clearly excessive, and would be held so in the general judgment of reasonable men," should a teacher be held liable in tort. And if the punishment is found to be excessive, he should be held liable even though he acted with good motives and considered in his own judgment the punishment to be necessary.[79]

A *Michigan Law Journal* article written in 1893 explains the shift in direction demonstrated by the *Lander* case as responsive to the historical changes of educational institutions themselves.[80] The article's author explains that the *Pendergrass* rule may have been viable in the era of small private schools, "when the instruction of each pupil was a question of direct contract between the parent and the master."[81] By the time of the *Randall* and *Lander* decisions, however, the educational landscape had changed, and parents had less control over the choice of the teacher or schoolmaster. Instead of being a mere agent of the parent, the teacher had become an agent of the state, "a public officer."[82]

The changing educational landscape—specifically, the new mission of the schools contemplated in the Common School Movement—also inspired an articulation of the powers of educators to suspend or expel. Of course suspensions and expulsions had occurred in the past for a variety of reasons. Teachers would send students traipsing home for the most minor infractions, and would work out the details with parents later. But as the Common School Movement pursued the objective of homogenization of the populace, the issue of the school's power to maintain the integrity of its curriculum and ideology when it was opposed by individual conscience naturally arose. It arose initially in the context of Bible reading in the schools, specifically in the conflict between Catholics and Protestants over the version of the Bible to be used. Of course such problems had not been seen before the common school's gathering together of religious and cultural groups; private educational endeavors of the past had fairly much occurred according to distinct, homogeneous groups. The initial authority for the common school's power to impose a consistent ideology and practice upon its students was the Maine case of *Donahoe v. Richards*.[83]

Donahoe was a tort action of trespass on the case against the local school board for the allegedly malicious, wrongful, and unjustifiable expulsion of a fifteen-year-old Catholic schoolgirl for refusing to read the Protestant version of the Bible in school. Counsel for the schoolgirl argued that the imposition of the Protestant Bible on an unwilling minority constituted "tyrannical democracy:"[84] "[I]f the majority of the school be protestants, the [board] may enforce such a system of instruction upon all; and Mahomedans[sic], catholics, or Mormons may follow their example if they get the power."[85] The Maine appellate court rejected such arguments and upheld the *Nisi Prius's* finding that the school board had not abused its authority. The basis for this holding was a broad view of the authority of the schools and school boards. For the decision that Miss Donahoe should be expelled for her failure to cooperate, the court held that the school board members could not be held liable in tort. As public officials acting in a judicial capacity, they could not be liable, civilly or criminally, even for erroneous judgments, "when their motives [were] pure and untainted with fraud or malice:"[86]

> The trustees have the power, and it is their duty to dismiss or exclude a pupil from the school, when in their judgment, it is necessary for the good order and proper government of the school so to do. They had no personal interest to gratify or benefit, they were acting for the public without salary or reward. They acted, as they believed, judiciously, in a matter of discretion, pertaining to the duties of their office. If they erred in judgment in such case, they ought not to be liable to an action.[87]

In addition, the state legislature had vested in the local school boards the power to determine the schools' curriculum. This right was meant to be general, unlimited, and final. This was so because of the necessity for continuity and for the general mission of the schools to promote homogeneity. To the court the distinctions between the Douay and King James versions of the Bible were not so significant as to suggest any substantial imposition of religious preference in the selection of one or the other. The choice of one Bible over another was found to be within the school board's authority to promote the learning of reading skills and the inculcation of Christian values. Certainly not everyone would agree with the choice, but the common school was premised on a certain degree of cooperation and compromise on the part of students, parents, and the schools themselves and this court was willing to enforce that cooperation and compromise for the greater good of society as a whole:

> Amid the various and conflicting differences on moral, political and religious subjects, there is need of mutual charity and forbearance—of mutual concession and compromise. Large masses of foreign population are among us, weak in the midst of our strength. Mere citizenship is of no avail, unless they imbibe the liberal spirit of our laws and institu-

tions, unless they become citizens in fact as well as in name. In no other way can the process of assimilation be so readily and thoroughly accomplished as through the medium of the public schools, which are alike open to the children of the rich and the poor, of the stranger and the citizen. It is the duty of those to whom this sacred trust is confided, to discharge it with magnanimous liberality and Christian kindness.[88]

Even so, the student was expected to make the greater compromise, and Miss Donahoe's expulsion was upheld as a valid exercise of school board authority.

Thus, on such broad principles as those stated in these early cases the mission of the schools as well as the authority of their personnel were predicated. In these cases—*Pendergrass, Lander, Donahoe*—commenced the themes that run through the rest of the history of education and student discipline.

Communalism and the Bureaucratization of Public Education

During the last part of the nineteenth century and the first half of the twentieth, public education came to fruition. After the Civil War the necessity of communalism, and the inculcation of national values became more urgent: the war itself demonstrated the need for some kind of homogenization of the country's diverse populace, and the liberation of a vast number of the population confronted the country with a new and troublesome problem of integration. The wars of the twentieth century, and their accompanying nationalism, only served to intensify these problems. Increasingly the community looked to the school as the vehicle for their resolution.

War and Nationalism: Class and Inequality

The quarter-century after the Civil War saw the Common School Movement that had started in the New England states reach the rest of the nation. In part, this growth of public education was a response to the initial vision of the pre–Civil War reformers—the homogenization of the country's diverse populace—a goal that loomed in greater importance as the country was torn with divisiveness. Consequently, in postwar institution building, schools occupied a large position. Informal educational opportunities had faded, and education had clearly become an economic, as well as political, necessity.[89]

By 1918 all the states had passed compulsory education laws, and schools were fast assuming many of the functions formerly performed by families, churches, and small homogeneous communities.[90] Even farm work and home skills were being taught at the nation's high schools and universities. As society became more complicated and technical, schools were expected to provide some quantification of ability. Thus, instruction became detailed and certified. The one-room schools gave way to graded schools, not only to answer the demands for quantification, but for efficiency. It was widely believed that arranging children into separate classes according to their age or accomplishment would make for a more carefully formulated curriculum and greater focus and specialization by teachers.[91]

The graded school was criticized for its factory-type approach to learning—some protested this new "academic lockstep"—but specialization and bureaucratization of the academic function continued to increase. The state legislatures, responding to state constitutional provisions for the establishment of free education enacted public school codes, vesting certain powers in local school boards to administer the economic, academic, and disciplinary requisites of the schools within their jurisdiction. Thus the school board acquired a new and important status as a legislative body empowered to make necessary regulations to govern the schools, and as a judicial body empowered to determine their infraction. With these new powers, the school board displaced with specific rules and regulations, and with more formal fact finding and decision making, the discretionary authority traditionally granted teachers and principals.[92]

This bureaucratization continued into the twentieth century as the schools confronted the shaping forces of modern America. Knowledge increased greatly with astounding advances in science and technology. Corporations and trade unions altered the face of the country's commerce. And people were swarming to the cities. As population centers grew and as the country became more mobile, schools grew in size and responsibility. More and more an extension of government, schools assumed the responsibilities of making children clean, well-nourished, healthy, athletic, and patriotic, in addition to making them literate.[93]

Increasingly, schools were expected to solve the country's problems. People like John Dewey continued to propound the necessity for communalism—as opposed to the aggressive individualism that typified commercial and industrial America. The role of the schools in fusing an immigrant society was still important. And some began to talk of the school as the site of reform for the social inequalities that persisted after the Civil War. Social equality, however, while talked of in glowing terms, would remain largely unrealized as long as individualism and the competitive ethic remained the reigning orthodoxy.[94]

Expanding School Board Authority: Suspension, Expulsion, and the Fourteenth Amendment

As noted above, the state legislatures empowered the school boards to provide for the efficient administration of schools within their respective jurisdictions. Part of this authority included the power to suspend or expel refractory students. The legislative grants of power were, at least in the early years, fairly broadly stated.[95] Therefore, the school board's actions were rarely questioned, and their ability to suspend or expel was nearly absolute. All that was required of a particular suspension or expulsion was that it be "reasonable"—a rather flexible standard. Nonetheless, courts were early capable of finding some limitations on the school board's authority.

Two methods of limiting school board authority were to construe the legislative grants narrowly, and to offset the authority against certain rights retained by parents. For example, an early case held the school board to be limited to its statutory authority, and required it to promulgate rules before attempting an expulsion.[96] An 1874 case, *Morrow v. Wood*, held that the reasonable dictates of parents as to the subjects their children would study could not be overridden.[97] This case seems to be an early exception to the general rule that the schools could determine the subject matter to be studied by its students. Part of its rationale was that students could not and should not be encouraged to disobey their parents. Yet, an underlying additional rationale probably was that the primary right to education was thought to reside in the parent.[98] This early notion derived from the fact that the historical responsibility for education of children was the parents'. The common school was simply delegated the responsibility traditionally required of the parent. However, the relationship between school and parent was eventually superseded by that between school and student, and though parental desires were given consideration, later cases spoke almost exclusively of the school–student relationship. For example, a school board could not impose the requirement of a dancing activity on an unwilling student,[99] nor could it prohibit a student's fraternity membership.[100] These cases spoke specifically of the student's rights to participate, or not to participate, in activity the school board attempted to regulate. Yet, certain activities the school board could enforce, even though students protested them as violations of individual conscience. These were activities perceived to be important to the inculcation of a uniform set of values— such as Bible reading and flag salutes.[101]

Otherwise, regulations and disciplinary actions by school boards, and by subordinate principals and teachers, were governed by "reasonableness" or "good faith," both of which granted a broad measure of authority to educators.[102] Early cases presumed "good faith" and "reasonableness" in the application of terribly vague rules and regulations. Thus a teacher could suspend a student for "general bad conduct"[103] or for refusal to participate in school activities.[104] A Catholic student's suspension for refusal to lay aside his books while the teacher read from the King James version of the Bible was held to be within the school board's authority to suspend or expel for "incorrigibly bad conduct" in the absence of evidence that the school board had suspended in bad faith.[105] A school rule that required students with knowledge of infractions by other students to report to the school authorities was held to be reasonable, as was the suspension of a student who refused to "snitch."[106]

This broad authority granted school boards and schools also extended to student conduct beyond the school grounds, as long as this conduct was significantly related to the operation of the school. Therefore, in one case, a school board could prohibit students from playing football off the school grounds where they did so in the school's name.[107] In another case, a principal was judged to have the authority to punish a schoolboy who had returned home after school, but who then came from his home to harass female classmates who were returning to their homes.[108]

Governed by whether it met the school's needs in reasonableness and good faith, a school board decision concerning a matter within its jurisdiction was considered final and not subject to question by either court or jury.[109] And at least one court denied mandamus where a complaining student had not exhausted the opportunity for appeal provided within the state educational hierarchy.[110] Only if evidence of a clear abuse of authority was shown, would a court intervene. One area, however, that has remained the exclusive prerogative of educators has been the determination of academic performance and imposition of academic sanction or award.[111]

Some legislative enactments included hearings for expulsions. Failure to meet the statutory requirements for a hearing could result in tort liability. Thus, even though the hearing required was not meant to be formal,[112] failure to hold a hearing to determine the facts was considered a breach of good faith sufficient to trigger judicial scrutiny and to impose liability.[113] These procedural provisions were only statutory, and would not achieve federal constitutional stature until the 1960s.[114] In fact, the 1926 case of *Flory v. Smith* confidently proclaimed that no property right to an education existed protectable by the Fourteenth Amendment to the federal Constitution.[115]

Corporal Punishment and the Changing Status of In Loco Parentis

Corporal punishment has persisted through the decades since the Civil War, as has a qualified judicial approval of its use. Unlike suspension and expulsion, the use of corporal punishment has traditionally been confined to teachers and principals.[116] Like suspension and expulsion, corporal punishment has come to be limited by legislative enactment and administrative regulation. However, applicable statutes have adopted common law doctrines; and where statutes are absent or vague, the courts have continued to rely on common law precedent. Principally, that precedent has consisted of doctrines enunciated by the initial cases of *State v. Pendergrass* and *Lander v. Seaver*.[117]

The *Pendergrass* malice rule persisted in some form until as recently as

1961.[118] Where it has recently appeared, it has done so in combination with the *Lander* reasonableness rule.[119] This is so even though in 1893 the *Michigan Law Register* spoke of the *Lander* rule as superseding the malice formula, and representing a more refined approach to corporal punishment.[120] The historical reason for this eventual mixing of the *Pendergrass* and *Lander* formulae is explained by the distinction that the courts perceived between the two cases in the fact that *Pendergrass* was a criminal assault and battery case, whereas *Lander* was an action for damages for tortious assault and battery.[121] Thus cases since *Lander* have followed *Pendergrass* where the charge is criminal,[122] and *Lander* where it is civil.[123] By 1937 some courts were combining the two doctrines into a configuration that would convict or hold liable a teacher only if the teacher's punishment of a student could be shown to be both unreasonable and malicious.[124] This development defied the original intent of the *Lander* holding, that an educator be held civilly liable or be convicted upon a criminal charge if the jury found from consideration of the surrounding circumstances that the punishment was unreasonable, malicious intent being only probative and not compulsory.

Other aspects of corporal punishment that have developed in the years between 1865 and 1950 are: 1) a teacher will be held guilty of criminal homicide for the death of a student who has been excessively punished;[125] 2) unjustified corporal punishment can serve as an offset against a parent or a student for assault and battery;[126] and 3) an additional, but indirect, remedy against a teacher for abuse of disciplinary authority is discharge from employment.[127]

THE THIRD PERIOD: "REFORMATION"—ENTER THE FEDERAL COURTS

In 1953, with the case of *Brown v. Board of Education*,[128] the Supreme Court of the United States announced its intent to supervise directly the affairs of the public school, at least in the area of racial segregation. Since that landmark case, a cascade of decisions has issued from the federal courts.[129] Of course, pursuant to *Brown*, the area into which the federal courts have been the most intrusive is the racial composition of the schools. The federal courts also have been accused of imposing themselves upon the area of student discipline. However, placed in the historical context recited above, the doctrinal changes pronounced by the Supreme Court in the area of student discipline have not been overly dramatic.

Parental Rights and the Rejection of Homogenization

The entrance of the federal courts upon the educational scene really begins in the 1920s, when the Supreme Court decided the cases of *Meyer v. Ne-*

braska[130] and *Pierce v. Society of Sisters*.[131] These two cases, which represent an early judicial skepticism of any governmental interference with the "rights" of citizens, embodied the tacit rejection of the common school reformers' zeal to homogenize the population by the imposition of a uniform and consistent educational program.

In *Meyer* the Supreme Court considered laws that between 1917 and 1921 had been enacted in thirty states, requiring all public school instruction to be in English. The specific law under consideration was a Nebraska statute that prohibited the teaching of any subject in a private, denominational, parochial, or public school in any language but English, and that prohibited even the teaching of foreign languages to any child who had not completed the eighth grade. The Supreme Court ruled that such a law was unconstitutional as a violation of the due process clause of the Fourteenth Amendment. The statute kept teachers from engaging in their "liberty" to make contracts to engage in the common occupations of life—Meyer being a German teacher in a Lutheran school—and it infringed upon the liberty of parents to educate their children as they saw fit. Though the Court found the state capable of making laws to compel the attendance of children at some school, and of making reasonable regulations for all schools, including the prescription of curriculum of institutions it supports, the state could not unreasonably interfere with the religious and private rights of parents to seek the kind of education they desire for their children, as it had done so in this case.[132] In dissent, Justices Holmes and Sutherland protested that the state did have the right to take appropriate measures to maintain the common welfare through using education as a means of preserving political unity.[133]

In *Pierce* a Roman Catholic teaching order brought suit against the state of Oregon to contest an initiative passed in 1922 that required all children of the state between ages eight and sixteen to attend public schools. Those who wished to attend private schools were required by this law to obtain permission, after examination, from the county superintendent of schools.[134] Over arguments that the public schools had to be preserved as the palladium of the republic, promoting the common good by countering the divisiveness created by the maintenance of parochial schools by religious groups and private schools by the wealthy, the Supreme Court unanimously held the state law to be unconstitutional. Also within the scope of Fourteenth Amendment substantive due process, this holding was based upon the grounds that the state could not deprive parents of the right to send their children to a private or religious school, so long as such a school was not inherently harmful to the child or the state, and so long as it met reasonable standards set by the state for curriculum and teacher qualification. The Court concluded:

As often heretofore pointed out, rights guaranteed by the Constitution may not be abridged by legislation which has no reasonable relation to

some purpose within the competency of the State. The fundamental
theory of liberty upon which all governments in this Union repose ex-
cludes any general power of the State to standardize its children by
forcing them to accept instruction from public teachers only. The child
is not the mere creature of the State; those who nurture him and direct
his destiny have the right, coupled with the high duty, to recognize and
prepare him for additional obligations.[135]

In response to the vindication of private rights represented by *Meyer*
and *Pierce,* state courts enthusiastically struck down school board regulations on the grounds that they went beyond the scope of the power delegated by state laws to school boards.[136] But, as noted by Professor Goldstein, this judicial skepticism and scrutiny of governmental action in the
area of education, eventually gave way to a general judicial deference to
administrative and other decision making.[137] The New Deal process, which
slowly seemed to extricate the country from the depths of the Great
Depression, also promoted an unquestioning faith in administrators and
specialists.

Judicial deference was reinforced in the school context by a specific faith
in the quality of American education. Thus, school regulations were
consistently upheld on the ground that they were not 'clearly arbitrary
and unreasonable,' although courts never explored whether or not the
rules performed a proper educational function. Moreover, even if a
court did inquire into the purposes and objectives of the rule, it would
invariably accept without question the school administration's conjec-
tures about the dangers to which the educational process would have
been exposed had the regulations in question not been adopted and
enforced.[138]

Yet recently the public and the judiciary have swung back to the initial
skepticism represented by *Meyer, Pierce* and their progeny. This skepticism has derived from the apparent failure of the professional administrators and specialists to attain their declared goals, and the apparent dehu-
manization of the groups of people they have sought to help.[139] In addition,
the faith in the ability of public education to educate has diminished. We
also seem to be experiencing the heyday of the individualism described by
the public school advocates of the turn of the century. Though the country's population is as diverse as before, the original mission of the public
school to weld those diverse parts into a homogeneous whole has given
way to a theory of self-actualization, in an age when individual constitutional rights have become the abiding concern of the federal and state judiciary.[140] The impact of this constitutionalism upon public education has
occurred in a number of areas. In 1954, with *Brown v. Board of Education,* the federal judiciary assumed a direct role in the desegregation of
public schools. Goldstein points to *Brown* as a significant step towards the
judiciary's later responsiveness in other areas: "It is not surprising that

their involvement in segregation problems made the courts more responsive to other problems of public education."[141] Another significant step occurred with the *In re Gault* decision.[142] There the Supreme Court declared that "whatever may be their precise impact neither the Fourteenth Amendment nor the Bill of Rights is for adults alone."[143] The most explicit application of this idea—that children enjoy constitutional rights akin to their parents'—to the educational context came in *Tinker v. Des Moines Independent Community School District*, decided in 1969, two years after *Gault*. There the Supreme Court declared that the public school student comes to school clothed with constitutional rights, and that these rights are not left at "the school house gate."[144] *Tinker* involved First Amendment rights, but the extension of its advocacy of constitutional rights for public school students to other areas of the public educational experience is the subject of the next chapter.

SUMMARY

This chapter reviewed the historical development of students' rights. There it was seen that the contemporary legal response to student discipline must rest upon several historical themes: the social consensus of what constitutes acceptable human activity and behavior; the perception of what the role of "common" education is in the reinforcement of that activity or behavior; the identity of the child vis-a-vis adults; the educational theories that grow out of that identity and, in turn, help define it; and the acceptable social sanctions for misbehavior. This chapter also charted the rise and fall of the doctrine of *in loco parentis* in the face of the early common-law remedies for children and parents against teachers and administrators for disciplinary abuses and the later recognition of childrens' rights under the federal Constitution.

REFERENCES

1. *See* Tinker v. Des Moines Independent Community School District, 393 U.S. 503, 506 (1969).
2. John C. Hogan, *The Schools, the Courts and the Public Interest* (Lexington, Mass: D. C. Heath, 1974), pp. 5–6.
3. 411 U.S. 1 (1973).
4. *See generally* C. Tribe, *American Constitutional Law* (1978).
5. *See generally* John Barnard and David Burner, eds., *The American Experience in Education* (New York: Franklin Watts, 1975); R. Freeman Butts and Lawrence A. Cremin, *A History of Education in American Culture* (New York: Henry Holt & Co., 1953).
6. *See* Sheldon S. Cohen, *A History of Colonial Education; 1607–1776, Studies in the History of American Education Series* (New York: John Wiley and

Sons, 1974), pp. 7–30. *See also*, Lawrence A. Cremin, *American Education, The Colonial Experience: 1607–1783* (New York: Harper & Row, 1970), pp. 109–12.

7. Cohen, pp. 30–36.
8. Cremin, pp. 123–37, 192–95.
9. Perry Miller, *The New England Mind, The Seventeenth Century* (New York: MacMillan, 1939), pp. 73–77.
10. Miller, pp. 101–102.
11. Cohen, pp. 51–54, 159–61, 169–70, 176–79, 190–91.
12. *Id.*, pp. 109–18.
13. *Id.*, pp. 52–58.
14. *Id.*, pp. 44–45.
15. *Id.*, pp. 45–46.
16. Quoted at *Id.*, pp. 47–48.
17. *Id.*, pp. 48–52.
18. Cremin, pp. 126–29.
19. Cohen, p. 51.
20. *See* Robert Francis Seybolt, *Apprenticeship and Apprenticeship Education in Colonial New England and New York, American Education: Its Men, Ideas, and Institutions* (New York: Arno Press, 1969) p. 38.
21. Cremin, pp. 126–36.
22. Massachusetts Records, III (1854), 101, in Robert H. Bremner, ed., *Children and Youth in America, A Documentary History*, 2 vols. (Cambridge, Mass.: Harvard University Press, 1970), p. 447.
23. Cohen, pp. 39–40.
24. Sanford Fleming, *Children and Puritanism, American Education: Its Men, Ideas, and Institutions* (New York: Arno Press, 1969), pp. 60–62.
25. William Perkins, *Christian Oeconomie* (London, 1609), p. 164, in Bremner, 1:27.
26. Proverbs 23: 13–14.
27. Cohen, pp. 59–60.
28. Seybolt, pp. 28–29.
29. Records and Files of the Quarterly Courts of Essex County, IV (Salem, 1914), 200, in Bremner, 1:108.
30. Records of the Suffolk County Court, 1671–1680, in SSM Publications XXIX (1933), 155, in Bremner, 1:109.
31. Records of Essex County, VII (1921), 302–3, in Bremner, 1:124.
32. L. H. Butterfield, ed., Letters of Benjamin Rush, 2 vols. (Princeton, N. J.: Princeton University Press, 1951), 1:388 in Lawrence A. Cremin, *Traditions of American Education* (New York: Basic Books, 1977), p. 42.
33. *See generally* R. Freeman Butts, *Public Education in the United States: From Revolution to Reform* (New York: Holt, Rinehart and Winston, 1978); R. L. Church & Michael W. Sedlak, *Education in the United States: An Interpretive History* (New York: The Free Press, 1976); David Madsen, *Early National Education: 1776–1830, Studies in the History of American Education Series* (New York: John Wiley & Sons, 1974).
34. Madsen, p. 4.
35. *Id.*, pp. 17–49; Cremin, pp. 41–87.
36. Madsen, pp. 19–20.
37. *Id.*, pp. 23–26.
38. *Id.*, p. 84.
39. *Id.*, pp. 17–49.
40. *Id.*, pp. 83–92.
41. *Id.*

42. Warren Burton, *The District School As It Was* (Boston: Carter, Hendee & Co., 1833).
43. For the source of the last three paragraphs see Burton, pp. 24–26, 42–45, 116–23.
44. Frederick M. Binder, *The Age of the Common School, 1830–1865, Studies in the History of American Education Series* (New York: John Wiley & Sons, 1974), pp. 3–9.
45. Bernard Wishy, *The Child and the Republic: The Dawn of Modern American Child Nurture* (Philadelphia: University of Pennsylvania Press, 1968), p. 17.
46. *Id.*, pp. 11–23.
47. Horace Bushnell, *Views of Christian Nurture* (Hartford, Connecticut: Hart, 1847).
48. Wishy, p. 22.
49. Binder, pp. 19–20.
50. *Id.*, pp. 42–54.
51. *Id.*, pp. 57–70.
52. *Id.*, pp. 76–83.
53. *Id.*, pp. 90–99.
54. *Id.*, pp. 140–41.
55. *Id.*, pp. 74–76.
56. *Id.*, p. 78.
57. James P. Jewett, *The Fight Against Corporal Punishment in American Schools.* 4 History of Ed. J. 2–3 (1952).
58. J. Orville Taylor, *The District School* (New York: Harper & Row, 1834), p. 99.
59. Jewett, p. 4.
60. *Id.*, pp. 5-8.
61. Boston School Comittee, *Rules of the School Committee and Regulations of the Public Schools*, 1841, p. 11, quoted in Jewett, 4 History of Ed. J. at 8.
62. *Id.*, pp. 8–9.
63. 19 N.C. 365 (1837).
64. *Id.* at 366.
65. *Id.* at 366.
66. *Id.* at 367.
67. *Id.* at 366.
68. *Id.* at 368.
69. *See, e.g.,* Commonwealth v. Seed, 5 Clark 78, 4 Am. Law J. (N.S.) 137 (Pa. 1852); State v. Ward, 1 Kan. L.J. 370 (Kan. 1855).
70. 4 Ind. 290 (1853).
71. *Id.*, pp. 292–93.
72. 4 Grey 36 (Mass. 1855).
73. 32 Vt. 114 (1859).
74. *Id.* at 114–19.
75. 1 W. Blackstone, Commentaries 453.
76. 32 Vt. at 123.
77. *Id.* at 122.
78. *Id.* at 123–24.
79. *Id.* at 124.
80. W. P. Borland, *The Law of Schoolmaster and Pupil as to Punishment*, 2 Mich. L.J. 198 (1893).
81. *Id.* at 201.
82. *Id.*
83. 38 Me. 379, 61 Am. Dec. 256 (1854).
84. *Id.* at 387, 61 Am. Dec. at 263.

85. *Id.*
86. *Id.* at 393, 61 Am. Dec. at 259.
87. *Id.* at 394, 61 Am. Dec. at 260.
88. *Id.* at 413, 61 Am. Dec. at 275.
89. *See generally* Patricia A. Graham, *Community and Class in American Education, 1865–1918, Studies in the History of American Education Series* (New York: John Wiley & Sons, 1974).
90. *Id.* at 7–8.
91. *Id.* at 16–17.
92. *See generally* S. R. Goldstein, *The Scope and Sources of School Board Authority to Regulate Student Conduct and Status,* 117 U. of Pa. L. Rev. 373 (1969).
93. See R. Freeman Butts, *Public Education in the United States: From Revolution to Reform* (New York: Holt, Rinehart and Winston, 1978). pp. 95–96.
94. *Id.* at 85–86.
95. *See, e.g.,* Flory v. Smith, 145 Va. 164, 134 S.E. 360 (1926). *See also* B. E. Packard, *The Lawyer in the School-room,* 7 Maine L. Rev. 176 (1914).
96. Murphy v. Board of Dir. Indep. Dist., 30 Iowa 429 (1871). *But cf.* State ex rel. Burpee v. Burton, 45 Wis. 150, 30 Am. Rep. 706 (1878) (teacher has inherent power *in loco parentis* to suspend).
97. 25 Wis. 59, 17 Am. Rep. 471 (1874). *Cf.* State ex rel. Andrew v. Webber, 58 Am. Rep. 30, 8 N.E. 708 (Ind. 1886) (statutory authority for proposition that parental desires as to curriculum, when only arbitrary and without good reason, must yield to school board authority).
98. See Board of Education of Cartersville v. Purse, 101 Ga. 422, 28 S.E. 896 (1897).

    The law providing for a public-school system was not intended to create any new right in, or give any new remedy to, a child. It being settled that the presence of the child in school depends absolutely upon the consent and will of the parent, the school authorities are justifiable [*sic*] in dealing with the child in light of this fact.

    101 Ga. at 433, 28 S.E. at 900.
99. Hardwick v. Board of School Trustees, 54 Cal. App. 696, 205 P. 49 (1921).
100. Wright v. Board of Education, 295 Mo. 466, 246 S.W. 43 (1922). See also Nutt v. Board of Educ., 128 Kan. 507, 278 P. 1065 (1929) (overturned expulsion of married girl who was expelled under statutory authority that school authorities may expel a student who becomes undesirable from physical malady or moral obloquy).
101. *See, e.g.,* Leoles v. Landers, 184 Ga. 580, 192 S.E. 218 (1937) (school has authority to compel devotion to the flag); People ex rel. Fish v. Sandstrom, 279 N.Y. 523, 18 N.E.2d 840 (1939) (flag salute); Shinn v. Barrow, 121 S.W.2d 450 (Tex. Ct. Civ. App. 1938) (flag salute).
102. *See, e.g.,* State ex rel. Burpee v. Burton, 45 Wis. 150, 30 Am. Rep. 706 (1878) ("While the principal or teacher in charge of a public school is subordinate to the school board or board of education of his district or city, and must enforce rules and regulations adopted by the board for the government of the school, and execute all its lawful orders in that behalf, he does not derive all his power and authority in the school and over his pupils from the affirmative action of the board. He stands for the time being *in loco parentis* to his pupils, and because of that relation he must necessarily exercise authority over them in many things concerning which the board may have remained silent."); Fertich v. Michener, 111 Ind. 472, 11 N.E. 605 (1887) (whether a rule is reasonable or valid is a question of law for decision of the

court, not a question of fact for the jury); Churchill v. Fewkes, 13 Ill. App. (13 Bradw.) 520 (1883) ("The general principle is established by an almost uniform course of decisions, that a public officer, when acting in good faith, is never to be held liable for an erroneous judgment in a matter submitted to his determination").

103. 45 Wis. at 151, 30 Am. Rep. 707 ("The specific cause for the suspension is unknown to the relator, except that the defendant informed him that it was 'general bad conduct' of his son").

104. Cross v. Board of Trustees, 129 Ky. 35, 110 S.W. 346 (1908) (student refused to play role in school play).

105. McCormick v. Burt, 95 Ill. 263, 35 Am. Rep. 163 (1880).

106. Board of Education v. Helston, 32 Ill. App. 300 (1890).

107. Kinzer v. Directors Indep. Sch. Dist., 129 Iowa 441, N.W. 686 (1906).

108. O'Rourke v. Walker, 102 Conn. 130, 128 A. 25 (1925).

109. See, e.g., Watson v. Cambridge, 157 Mass. 561, 32 N.E. 864 (1893) (student excluded because of such "weak mind" that it was perceived that he did not benefit from instruction sufficiently to justify his attendance) (jury composed of men of no special fitness to decide educational questions should not be permitted to say that the school committee's answer is wrong); Cross v. Board of Trustees, 129 Ky. 35, 110 S.W. 246 (1908) (high duty upon trustees to maintain integrity of common school system by enforcement of wholesome and reasonable discipline, and court will never interfere while they act within their legal province).

110. Lamme v. Buckland, 84 Colo. 240, 269 P. 15 (1928).

111. See, e.g., Barnard v. Shelburne, 216 Mass. 19, 102 N.E. 1095 (1913) (high school student expelled according to rule that called for exclusions of freshmen whose standing was below 60 percent in two or more subjects).

112. See, e.g., Vermillion v. Englehardt, 78 Neb. 107, 110 N.W. 736 (1907) (the hearing required by statute is administrative, not judicial, hearing; notice not required); Morrison v. City of Lawrence, 181 Mass. 127, 63 N.E. 400 (1902) (as long as school committee acted in good faith, failure to compel fellow students of accused to give testimony at hearing not sufficient to give rise to cause of action).

113. Bishop v. Rowley, 165 Mass. 460, 43 N.E. 191 (1896) ("If a school committee acts in good faith in determining the facts in a particular case, its decision cannot be revised by the courts. . . . But the power of exclusion is not merely arbitrary power, to be exercised without ascertaining the facts.) (facts of case in dispute).

114. See Chapter Three.

115. 145 Va. 164, 134 S.E. 360 (1926).

116. See, e.g., Rogers v. Board of Educ., 125 W. Va. 579, 25 S.E.2d 537 (1943) (professionally trained teachers, principals and superintendents and not members of boards of education have exclusive control of methods of instruction and discipline); Prendergast v. Masterson, 196 S.W. 246 (Tex. Ct. Civ. App. 1917) (superintendent of schools could not chastise student because he was not considered a "teacher" within the meaning of the law that authorizes a teacher to chastise his pupil).

117. State v. Pendergrass, 19 N.C. 365, 31 Am. Dec. 416 (1837); Lander v. Seaver, 32 Vt. 114, 76 Am. Dec. 156 (1859).

118. See Tinkham v. Kole, 110 N.W.2d 258 (Iowa 1961).

119. While teachers are clothed with a discretionary authority with respect to the infliction of corporal punishment on their pupils, the punishment must be reasonable and confined within the bounds of moderation; that is, it must not be cruel or excessive, and

the teacher must not act wantonly or from malice or passion. . . . [N]o precise rule can be laid down as to what is excessive or unreasonable punishment. Each case must depend on its own circumstances.

Id. at 261 (quoting 47 Am. Jr. *Schools* § 175 (1943)). See also Andreozzi v. Rubano, 145 Conn. 280, 141 A.2d 639 (1958).

120. W. P. Borland, *supra* note 80, at 201.
121. 19 N.C. at 365; 32 Vt. at 114.
122. *See* State v. Thornton, 136 N.C. 610, 48 S.E. 602 (1904); Holmes v. State, 39 So. 569 (Ala. 1905); Dodd v. State, 94 Ark. 297, 126 S.W. 834 (1910); Roberson v. State, 22 Ala. App. 413, 116 So. 317 (1928).
123. *See* Patterson v. Nutter, 78 Me. 509, 7 A. 273 (1886); Haycraft v. Grigsby, 99 Mo. App. 354 (1901); Calway v. Williamson, 130 Conn. 575, 36 A.2d 377 (1944). *But see* Vanvactor v. State, 113 Ind. 276, 15 N.E. 341 (1888) (criminal assault and battery case following *Lander*).
124. *See* Harris v. Galilley, 125 Pa. Super. 505, 189 A. 779 (1937); People v. Mummert, 183 Misc. 243, 50 N.Y.S.2d 699 (1944); Marlar v. Bill, 181 Tenn. 100, 178 S.W.2d 634 (1944); Suits v. Glover, 71 So. 2d 49 (Ala. 1954).
125. Johnson v. Commonwealth, 69 S.E. 1104 (Va. 1911).
126. *See* Cook v. Neely 143 Mo. App. 632, 128 S.W. 233 (1910); State v. Loftin, 230 S.W. 338 (1921).
127. *See, e.g.*, Houeye v. St. Helena Parish School Board, 223 La. 966, 67 So.2d 553 (1953).
128. 347 U. S. 483 (1954) (Brown I).
129. *Compare* 26 Sixth Dec. Dig. *Schools & School Dist.* §§ 169–77 (1946–1956) *with* 36 Eighth Dec. Dig. *Schools & School Dist.* §§ 169–77 (1966–1976).
130. 262 U.S. 390 (1923).
131. 268 U.S. 510 (1928).
132. 262 U.S. at 396–403.
133. 262 U.S. at 403 (opinion printed at 262 U. S. 412–413).
134. 268 U.S. at 530–31.
135. *Id.* at 535.
136. Goldstein, *Reflections on Developing Trends in the Law of Student Rights,* 118 U. Pa. L. Rev. 612, 612–13 (1970). (courts struck down school board regulations concerning compulsory vaccinations, membership in secret societies, and penalities for accidentally damaging school property).
137. *Id.* at 613.
138. *Id.*
139. *Id.*
140. There is no doubt, however, that the schools are still perceived as socializing agents, inculcating in the young some narrow set of values that preserves society. Individualism is simply a dominant theme. Students involved in the very social exercise of education are nonetheless to exercise individual choice in what they will learn. As Goldstein states:

There is a growing recognition that students cannot be regarded as merely passive vessels into which education is poured, but must, at least to a limited extent, be regarded as active participants in the educational process. To oversimplify, education can be divided, for analytical purposes, into two models: prescriptive and analytic. In the prescriptive model, information and accepted truths are furnished to a theoretically passive, absorbent student. The teacher's role is to convey these truths rather than to create new wisdom. Both teacher and student appear almost automatons. Analytic education, however, signifies the examination of data and values in a way that involves the student and teacher as active participants in the search for truth. While these polar models represent only a theoretical paradigm that can never exist in pure form, we have traditionally conceived of pre-college public education as essentially prescriptive, and college and post-graduate students as analytic.

Paradoxically, and more important from the point of view of student "rights," a strong movement exists at the moment to make high schools more analytic. *Id.* at 615–16.

141. *Id.* at 614.
142. 387 U.S. 1 (1967).
143. *Id.* at 13.
144. 393 U.S. 503, 506 (1969).

CHAPTER THREE

Students in the Schools: A Case Analysis of Rights, Responsibilities, and Remedies

INTRODUCTION

This chapter brings us into the contemporary climate of students' rights: a climate of constitutional enthusiasm. In the past two decades there has evolved a fervent advocacy of individual rights, a corollary of which has been the advocacy of childrens' rights under the Constitution.[1] Consequently, the schoolhouse, long the dominion of teachers and administrators, has been invaded by the federal courts, and the disciplinary hand of teachers and administrators has been checked by constitutional doctrines. Primary among these doctrines in the area of school discipline is due process. Due process, which involves substantive and procedural rights accruing to individuals who are affected by government activity, will be reviewed briefly before our investigation of the salient cases that define contemporary school discipline.

A FEW CONSTITUTIONAL PRINCIPLES

Due Process

Though due process matters will later be dealt with at a greater length, it will be helpful to attempt a definition of the term *due process* in order that the cases to be reviewed will be better understood. Due process of law is most simply a principle of fundamental fairness in dealing with the inevitable deprivations that occur in the course of governmental activity.[2]

The substantive element of the due process concept is that if certain rights involving individuals' dignity have been determined to be "fundamental," these rights cannot, in the absence of a countervailing governmental purpose, be subordinated to the social order.[3]

The procedural element consists of institutional requirements, or checks—normally notice and a hearing—that must attend any governmental infringement or deprivation of personal rights generally comprised in the categories of "life," "liberty," and "property." Procedural safeguards, as stated by the Supreme Court, are primarily intended to afford the individual "the right to be heard before being condemned to suffer grievous loss of any kind" that results from governmental choices.[4] Procedural due process corresponds to the nature of the threatened loss: it is a flexible principle that depends upon the range of personal interests involved that qualify as "life," "liberty," or "property."[5] For example, the discipline aimed at a disruptive student reasonably requires fundamental fairness. The elements of that fairness are the procedural safeguards of notice and a hearing. The exact nature of these depends upon the degree of deprivation contemplated by the disciplinary action.[6] Whether the hearing provided consists of a brief interchange between student and disciplinarian, or a full-blown adversarial procedure will depend upon whether the deprivation intended is after-school detention or transfer to a special educational facility.[7]

There exists two views of the purpose of due process: the intrinsic view and the instrumental view.[8] These are worthy of brief consideration for their implications in the educational environment. The first view contemplates that there is intrinsic value in the due process right to be heard. A hearing respects the dignity of individuals by allowing them to voice their concerns in the process of a decision that may vitally affect them. In relation to the maintenance of social order, an individual is considered a person rather than a thing. Accordingly, a person's social sense is affected in such a hearing: the feeling, so important to popular government, is generated "that justice has been done."[9] The instrumental approach, on the other hand, focuses upon the legal content of due process. By this view, due process is required to avoid " 'substantially unfair or mistaken deprivations' of the entitlements conferred by the law upon individuals."[10] The principles of due process are therefore constitutionally identified and valued for their role in the consistent enforcement of society's rules of conduct and in the fair distribution of the benefits conferred by the state. As Professor Tribe states, the instrumental justification of due process is "less to assure participation than to use participation to assure accuracy."[11] The Supreme Court has not adopted the intrinsic view, but instead has emphasized the instrumental purpose of due process—necessarily because an emphasis on the intrinsic value of due process would require of the courts a political role unintended by the Constitution.[12] Nonetheless, the intrinsic qualities of due process are a certain result of any fair procedure, and should be considered as an important effect of procedures that accompany student discipline.

The Fourteenth Amendment and Selective
Incorporation of the Bill of Rights

Another matter of importance at the outset is the explication of the authority by which the federal courts enforce constitutional principles. There are two due process clauses in the Constitution: the first appears in the Fifth Amendment; the second appears in the Fourteenth Amendment. As a matter of constitutional history, the Fifth Amendment was adopted as part of the Bill of Rights in 1791 and was meant to protect citizens of the union against federal impositions.[13] The Fourteenth Amendment was adopted in 1868 in response to the intransigence of the states in extending human liberties to blacks. With its adoption, the federal courts gained the authority to act as watchdogs over the states—at least as far as blacks and the utterly vague term "due process" were concerned.[14]

Therefore, the authority of the federal courts to enforce the constitutional rights of school students rests upon the authority extended by the Fourteenth Amendment to insure that any state-sponsored activity does not deprive "any person of life, liberty, or property, without due process of law."[15] Just what due process the federal judiciary would enforce against the states has been a matter of controversy from the outset, but suffice it to say that the Supreme Court has given substantive content to Fourteenth Amendment due process by "selective incorporation" of the other constitutionally prescribed liberties of the Bill of Rights.[16] Rights absorbed into the Fourteenth Amendment due process clause include the right to just compensation;[17] the First Amendment freedoms of speech,[18] press,[19] assembly, [20] petition,[21] free exercise of religion,[22] and nonestablishment of religion;[23] the Fourth Amendment rights to be free of unreasonable search and seizure[24] and to exclude from criminal trials evidence illegally seized;[25] the Fifth Amendment rights to be free of compelled self-incrimination[26] and double jeopardy;[27] the Sixth Amendment rights to counsel, [28] to a speedy[29] and public[30] trial before a jury,[31] to an opportunity to confront opposing witnesses,[32] and to compulsory process for the purpose of obtaining favorable witnesses;[33] and the Eighth Amendement right to be free from cruel and unusual punishments.[34]

In the process of outlining the content of the due process clause, the Court has relied upon reasoning that its search was for the "principle[s] of justice so rooted in the tradition and conscience of our people as to be ranked as "fundamental" and thus "implicit in the concept of ordered liberty."[35] It has been argued that these principles of justice include and are confined to those enumerated in the Bill of Rights.[36] But it has also been argued that the Fourteenth Amendment must go beyond the Bill of Rights and comprehend other liberties.[37] It has been strongly asserted that:

> [T]he full scope of the liberty guaranteed by the Due Process Clause cannot be found in or limited by the precise terms of the specific guarantees elsewhere provided in the Constitution. This 'liberty' is not a series of isolated points pricked out in terms of the [rights enumerated in the Bill of Rights]. It is a rational continuum which, broadly speaking, includes a freedom from all substantial arbitrary impositions and purposeless restraints, . . . and which also recognizes . . . that certain interests require particularly careful scrutiny of the state needs asserted to justify their abridgement.[38]

Thus the Court has found due process rights to be protected in unenumerated aspects of liberty: the right to teach one's child a foreign language,[39] the right to send one's child to a private school,[40] the right to procreate,[41] the right to be free of certain bodily intrusions,[42] the right to travel abroad,[43] and the right to privacy in sexual matters.[44]

Compulsory Education As a Right

Initially, it is also important to understand to what degree the Supreme Court considers education—or the opportunity for education—to be a right. Though the statement of a right to compulsory education seems oxymoronic, education is considered by the law to be at once enforceable upon the populace as well as a "property" right to be protected by constitutional principles of due process. Both principles, education as right and compulsoriness, are products of the Common School Movement discussed in Chapter Two.[45] Though there is an interesting interplay between these two principles,[46] what is important for our purposes is the definition of the right to education.

State laws give such a definition. Every state constitution except Connecticut's contains a provision for public education, authorizing the legislature to establish and maintain a system of free public education.[47] The statutes enacted in response to these constitutional mandates provide for free public education for all resident children between certain ages.[48] Additionally, some state court decisions explain more specifically the legal right to an education. For example, the California Supreme Court, in the case of *Ward v. Flood*, described the right to an education as a property right deserving of the protection given legal rights in general:

> The advantage or benefit thereby vouchsafed to each child, of attending public school is therefore, one derived and secured to it under the highest sanction of positive law. It is therefore, a right—a legal right—as distinctively so as the vested right in property owned is a legal right, and as such is protected, and entitled to be protected by all the guarantees by which other legal rights are protected and secured to the possessor.[49]

Overarching declarations of the right to an education have been made by the Supreme Court of the United States. Yet, even with these declarations, the specific content of an educational right is less than clear. In *Brown v. Board of Education*,[50] the landmark school desegregation case, the Supreme Court applied the Fourteenth Amendment's equal protection clause to find state-sanctioned segregation in public schooling unconstitutional. On its way to finding that separate educational facilities are "inherently unequal," the Court explained the role and the right of education:

> Today, education is perhaps the most important function of state and local governments. Compulsory school attendance laws and the great

expenditures for education both demonstrate our recognition of the importance of education to our democratic society. It is required in the performance of our most basic public responsibilities, even service in the armed forces. It is the very foundation of good citizenship. Today it is a principal instrument in awakening the child to cultural values, in preparing him for later professional training, and in helping him to adjust normally to his environment. In these days, it is doubtful that any child may reasonably be expected to succeed in life if he is denied the opportunity of an education. Such an opportunity, where the state has undertaken to provide it, is a right which must be made available to all on equal terms.[51]

Despite this encomium, the Court later refused to find an absolute right to education in the case of *San Antonio Independent School District v. Rodriguez*.[52] There it is said that education is not a "fundamental right,"[53] a right of the magnitude that requires a necessary relationship between the state's depriving someone of the right and a "compelling" governmental purpose[54] in order for the deprivation to be found constitutional. Though recognizing the importance of the service of public education provided by the states, the Court was unwilling, for equal protection purposes, to find that education was a right of constitutional (i.e., fundamental) stature. Basic to its reasoning was the fact that "[e]ducation . . . is not among the rights afforded explicit protection under [the] Federal Constitution."[55]

Although the opportunity for education is not a right specifically protected by the Constitution, this is not to say that there is no protectable rights to education. If a state or local government provides educational services, it still must do so with some degree of continuity across the populace as a whole. (Read broadly, *Brown* indicates that this continuity is accomplished partially by racial integration.)[56] And even if not a fundamental right, as a benefit extended by government, the opportunity for education cannot be revoked capriciously. Before any governmental benefit can be interfered with by governmental action, it is necessary to comply with individual rights to due process.[57] This kind of due process—"procedural due process"—generally requires notice of a potential governmental imposition and its grounds, as well as a hearing in which the individual can contest both imposition and grounds. (The dynamics of procedural due process will become clearer in our inspection of the landmark school due process case, *Goss v. Lopez*, below.)[58]

If education were a "fundamental right," any governmental imposition on it, even if accompanied by procedural due process, would have to be justified by a "compelling" state interest and would probably be found unconstitutional. The imposition would be found unconstitutional because any deprivation of the right would require the "strict scrutiny" of the federal courts, and "strict scrutiny" has generally been fatal. This would mean a much greater degree of judicial intervention in educational decision making. The fact that the Court has declined to recognize education as a "fundamental right" indicates a certain measure of restraint and a judicial awareness that effective educational procedure requires the flexibility of spontaneous decision making and action, unconstrained by the possibility of constitutional enforcement.

A Word About the Dynamics of State and Federal Courts

It may be helpful to briefly define what roles the state and federal courts actually play in the educational process. Simply stated, the federal courts have jurisdiction over "federal questions"[59] that arise in the educational context. This jurisdiction derives from the Constitution itself where "the judicial Power" is described as "extend[ing] to all Cases, in Law and Equity, arising under [the] Constitution, the Laws of the United States, and Treaties."[60]

State courts, on the other hand, generally have jurisdiction over cases involving their own laws and constitutions. With a few exceptions,[61] a state may also consider federal questions. Should a state's highest court invalidate a federal law, there exists a right of appeal to the Supreme Court of the United States.[62] Similarly, there exists a right of appeal to the Supreme Court if a state statute is validated by a state's highest court in response to a controversy over its incompatibility with the federal constitution or federal laws.[63]

This overview is necessarily simplistic. For example, there is a superficial conflict between federal jurisdictional statutes. One statute purports to grant federal court jurisdiction over suits brought by individuals against states or their agencies only if there is a federal question and an amount in controversy of $10,000.[64] But another section of the federal statutes provides for federal court jurisdiction in the absence of an amount in controversy if the ground for suit is a violation of the Civil Rights Act[65] or a state deprivation of any "right, privilege or immunity secured by the Constitution of the United States or by any Act of Congress providing for equal rights of citizens or all persons within the jurisdiction of the United States."[66] However, for purposes of this analysis of rights and remedies in regard to student discipline, it is only necessary to understand that the traditional remedies for disciplinary abuses[67] will generally be attached only in the state courts. If those abuses can be described as violations of federal constitutional or statutory rights, remedy may be sought in either the state or federal courts.

STUDENT RIGHTS IN GENERAL

There has been a perennial conflict between education and individual rights. On one side of the conflict persists the doctrine of *in loco parentis*, which supports the notion that to maintain its effectiveness, education must be free of the enforcement of individual rights guaranteed to citizens in general. On the other side is the sentiment that individual freedoms must extend to all members of society, especially children, who should be given the opportunity to determine their own destiny.[68] Traditionally, the former notion was dominant and the educational sphere was preserved as the domain of educators—the specialists.[69] But contemporary sentiments favor the latter position, and the Supreme Court, though conceding that there is a necessity for flexibility and independence in school administration, has made it clear that the school is not a closed environment and that the student does not forsake individual rights by submitting to the educational process. The most epigrammatic declaration of this policy is in the 1969 case of *Tinker v. Des Moines Independent School District*.[70]

Within the Schoolhouse Gate: Tinker and the First Amendment

It was in *Tinker* that the Court said that students do not "shed their constitutional rights to freedom of speech or expression at the schoolhouse gate."[71] The Court also made this more general statement:

> In our system, state-operated schools may not be enclaves of totalitarianism. School officials do not possess absolute authority over their students. Students in school as well as out of school are "persons" under our Constitution. They are possessed of fundamental rights which the State must respect, just as they themselves must respect their obligations to the State.[72]

Of course these statements were made in the context of a First Amendment case. Mary Beth Tinker was one of a number of junior and senior high school students who engaged in a silent protest of the Vietnam war by wearing black armbands to school. The students' protest was part of a more general protest by them and their parents, decided upon and planned for at an earlier meeting at a private residence. Having learned of the group's intentions before the day of the protest, the principals of the schools the students attended met and adopted a policy that students wearing armbands would be asked to remove them. The policy also provided that if the student refused to remove the armband the student would be suspended until he or she returned without the armband. Tinker and others appeared at their schools wearing the armbands and were consequently sent home, where they remained until the time planned for wearing the armbands had passed.[73]

The Supreme Court held the suspensions to be violations of the students' First Amendment rights. For the reasons recited above and for the additional reason that schools are public places where public dialogue should occur,[74] the Court declared that more than "undifferentiated fear or

apprehension of disturbance" was required "to overcome the right to freedom of expression."[75] Only if the particular expression of an opinion could
be shown by the state in the person of school officials to be "materially"
disruptive of classwork, to be the cause of "substantial" disorder, or to be
an invasion of the rights of others, would school officials be justified in its
infringement.[76]

   Tinker is significant for the introduction of the notion that schoolchil-
dren do not forsake their constitutional rights in coming to school. This of
course does not necessarily mean that everything a child would be privileged to do off the school grounds may now be done on them. Though
students enjoys at school the same constitutional rights, in kind and degree, as they do elsewhere, once within the schoolhouse gate, students
may expect those rights to be subject to the peculiar necessities of the
communal enterprise of education. As *Tinker* clearly states, these constitutional rights comprehend First Amendment rights. As explained above,
First Amendment rights have been incorporated into the Fourteenth
Amendment; therefore, a state (or its school authorities) may not infringe
upon them without substantial justification—which justification is found in
the necessities of the educational process.

   But the Supreme Court's perception of educational necessity must depend upon its conception of education, its educational theory. Therefore,
the Court, while prescribing constitutional rights in the schoolhouse, must
engage in educational theorizing. This theorizing is well-illustrated by the
Tinker decision. The *Tinker* Court postulates that the educational process
must be tolerant of student expression, even in the form of dissent, until
it becomes disruptive of classwork or infringes upon the rights of others.
Thus the tolerance for student expression that has traditionally characterized the university, is required in *Tinker* for junior and senior high schools
as well.

   The distinction between traditional educational theory and that suggested by *Tinker* is explained by Professor Goldstein as the difference between prescriptive and analytic education.[77] Prescriptive education perceives the student as a "passive vessel" into which information and
accepted truths are poured; analytic education demands of the student participation with the teacher in the "search for truth." Analytical education
being more experiential, participation in dissent—the wearing of black
armbands—is to be encouraged because it is part of the exchange of ideas
that is at the heart of the First Amendment and is the ideal of classical
education. Though it may be argued that a junior or senior high school
student lacks the maturity and sophistication that make the exchange of
ideas a "search for truth," schools are nonetheless required to be tolerant
of student expression. As Justice Fortas said for the Court: "In our system,
students may not be regarded as closed-circuit recipients of only that
which the State chooses to communicate. They may not be confined to the
expression of those sentiments that are officially approved."[78] A discipli-

nary decision must therefore be sensitive to the potential infringement of First Amendment rights. The degree to which these rights of self-expression must bend to the necessities of the educational process is determined in the meaning of "materially and substantially interfering with . . . appropriate discipline in the operation of the school,"[79] to which we will now turn.

Many courts have struggled with the *Tinker* language that student conduct that would ordinarily be protected by the First Amendment may be infringed if school authorities can make a legitimate prediction that the conduct will cause a substantial disruption of the educational process. Courts have disagreed on the question of whether the prohibition of First Amendment activity can be justified when a disruption occurs as a reaction to the student activity, even though the activity itself is inoffensive. Clearly, if the conduct is itself disruptive it will come within the *Tinker* exception: if a student screams political diatribe during a class period, interrupting the teacher's presentation, the *Tinker* privilege may be overcome. But what if the student simply wears a political pin, or sports shoulder-length hair? This problem is represented by *Guzick v. Drebus*[80] and *Crews v. Cloncs*,[81] both federal courts of appeal cases.

Guzick represents the majority position that it is enough that disruption is caused by those who react to a certain student's conduct or appearance. This case involved a long-standing rule forbidding the wearing of buttons, badges, scarves, and other marks or apparel that identified students with a cause or bore messages unrelated to their education. The rule originated in response to disruptions caused in the past when fraternities competed for members. The rule persisted after fraternities were displaced by informal clubs, and the contemporary justification for the rule as pleaded before the court was that the defined racial populations in the school could flare into conflict with the wearing of buttons or apparel bearing racial symbols or messages. The prohibition was also explained by the reasoning that such symbols or messages "[magnified] the differences between students [encouraged] emphasis on these differences and [tended] to polarize the students into separate, distinct, and unfriendly groups."[82]

Though the button in question did not bear a radical message—it only announced an antiwar rally—the court of appeals upheld the school rule and Thomas Guzick's suspension. The court distinguished this case from *Tinker* in that the rule before it was one of long-standing, its genesis was an actual experience of disruption, and it had universal application. By contrast, the rule in *Tinker* was trumped up overnight and singled out only one symbol—black armbands—while allowing others to be worn. The *Guzick* case also was distinguished by a background of racial tension: "In our view," the court wrote, "school authorities should not be faulted for adhering to a relatively non-oppressive rule that will indeed serve our ultimate goal of meaningful integration of our public schools."[83] Given the school's specific experiences with disruption, the court upheld the finding that more than an "undifferentiated fear or apprehension" of disturbances justified the rule[84] and Guzick's suspension. This was so even though the potential disturbance was only in reaction to the wearing of a button or other symbol. And the universal prohibition was appropriate because "to allow some buttons and not others would create an unbearable burden of selection and enforcement."[85]

The *Crews* case, on the other hand, represents the proposition that the disturbance must comprise the actual conduct, not simply the reaction to it, to justify a school infringement of constitutional rights. In other words, disciplinary action should be directed towards the reactors, those who react, not towards the actor, the individual who is exercising freedom of expression. In *Crews,* the disciplined student was one who refused to abide by the school rules prescribing hairstyle. The court first found that he enjoyed a constitutional right to wear his hair the length he desired.[86] Though this right is not specifically a First Amendment right, the court grounded it in the right of privacy that is implicit in the " 'fundamental rights specifically mentioned in the first eight amendments.' "[87] The infringement of this constitutional right was not justified by the school's arguments that 1) Crews's hair actually caused distraction of other students and disturbance of the educational process and that 2) short hair was required for health and safety reasons. The second of these arguments was dismissed by the reasoning that the health and safety objectives could be accomplished by narrower rules and that girls, who apparently presented the same health and safety problems, were not affected by the regulation. The dismissal of the first argument illustrates the actor-reactor problem. Though there had been a showing of actual disturbance in response to Crews's hair length, the reaction to his constitutionally privileged conduct was not enough to justify the disciplinary measures taken against him.[88] "We agree with the sentiments voiced by Professor Chafee," the court wrote, "when he observed that it is absurd to punish a person 'because his neighbors have no self-control and cannot refrain from violence.' "[89]

In addition to the actor–reactor problem, there exists some question of what constitutes protectable First Amendment expression. For example, a federal district court found that leaflet distribution and button wearing by high school students for the purpose of boycotting a school candy drive as a protest of the school dress code was distinguishable from the conduct in *Tinker*. The candy drive boycott and dress code protest did not rise to the constitutional proportions of the *Tinker* protest, which involved an important national issue and was part of a national movement.[90] The court of appeals overturned such reasoning with this declaration: "That these policies may not directly affect the adult community or concern the nation as a whole is of no moment. . . . It is not for this or any other court to distinguish between issues and to select for constitutional protection only those which it feels are of sufficient social importance."[91]

Other areas of student conduct besides the wearing of buttons or long hair that may demand *Tinker* protection are student publications and student organizations.[92] Student publication involves First Amendment rights of self-expression; organization involves First Amendment rights of association. It is fairly clear that publication rights should be confined to student publications only. Students have been prohibited from distributing leaflets and soliciting funds for outside organizations who attempt to exploit the "captive audience" of the student community.[93] On the other hand, dissemination of student-produced materials—leaflets, newspapers, etc.— may not be prohibited unless it creates the disturbance by which *Tinker* justifies infringement.[94] This is true whether the publication occurs on or off the school grounds.[95] At least one appellate court has declared that criticism of the school administration or bad taste are insufficient to constitute the justifying disturbance.[96] The area of regulation of student organizations on the high school level is not as clearly defined. On the college level the Supreme Court has held that administrators could not prohibit the formation of a campus organization simply because they disagreed with the organization's stated objectives and feared disruption.[97] The college could, however, require that the organization state in advance its willingness to abide by reasonable campus law, since such a requirement does not impose an "impermissible condition on the students' associational rights."[98] Though there has been no similar statement of the rights of high school students to organize, the rules for colleges will likely be applied by analogy to high schools, since *Tinker* has postulated secondary schools to be a "public forum" akin to the college or university.

The Nonprocedural Right to Freedom from
Unreasonable Search and Seizure: Schools and the
Fourth Amendment

The Fourth Amendment right against unreasonable search and seizure fits within the *Tinker* logic: a student comes to school additionally clothed with a right against unreasonable search and seizure; however, this right may be subject to the special necessities of educational process. This principle is illustrated by a recent New York delinquency case, *In re Ronald B*.[99] In that case, Ronald, a high school student, was conversing with one of his school's officials in the school hallway. During the conversation another school official approached and told Ronald that he had been informed that Ronald had a gun. Ronald denied the allegation and refused to be searched. As he spoke with Ronald, the second official noticed that Ronald's hand was in his pocket, and he asked him to withdraw it. When Ronald made a sudden movement, the two officials grabbed his arm, and, upon withdrawing it from Ronald's pocket, saw that he was holding a .32 caliber pistol. Ballistics tests later showed the gun to be operable. In the resulting delinquency hearings, Ronald arqued that his Fourth Amendment rights to be free of unreasonable search and seizure were violated by the school officials' actions.[100]

In dismissing Ronald's argument, the court relied upon language from *Tinker*—"the court has repeatedly emphasized the need for affirming the comprehensive authority of the States and of school officials, consistent with fundamental constitutional safeguards, to prescribe and control conduct in the schools"[101]—to support the state's *in loco parentis* doctrine.[102] The court explained that even though the concept of *in loco parentis* was limited, it did allow school personnel to exercise such power, restraint, and correction over students as was reasonably necessary to facilitate the educational functions of the school. Acting upon suspicion only, a school official could take reasonable steps to remedy a dangerous situation:[103]

> A school is a special kind of place in which serious and dangerous wrongdoing is intolerable. Youngsters in a school, for their own sake, as well as that of their age peers in the school, may not be treated with the same circumspection required outside the school or to which self-sufficient adults are entitled.[104]

Searches that are unjustified, the court noted, are random ones that may psychologically harm a child.[105]

Similarly, it is clear that school officials, acting upon suspicion of a dangerous condition that threatens the safety of other students, may search student lockers.[106] A high school official has also been found to have the authority to consent to what would otherwise be an impermissible search by police officers.[107] Without the consent of a school official, or a waiver of right by the student, police use of seized evidence in a criminal prosecution is problematic. At least at the college level it has been held that in a search of a dormitory room by school officials and police in concert, evidence seized could at least stand as the basis for school disciplinary proceedings.[108] This was so because the special necessities of the educational environment required of school officials only a "reasonable belief" of impropriety to justify a search.[109] But without a warrant, and without probable cause based upon a reasonable view of the circumstances or the reliability of an informer, police officers could not use the seized evidence in a criminal proceeding.[110] Given the *in loco parentis* responsibilities of primary and secondary school officials for their charges, the application of these college principles to the primary and secondary school is improbable. Doubtless, upon something equal to or less than "reasonable belief," a public school official may search, seize, and discipline. Whether the school official's search and its products may in turn be the basis for criminal prosecution is uncertain.[111] Though there is logic to the holding that school officials, by virtue of their responsibility for students and school property, may consent to a police search of a student locker, it also may be argued that restrictions upon police access to a high school locker should be more strict than those placed upon a college dormitory room, since educators have become more tolerant of youthful folly and since students may become hardened by this use of criminal procedure. But then it may be more forcefully argued that youth correction should be the role of the juvenile courts, not the schools. Nonetheless, police officials looking for a prosecution may be well adivsed to apply the conventional "adult" standards of probable cause to the search of students or their lockers, whether or not assisted by school officials.

Procedural Rights: The Rest of Due Process

As explained above, the due process clause of the Fourteenth Amendment incorporates procedural and nonprocedural elements of the Bill of Rights. The substantive-procedural requisites of primary and secondary school disciplinary methodology may include rights that correspond to those constitutionally reserved for criminal proceedings: the Fifth Amendment rights against self-incrimination and double jeopardy; the Sixth Amendment rights to counsel and to confront opposing witnesses; and the Eighth Amendment right to be free from cruel and unusual punishments. Remember that in addition to these substantive rights, the due process clause itself comprehends rights of fair procedure. Procedural due process classically means notice and a hearing before the governmental deprivation of "life," "liberty," or "property" interests. But procedural due process is a flexible concept that demands only those safeguards adequate to protect the individual interest involved while at the same time accounting for the opposing governmental interests. Thus, procedural due process required of school administrators does not rise to the level of that required in criminal proceedings, given that school disciplinary measures are noncriminal and that school personnel must be given some measure of flexibility in performing their educational duties towards their students. It is possible, however, that student discipline involving a severe personal deprivation would require more formal notice and a hearing that allows for the exercise of procedural rights akin to those guaranteed criminals in the Fifth and Sixth amendments. We turn, then, to the procedural requirements the federal courts have charted for school disciplinary measures. Axiomatic of any fair procedure is the existence of a reasonably clear, pre-existing rule by which institutional expectations are announced and individual responsibilities are defined.

The Need for Reasonably Clear, Pre-existing Rules

The requirement of clear pre-existing rules in the educational context became evident in college and university desciplinary proceedings at the height of the Vietnam era protests. However, some disagreement developed among the federal circuits over just what specificity was required of school rules and regulations: whether it was enough that the rules defined generally the expected behavior, or whether greater specificity was required. The problem is illustrated with a comparison of the federal courts of appeal cases of *Soglin v. Kauffman*[112] and *Esteban v. Central Missouri State College*.[113]

In *Soglin* the seventh circuit required specificity. In that case members of the Students for a Democratic Society (SDS) were charged by university officials with "misconduct" in the obstruction of doorways and corridors of a university building. The SDS members argued upon their suspension that the unwritten university doctrine that proscribed "misconduct" was vague and overbroad in violation of due process. The university, on the other hand, argued that the doctrine of "misconduct" represented the "inherent power of the University to discipline students."[114] In rejecting the university's argument, the court cited *Tinker* to support the assessment that "[t]he proposition that government officers, including school administrators, must act in accord with rules in meting out discipline is so fundamental that its validity tends to be assumed by courts engaged in assessing the propriety of specific regulations."[115] Due process, the court held, required reasonably clear and narrow rules "whose coherence and boundaries may be questioned"[116] as well as regulations, "properly promulgated."[117] The fault of the "misconduct" standard, the court wrote, was that it did not provide "clues which could assist a student, an administrator or a reviewing judge in determining whether conduct not transgressing statutes is susceptible to punishment by the University as 'misconduct.' "[118]

Esteban, by contrast, specifically disagreed with the *Soglin* result.[119] *Esteban* differed from *Soglin* by the existence of previously promulgated regulations. The regulations, however, contained language as broad as "[a]ll students are expected to conform to ordinary and accepted social customs."[120] The regulations also contained a prohibition of "unruly or unlawful" mass gatherings, and assumed that any student who enrolled at the college accepted the obligation of abiding by its rules and regulations. In rejecting as vague and overly broad the arguments of two suspended students who had been charged with violation of these regulations, the court noted that a college disciplinary proceeding was not the same as a criminal proceeding, since the standard of conduct sought to be enforced by the college was one relevant to its mission as an educational institution.[121] Given this mission, the court found nothing wrong with a criterion of flexibility and reasonable breadth—rather than "meticulous specificity."[122] The college, the court said, could expect its students to adhere to generally accepted standards of conduct. The court rejected the students' argument that "young people should be told clearly what is right and what is wrong, as well as the consequences of their acts" by observing that all that was required of the students was the exercise of common sense and minimum

intelligence in a situation the students understood very well for its implications and consequences. "Their [the students'] respective protestations
of young and injured innocence have a hollow ring," the court wrote.[123]

Though the argument that "young people should be told clearly what is
right and what is wrong" has more appeal at the primary and secondary
level, where behavior development assumes a more prominent educational
role, high school disciplinary procedures have been upheld according to
Esteban rationale in cases where there may be no promulgated rule or
regulation, or where the rule or regulation is broad in its language. In the
federal district court case of *Hasson v. Boothby*,[124] for example, the discipline of high school students for drinking was upheld, though the prohibition against drinking could only be typified as a custom. The court noted
the growing recognition of the desirability and possible constitutional necessity of previously promulgated rules, as represented by *Soglin*, but followed the opposite, *Esteban* view, which "retains great vitality."[125] Where
the offending student had prior knowledge of the wrongfulness of his conduct and the public policy involved is clear, and considering the potential
chilling of First Amendment rights, as well as the severity of the penalty
involved, the court found the discipline to be constitutional in the absence
of a published rule.[126] In this case, the drinking could not be considered to
be a First Amendment activity, and the disciplinary measures consisted
only of "probation"—exclusion from school activities, but not school
itself—and ouster from athletic teams.[127] However, the court admitted that
the imposition of a more severe penalty without a specific promulgated
rule might be constitutionally deficient "under certain circumstances."[128]

Under what circumstances the absence of a specific promulgated rule
will cause a constitutional defect in the discipline of students may never
be clearly defined. The standard that emerges from the applicable cases is
that the absence of a rule will not be defective if students are chargeable
with the knowledge that their behavior is unacceptable, if fundamental
First Amendment rights are not involved, and if the contemplated sanction
is not unduly severe. This, in fact, may be the best standard, since placing
some burden of moral consciousness on the student surely has the effect
of reinforcing social norms of acceptable behavior. But, as noted in *Hasson*, the prerogative of school officials to assume student awareness and to
discipline in the absence of a specific rule is limited.[129] What that limit
might be is further illustrated by a state supreme court case, *Clements v.
Board of Trustees of Sheridan County School District*.[130]

Clements involved disciplinary measures more severe than probation.
In that case, a high school student was suspended for ten days and placed
on a semester of probation for harassing a school bus on the public high-
way. In his own vehicle, the student passed in front of the school bus and
prevented it from going at a normal speed or passing. Arguing that this
behavior created a dangerous situation, the school board suspended the
student upon the basis of the statutory authority to suspend or expel for

"[a]ny behavior which in the judgment of the local board of trustees is clearly detrimental to the education, welfare, safety or morals of other pupils."[131] The student argued that this statute was void for vagueness as it applied to him, that there was no specific school board regulation prohibiting his conduct, and that the school board did not have the authority to regulate his conduct on the public highways. The court rejected the vagueness argument with the explanation that the language of the statute was sufficiently clear and definite to apprise the student of the type of conduct prohibited.[132] Not questioning the authority of the school administration to regulate the student's conduct in this situation, the court found that a rule specifically prohibiting this conduct was unnecessary. After referring to the limitations suggested by *Hasson,* and to the necessity of due process for the deprivation of the student's property interest in public education,[133] the court upheld the school board's authority to suspend the student where he was chargeable with the knowledge of the public policy involved and was aware that his conduct was unacceptable and dangerous: "Students should know, and are chargeable with the knowledge, that interference with the school's transportation of other students to and from school is wrong and unacceptable."[134]

The Right to Notice and a Hearing: Goss v. Lopez and Its Progeny

With the possible exception of *Tinker, Goss v. Lopez*[135] is presently the most significant judicial pronouncement in the area of student discipline. But it is not a pronouncement without ambiguity. Children's rights advocates have hailed it as a significant step in the advancement of children's constitutional stature, but have also criticized it for not going far enough.[136] School administrators, on the other hand, have sighed with relief that it went no further than it did, but have complained that it is an unwarranted intrusion upon their discretion and into the area of their expertise.[137] The *Goss* finding was that due process protection should be afforded students threatened with suspensions of ten days or less. This finding should have been a surprise to no one, given the background of *Tinker* and the result of a much earlier college case, *Dixon v. Alabama State Board of Education.*[138] In *Dixon,* the court found education to be a constitutionally protectable property interest to be afforded due process protection in the face of expulsion. In fact, the *Goss* Court noted that since *Dixon,* and before *Goss,* the lower federal courts had "uniformly held the Due Process Clause applicable to decisions made by tax-supported educational institutions to remove a student from the institution long enough for the removal to be classified as an expulsion."[139]

Dixon involved the expulsion from a state-supported college of several students who had participated in an unsanctioned demonstration. The issue faced by the court was whether students had a right to any notice or hearing before their expulsion. The court noted that the Supreme Court had recently held in the case of *Cafeteria & Restaurant Workers Union v. McElroy*[140] that where governmental power was almost absolute and individual interests slight, due process was not required. But that case had involved the expulsion as a security risk of a short-order cook working for a privately operated cafeteria on the premises of a naval gun factory. The *Dixon* students, by contrast, were found to have a "vital" interest in their education, one that would be injured by interruption at midterm and by the prejudice that might arise from the stigma of expulsion. Nor could the governmental power in this case be considered absolute. The power to expel the students was not absolute and the possibility of arbitrary action was not excluded by the existence of reasonable regulations. Therefore, some measure of due process was required: "In the disciplining of college students there are no considerations of immediate danger to the public, or of peril to the national security, which should prevent the [state board of education] from exercising at least the fundamental principles of fairness by giving the accused students notice of the charges and an opportunity to be heard in their own defense."[141] The court held that the process due should include notice containing a statement of the specific charges and grounds that would justify expulsion, if proven, under the regulations of the educational entity, and a hearing. Though the hearing would vary with the circumstances of the particular case, expulsion required more than an informal interview with a school administrator. This did not mean a full-blown adversarial hearing, but at least the rudiments of one.[142] The court found that the *Dixon* students should be allowed the names of the witnesses against them, a report, oral or written, of the facts to which each witness would testify, an opportunity to present their own defense, and, in case the hearing was not directly before the board of education, a report that contained the board's findings and conclusions.[143]

The applicability of the *Dixon* due process principles to the high school level was made clear by the *Goss* decision. *Goss* involved a statute that authorized a school principal to suspend students for misconduct for up to ten days or to expel them. With either procedure, the principal was required to notify the students' parents within twenty-four hours, stating the reasons for the disciplinary action. An expelled student could appeal the principal's decision to the board of education and appear and speak at a board meeting. After this appeal, the board could reinstate the student. A suspended student, on the other hand, was afforded no similar procedure. The students in the *Goss* case had been suspended for the maximum ten days for participating in student disturbances and demonstrations.[144] They were not given a hearing of any kind. In response to this treatment, they filed an action in the federal courts, complaining that they had been deprived of their rights to an education without the procedural due process required of the Fourteenth Amendment.[145]

As noted above, the United States Supreme Court accepted the students' argument and held that they could not be suspended for ten days or less without the observance of due process protections. To support its decision that procedural due process was required in such a circumstance, the Court first explained that the Fourteenth Amendment forbids a state to deprive any person of life, liberty, or property without due process of law. Protected interests in property, it said, were created and defined by state statutes or rules entitling citizens to certain benefits.[146] Thus, school students had legitimate claims of entitlement—property interests—in the public education that state statutes required local authorities to provide free to all residents between five and twenty-one years of age.[147] Therefore, since it had extended the right to an education to students, the state could not withdraw it without fundamentally fair procedures to determine whether misconduct had actually occurred. Though the state's authority to prescribe and enforce standards of conduct in the schools was seen as very broad, the Court declared that this authority must be exercised consistently with constitutional safeguards.[148] In exercising this authority, the state is required not only to recognize students' property interest in their education, but also the liberty interest to be free of governmental action that may damage their good name, reputation, honor, or integrity.[149] Arguing that it is the "nature," not the "wieght," of the private interest that is important, the Court rejected the state's claim that because the students were not subjected to "a severe detriment or grievous loss," procedural due process was not required. The weight of the property interest was seen as irrelevant to the question of whether process was due, so long as its deprivation was not de minimis.[150] The Court did not consider a ten-day suspension from school to be de minimis.

Having once decided that due process was required, the Court then turned to the question of what due process to protect the interests of students facing a ten-day suspension would entail. First, the Court reviewed the classical notion that a fundamental requisite of due process is the opportunity to be heard, which contemplates adequate notice and a hearing of some sort.[151] But the Court also recited the traditional litany that "[t]he very nature of due process negates any concept of inflexible procedures universally applicable to every imaginable situation."[152] And it admitted that "care and restraint" were required of any judicial interposition in the operation of the public schools, for public education was committed to the control of state and local authorities.[153] Therefore, the procedure required of a school disciplinarian would have to accommodate the competing interests involved: the individual interest in the accuracy of the disciplinary process; the institutional interest in achieving this accuracy without prohibitive costs or interference with the educational process; and the social interest in accomplishing through disciplinary methodology communal consciousness and socially appropriate behavior. Excessive and formalistic procedures could detract from these interests, but some modicum of fair procedure could only enhance them: "[I]t would be a strange disciplinary system in an educational institution if no communication was sought by the disciplinarian with the student in an effort to inform him of his dereliction and to let him tell his side of the story in order to make sure that an injustice is not done."[154]

The Court then outlined its expectations of what procedures should be provided a student threatened with a ten-day suspension. Generally, "in connection with a suspension of 10 days or less, . . . the student [should] be given oral or written notice of the charges against him and, if he denies them, an explanation of the evidence the authorities have and an opportunity to present his side of the story."[155] Specifically, this did not mean that there needed to be delay between the notice and hearing; rather, what the Court had in mind was an informal "give-and-take" between the student and the disciplinarian moments after the misconduct, but before the suspension. Yet, the Court also admitted that this conversational approach to discipline should not apply in every case. With *Tinker* logic, it allowed that there were times when prior notice and a hearing, no matter how informal, could not be insisted upon. When a student's conduct and presence posed a continuing danger to persons or property, or an ongoing threat of disrupting the adademic process, the student could be removed immediately from school. The notice and hearing, however, would follow as soon as practicable.[156] Otherwise, the Court meant this informal procedure to follow every infraction, and precede every suspension, even when the disciplinarian has personally witnessed the alleged misconduct. Though in that situation the informal give-and-take would perform less of a fact-finding function, it would at least allow students the opportunity to characterize their conduct and put it in proper context.[157]

The Court specifically refrained from requiring greater formality than this: "further formalizing the suspension process and escalating its formality and adversary nature may not only make it too costly as a regular disciplinary tool but also destroy its effectiveness as part of the teaching process."[158] Therefore, the Court did not require the usual due process formalities of affording the opportunity to secure counsel, allowing the accused to confront and cross-examine witnesses or to call their own witnesses, though the disciplinarian, in his or her own discretion, could allow these elements.[159] The Court also warned that these informalities were meant for temporary suspensions of ten days or less; longer suspensions or expulsions could require greater formality.[160]

Of course, the immediate criticism of the *Goss* decision was that its standards were ambiguous, that it provided no clear vision of the minimums and the maximums of this informal constitutional protection. Furthermore, the Court provided no definition of the disruptive conduct that would trigger the exception to its holding. As for minimums, what in the educational context could be taken from a student without infringing some property or liberty interest that requires due process protection? What of suspensions from class attendance accompanied by in-school detention, or exclusions from extracurricular activities? As for maximums, what deprivations are more serious than short suspensions and trigger more formal procedures than those contemplated by the *Goss* Court? What about academic sanctions for misbehavior, or, by contrast, what about deprivations like transfer or expulsion based upon academic performance alone? What of lateral transfers based on nothing more than administrative requirements? And what of corporal punishment? Lower court cases subsequent to *Goss* provide some reference points in this still uncharted area.

Almost immediately the fifth circuit court of appeals illustrated an exception to *Goss* with the case of *Sweet v. Childs*.[161] In that case, high school students had engaged in a "sit-in" after fellow students had been expelled for fighting. Trying to control an atmosphere of racial violence, the principal of the school conferred with the protesting students, giving them a choice of returning to class or leaving the school grounds and taking a zero for the day. The protesters chose to leave the school for the day, but in the process violated their agreement with the principal by encouraging other students to leave with them. In response, the principal announced over the radio that the students—all 124 of them—were suspended for ten days. However, within three days conferences were held with the students' parents, and within the ten-day suspension period the suspension was lifted and the students were reinstated in school. In response to the students' due process violation claim, the court held that this procedure had not violated the requirements of *Goss*.[162] Though *Goss* called for notice and a hearing before suspension, it also recognized that students must sometimes be removed immediately from school where their presence "poses a continuing danger to persons or property or an ongoing threat of disrupting the adademic process."[163] Considering the circumstances of the students' suspension in the *Sweet* case, the fifth circuit held that the procedural protections provided were within the guidlines of *Goss*. The students had created "more than an 'ongoing threat of disrupting the academic process.' "[164] And the postsuspension hearings had been sufficient "give-and-take" sessions.[165]

Prior notice and hearing have been held to be required, however, when a student is threatened with transfer to another school, whether for disciplinary or administrative reasons. In *Jordan v. School District of City of Erie*,[166] the third circuit held that *Goss* required that where the school's disciplinary procedure included transfer to a correctional school for disruptive students, notice and a hearing were required before the student could be removed from class. In that case the school's disciplinary regulations provided that if, in the teacher's judgement, a student's conduct created a continuing threat of disruption to the academic process, the student could be "immediately" removed from the classroom. Immediate removal, however, constituted a recommendation of transfer to the correctional school. Given the rather severe consequences of immediate removal, the court held that a student not actually posing a danger to persons, property, or the academic process could not be removed without notice and an informal hearing with the building principal.[167] A federal district court in *Everett v. Marcase*[168] held that *Goss*-type procedures were required in nondisciplinary "lateral transfers." Each year a substantial number of pupils were involuntarily transferred from one public school to another for administrative reasons. The school district argued that due process did not apply to these "lateral transfers" since the transfer did not deprive students of the constitutionally cognizable rights recognized in *Goss*. The district court disagreed. Adopting *Goss* language, it found that the transfers involved protectable property interests in "a serious event in the life of the [transferred] child."[169] A transfer could be terrifying, since it was possibly dangerous for students to pass through different neighborhoods on their way to a new school;[170] also, any disruption of the educational process constituted a loss of benefits and opportunities. Therefore, the court required the school district to provide due process protections. Though an attorney was not required, the school district had to provide for notice and a hearing before an impartial hearing officer, one other than the principal who holds the initial informal hearing and recommends transfer.[171]

Notice and a hearing were not required where the student was placed on in-school probation. In *Fenton v. Stear*,[172] a federal district court held that in-school probation that consisted of forcing the student to sit in a certain chair in a room of the school, studying under the supervision of a school official, did not require the due process of prior notice and a hearing. Nor have due process protections been extended to exclusions from extracurricular activities, including sports.[173] In *Pegram v. Nelson*, a federal district court case, *Goss*-type procedures had accompanied a ten-day suspension and a semester-long exclusion from extracurricular activities.[174] The issue presented the court was whether, because of the exclusion from activities imposed in addition to the suspension, more extensive process than that required by *Goss* was due. In finding that *Goss*-type procedures had been adequate, the court relied upon the doctrine expressed in *Goss* that constitutionally protectable property interests are defined by state law. Since no state statute created a right to participate in extracurricular activities, Chester Pegram was not deprived of a property interest. Therefore, procedures more formal than, or in addition to, those employed in the process of his suspension could not be required.[175]

When deprivations more severe than temporary suspension are contemplated, more formal procedures may be required. For example, a court could find that the Constitution requires the aid of counsel, an impartial tribunal, opportunities to present and cross-examine witnesses, and more formal evidence rules to protect a student from the misapplication of the threatened sanction. As for representation by legal counsel, however, courts have generally rejected the existence or necessity for such a right.

The argument has been that legal representation would turn what is meant to be a cooperative, conciliatory, and educational experience for a student into an adversarial proceeding.[176] The context in which the right to legal representation has developed has been the criminal trial, and a disciplinary proceeding is certainly not a criminal proceeding. As the Second Circuit Court of Appeals has said, "[l]aw and order in the classroom should be the responsibility of our respective educational systems. The courts should not usurp this function and turn disciplinary problems . . . into criminal adversary proceedings—which they definitely are not."[177] Of course the same argument could be made for the other possible procedural requirements. But in several circumstances courts have found them to be required.

For example, in *Gonzales v. McEuen*[178] a federal district court found that when faced with expulsion, high school students were entitled to more than *Goss* due process protection. Where a state statute required an impartial tribunal for an expulsion proceeding, a hearing before the school district's board of trustees was prejudiced by the district superintendent's presence during the board's deliberations. In addition, the school district's attorneys' multiple roles as counsel to the board of trustees and as the students' prosecutors biased the board and therefore denied the students due process.[179] The court also held that the hearsay evidence introduced at the hearing did not form an appropriate basis for the board's decision and that the students should be allowed to confront and cross-examine their accusers.[180] In addition, the prosecutors' commentary on the students' refusals to testify was found to be a violation of their Fifth Amendment rights against self-incrimination.[181] The court required these procedural protections because "a high school student who is punished by expulsion might well suffer more injury than one convicted of a criminal offense."[182]

Other courts have not been so strict. In *Long v. Thornton Township High School District*,[183] a student faced with expulsion was not denied due process by the name of his accuser being omitted from the notice of misconduct and hearing; nor was the student denied an impartial tribunal with the principal of the school. The principal's mere involvement with the case prior to hearing did not necessarily bias him. In order to show the denial of due process, the student was required to prove prejudice by the principal stemming from a source other than the principal's knowledge of the case.[184] Other courts have been less inclined than the *Gonzales* court to allow students the right to confront those whose accusations have led to the disciplinary proceeding[185] for the reason that reprisals against fellow students could result. In *Dillon v. Pulaski County Special School District*,[186] these concerns were held to be unfounded where the individual bringing the complaint was a teacher or administrator, "who would not be subject to the ostracism and psychological trauma that a student accuser might suffer at the hands of his peers."[187] Therefore, the student was entitled to the due process protection of confronting and cross-examining the teacher who had complained of disrespect.

Academic Sanctions and Due Process

Similar due process protection has not been extended to deprivations related purely to academic performance. For example, process will not be due a student who is held back a year for failing, who is moved to a different reading group, or who is given a B rather than an A. The reason for the courts' reticence to enter this area of apparent deprivation is that academic evaluation is at the very heart of educator discretion, and is an area of expertise for which the courts are unsuited.

Deprivations related to academic evaluation are to be distinguished from academic sanctions that are related to misconduct. As noted above, academic evaluation is based upon academic performance alone, and since it is accepted as fundamental to the educational process, incidental deprivations are tolerated; therefore, the notice and hearing afforded suspensions and expulsions do not similarly apply. Academic sanctions for misconduct, however, make the grading system a tool of discipline alternative or additional to suspension and expulsion. Where the question has arisen, this practice has been discouraged with the argument that the grading system already has serious inherent limitations and must not be handicapped further by also being made to serve disciplinary purposes.[188]

The judicial hesitancy to enter the realm of academic evaluation is most authoritatively expressed in the Supreme Court case of *Board of Curators of the University of Missouri v. Horowitz*.[189] That case involved the dismissal of a medical student in the final year of her program for failure to meet academic standards. To her *Goss*-based argument that she has been denied due process, the Court replied that academic dismissals required less stringent procedural protection than dismissals for misconduct, since there is a "significant difference between the failure of a student to meet academic standards and the violation by a student of valid rules of conduct."[190] This difference lay in the fact that a school is an academic institution, "not a courtroom or administrative hearing room."[191] The *Goss*-type hearings were meant to resolve factual issues upon which the disciplinary decision turned. Resolution of these issues in a hearing where the student is given the opportunity to present her side of the factual issue was meant to be a hedge against erroneous action. The decision to dismiss a student, by contrast, rests upon the academic judgement of school officials, "a judgment [that] is by its nature more subjective and evaluative than the typical factual questions presented in the average disciplinary decision."[192] The Court therefore declined to further enlarge the judicial presence in the academic community and thereby risk deterioration of many beneficial aspects of the faculty-student relationship. "We recognize, as did the Massachusetts Supreme Judicial Court over 60 years ago, that a hearing may be 'useless or even harmful in finding out the truth as to scholarship.' "[193]

An area related to academic evaluation is access to educational records. Because of concerns for privacy and the logical necessity for accuracy of records used in both academic and disciplinary decision making, Congress has enacted the Family Educational Rights and Privacy Act (FERPA), commonly known as the Buckley Amendment.[194] The Act not only increases student and parent access to school records, it restricts the availability of school record information to third parties. Enforcement is achieved by FERPA's authorization of the Secretary of the Department of Education to withhold all federal education monies to institutions that: 1) prevent or prohibit parents or students from examining and reviewing school records maintained on students; or 2) do not provide opportunities for parents or students to challenge those record data which are "inaccurate, misleading, or otherwise inappropriate;" or 3) allow the release of student record information to third parties without student or parental consent; or 4) do not provide parents and students information concerning record-keeping procedure and their rights under FERPA. In response to a challenge to the record-keeping procedure, to third-party access, or to the accuracy of the records themselves, a school must provide a formal hearing before a disinterested party, in which parents or students must be allowed to present all relevant evidence. Provision also is made for judicial review of the hearing's result if the parents or students remain dissatisfied.[195]

Corporal Punishment and Due Process

The courts also have been hesitant to extend *Goss's* prior notice and hearing requirements to the area of corporal punishment. This hesitation has been surprising in light of the liberty interest language of the *Goss* decision. It is not difficult to consider the pain and embarrassment incident to corporal punishment as equal to the potential damage to "good name, reputation, honor, or integrity"[196] of suspension that *Goss* protected against. But the courts have not declared the existence of a liberty interest when pain results from corporal punishment, or at least an interest significant enough to require schools to hold a prior hearing. Nor have the courts been willing to find that corporal punishment in the schools is "cruel and unusual" within the meaning of the Eighth Amendment. The most significant judicial pronouncement in this area has been by the Supreme Court in the case of *Ingraham v. Wright*.[197]

Ingraham considered a state statute that authorized corporal punishment of students by teachers or other members of the school staff, as well as regulations promulgated by the county school board. The regulations authorized punishment that consisted of one to five "licks" on the buttocks with a flat wooden paddle no more than two feet long, three to four inches wide, and about one-half inch thick. Students alleged to have been subject to even more severe punishment than that authorized brought suit on the grounds that the statute and the regulations violated the Eighth Amendment, by authorizing "cruel and unusual punishment," and the Fourteenth Amendment, by denying liberty interests without due process of law.[198]

In response to the Eighth Amendment argument, the Court relied upon history and prior cases in deciding that the amendment was meant to apply to criminal cases and not to "the paddling of children as a means of maintaining discipline in public schools."[199] The practice was defended as one that retained significant inertia: though there exists a sharp division of opinion on its effectiveness, it is an historic practice, the elimination of which does not appear imminent. In fact, only two states have statutes that prohibit its use.[200] Since *Blackstone* the application of "moderate correction" to school children has been justified to achieve educational purposes. Today, the practice of corporal punishment continues to be governed in the common law by "reasonableness:"

> Although the early cases viewed the authority of the teacher as deriving from the parents, the concept of parental delegation has been replaced by the view—more consonant with compulsory education laws—that the State itself may impose such corporal punishment as is reasonably necessary 'for the proper education of the child and for the maintenance of group discipline.' 1 F. Harper & F. James, Law of Torts § 3.20, p. 292 (1956). All of the circumstances are to be taken into account in determining whether the punishment is reasonable in a particular case. Among the most important considerations are the seriousness of the offense, the attitude and past behavior of the child, the nature and severity of the punishment, the age and strength of the child, and the availability of less severe but equally effective means of discipline.[201]

Besides these common-law rules of reasonableness, some states have provided further protections such as notification of parents and infliction of punishment only in the presence of an adult witness.[202] If corporal punishment is considered to be excessive or unreasonable, an educator is subject to possible civil or criminal liability.[203]

To further support its argument that the Eighth Amendment does not apply in the school context, the Court distinguished between the relative situations of students and prisoners. Unlike a prisoner, who is deprived of the freedom to associate with friends and family, a student attends an "open" institution. Students come to school with the support of family and friends; teachers and fellow students may protest any mistreatment; students are free to leave, in most cases, at any time; and every night they return home. Parents and other members of the community participate in the school's supervision and where informal safeguards leave off, the formal safeguards of the legislative and common law take over.[204]

With these informal and formal safeguards in mind, the Court next turned to the due process issue. Though the Court admitted that students enjoy a strong liberty interest in avoiding bodily restraint and punishment, it refused to find that prior notice and hearing were necessary. Instead it found that this liberty interest was adequately protected by the common-law rules of reasonableness. Considered in light of the openness of the school environment, the civil and criminal proceedings for abuse were seen as affording significant protection against unjustified corporal punishment. In addition, the practice of inflicting corporal punishment without prior notice and hearing was considered analogous to the warrantless arrest: the benefit of allowing authorities to act spontaneously and immediately outweights the possible error that may result from the absence of prior procedural safeguards.[205] In other words, prior procedural safeguards would "significantly burden the use of corporal punishment as a disciplinary measure." . . . "Hearings—even informal hearings—require time, personnel, and a diversion of attention from normal school pursuits. School authorities may well choose to abandon corporal punishment rather than incur the burdens of complying with the procedural requirements."[206] Though this appeared to be an implicit endorsement of the practice, the Court warned that the value judgment required in abolishing it was one to be made through the political process and not in the Court.[207] This reticence was especially called for where the private interests involved were apparently outweighed by the societal costs that would result from finding the state statute and the school district's regulations unconstitutional.[208]

The *Ingraham* decision was immediately criticized by the legal and educational communities alike. Legal commentators questioned the Court's interpretation of the Eighth Amendment, saying that history and precedent had been misinterpreted. They also questioned the assumption that schools, at least as compared with prisons, were "open" institutions. Students are compelled to attend school by state authority, and leaving during school hours might constitute the basis for juvenile court truancy or incorrigibility charges. Nor are members of the community really free to visit schools when they like, since statutes in some jurisdictions require written permission from school authorities before visiting the school premises. The Court also was criticized for assuming that teachers would break rank to question the actions of their colleagues and supervisors, and for assuming that the community would react against the beating of a minority of children any more quickly than it had responded to inhumane prison conditions. The Court's reluctance to follow *Goss* was especially troublesome, since the interest in freedom from "infliction of appreciable physical pain," unlike property interests, could not be restored by a postdeprivation hearing. Besides the fact that the liberty interest involved was truly protectable only by a prior hearing, the inadequacy of postdeprivation remedies was made more acute by the fact that, to pursue them, parents and students had to secure an attorney and submit to the endless process of state court litigation. But most ironic was the Court's acknowledgement of its own inability to make the subjective judgments involved in the case, while at the same time requiring the nation's schoolteachers to make decisions about reasonableness that, if erroneous, could lead to tort or criminal liability.[209] Educational commentators, on the other hand, spoke of actual defects in the practice of corporal punishment itself and suggested alternative means of behavioral control.[210]

Though these criticisms are logical and appealing, and though it may be argued that the abolition of corporal punishment in the schools would be a cultural advance, *Ingraham* indicates that for the present, change must occur on the state and local level. Meanwhile, *Ingraham* stands as good constitutional law in which those states that choose to retain the practice of corporal punishment in their schools may find justification.[211] State courts also may rely on the federal district court decision of *Baker v. Owen*,[212] which the United States Supreme Court affirmed without opinion, for the proposition that the *Ingraham* holding even stands up against the rights of parents to determine the disciplinary methods used with their children.

In the *Baker* case, a sixth grader, who had violated his teacher's announced rule against throwing kickballs outside designated play periods, was given two strikes with a wooden drawer divider in the presence of a second teacher and other students. The student received this punishment even though his mother had requested that he not be the subject of corporal punishment, since she opposed it on principle. In response to the mother's arguments, the court held that her right to determine the means of discipline of her child was offset by the state's countervailing interest in the maintenance of order in the schools.[213]

REMEDIES AVAILABLE TO STUDENTS FOR DISCIPLINARY ABUSES: IMMUNITY AND MONETARY DAMAGES

As indicated in the previous discussion, school administrators and teachers may be liable both civilly and criminally for abuses of discretion in disciplinary matters. These are remedies provided by state law, and they were sufficiently described in Chapter Two as to not require repetition here. What is important at this point is consideration of potential remedies for deprivation of the constitutional rights described in this chapter. Since the Supreme Court has explicitly stated that remedies already provided by the legislative and common law of the states are sufficient due process protection against abuses in the application of corporal punishment, remedy for deprivation of constitutional rights must be limited to the denial of procedural due process in suspensions and expulsions, and possibly unreasonable search and seizure.[214] The most significant statement on student remedies for due process violations is the case of *Wood v. Strickland*,[215] argued the same day as *Goss v. Lopez* before the United States Supreme Court.

The *Wood* case dealt with the question of immunity for school officials against actions brought for violation of constitutional or legal rights under Section 1983 of the Civil Rights Act.[216] The *Wood* action itself was based on the expulsion without due process of three high school girls who surreptitiously "spiked" the punch at a school-sponsored function in violation of a school regulation that prohibited the use or possession of intoxicating beverages at the school or at school-sponsored activities.[217] The students sued for injunctive relief that would allow them to return to school without further sanction and that would restrain enforcement of the regulation by which they were expelled. They also demanded the expunction of any notation of the expulsion from their records and declaratory judgement that the regulation was unconstitutional. In addition to equitable and declaratory relief, the students further sought compensatory and punitive damages.[218] The federal district court, where relief was first sought, decided against the students, claiming that the school officials were immune from damages unless malice was shown. The federal court of appeals reversed this decision and granted the injunctive relief prayed for, as well as a new trial on the question of damages. To the court of appeals, immunity depended upon "good faith" instead of malice or ill will. If the students could show that the school officials had not acted in good faith, the school officials would be without an immunity defense and liable for damages under Section 1983.[219] The Supreme Court affirmed the court of appeals decision and then elaborated upon the immunity standard it expected to be applied to school officials.

In finding that a "qualified good faith immunity" should extend to school officials, the Court reviewed the immunity traditionally given other governmental officials whose duties require uncoerced decision making. State courts, the Court observed, have generally recognized that school officials should be protected from tort liability for good-faith, nonmalicious action taken in the performance of their duties. And it found no indication in the legislative record that Congress meant to abolish wholesale these common-law immunities in the enactment of Section 1983. Rather, it found that the common-law tradition and strong public policy reasons militate in favor of a construction of Section 1983 that extends to school officials a qualified good-faith immunity. Instead of the absolute immunity argued for by the school officials themselves, this qualified immunity would at once protect the student's constitutional rights and preserve the values of "principled and fearless decision-making."[220] Absolute immunity, the Court said, would not be justified by any significant increase in the ability of school officials to exercise their discretion in a forthright manner. But qualified immunity would save them from liability when they acted sincerely with a belief that they were doing right. An act violating a student's constitutional rights, however, could not be "justified by ignorance or disregard of settled, indisputable law on the part of one entrusted with supervision of students' daily lives."[221] One who has undertaken such a responsibility must be held to a standard of conduct "based not only on permissible intentions, but also on knowledge of the basic, unquestioned constitutional rights of his charges:"[222]

> Therefore, in the specific context of school discipline, we held that a school board member is not immune from liability for damages under § 1983 if he knew or reasonably should have known that the action he took within his sphere of official responsibility would violate the consti-

tutional rights of the student affected, or if he took the action with the malicious intention to cause a deprivation of constitutional rights or other injury to the student.[223]

The Court refined its *Wood* holding in the subsequent case of *Carey v. Piphus*.[224] In that case, where students had been suspended from school without notice or hearing, the Court held that in the absence of proof of actual damages, the students were not entitled to recover compensatory damages.[225] In other words, a showing that the students would have been suspended even with procedural protections would defeat any student claim of actual damage.[226] In such a situation, where the deprivation was justified but the procedures deficient, students could get a damage reward only if they could produce evidence that their "mental and emotional distress actually was caused by the denial of procedural due process itself" and not by the justified deprivation.[227] However, the Court did hold that nominal damages were recoverable where procedural rights had been violated, even if the suspension would have nonetheless occurred.[228] The Court considered the award of at least nominal damages for failure to provide due process protections to be symbolic of its constitutional objectives: "By making the deprivation of such rights actionable for nominal damages without proof of actual injury, the law recognizes the importance to organized society that those rights be scrupulously observed."[229]

The clarifications of the *Carey* decision notwithstanding, the *Wood* decision has been criticized for placing a greater burden on educators than that placed on other public officials,[230] and for enunciating an ambiguous standard.[231] Of course any decision will be fraught with some degree of ambiguity, and its readers can only be required to conscientiously interpret and apply its language. The requirements the Supreme Court has placed upon educators in their application of disciplinary measures are not really very difficult or ambiguous. They are requirements that would not surprise reasonable and fair-minded educators. Nor should it seem onerous that the Court would require educators to maintain an awareness of the constitutional rights of their students. Constitutional law is not so obscure as some may think, nor is it pronounced by an obscure court. In addition to the media coverage that invariably accompanies the Supreme Court's proceedings, educators are further aided by legal counsel and by a number of publications that report legal developments. Since educators are reasonably expected to maintain an awareness of the world they interpret to their students, it does not seem too much to require them to maintain some awareness of the law.[232]

SUMMARY

The recognition of student constitutional rights is fairly recent. The real beginning point was probably the 1954 case of *Brown v. Board of Education*, where education was described in sublime terms. But the *Tinker* decision of the late 1960s also achieves transcendent status as a point of departure for the development of student rights. *Tinker* recognized First Amendment rights of students to free speech. Since *Tinker*, other First Amendment student rights, such as the right of association and the free exercise of religion, have been recognized. Students also have been found to have Fourth Amendment rights to be free of unreasonable search and seizure. They are recognized as having rights to due process: the right to be at least apprised of school policies, the right to notice and a hearing prior to suspension or expulsion, and the right to postinfliction remedies for abuses in corporal punishment. The Supreme Court also has made it clear that school officials, as state officials, do not enjoy an absolute immunity against student actions for damages through either traditional state common-law or legislative remedies or federal civil rights legislation. All of these rights are subject to the special necessities of education, however; a constitutional right may bend to the requirements of nondisturbance, group discipline, and personal or property safety. None of these rests upon ultrafine distinctions. Rather, they represent general notions of fair play in a society that places great value and emphasis on education.

Of course these developments have not been achieved without controversy. Some educational commentators have recognized the symbolic quality of decisions like *Tinker*, *Goss*, and *Wood*, and have hailed their enunciation of fairness in the educational context. In turn, they have recognized the Court's restraint in the sensitive balancing of competing values of individual rights and educational purpose.[233] Others have criticized the Supreme Court's decisions as significant intrusions upon educator discretion.[234] Still others have criticized the decisions for their potential damage to the teacher-student relationship, transforming it from one that is cooperative and trusting, to one that is adversarial.[235] Regardless of the criticism, the Court's decisions are the law of the land and must be accommodated by every educator. Educators can avoid constitutional problems by taking preventative measures: for example, more explicit student codes,[236] student involvement in decision making,[237] and student grievance procedures.[238] At the same time, however, an educator must be aware of the principles the courts have prescribed and must be willing to respect the individual-student rights that they represent.

REFERENCES

1. *See generally* Foster & Freed, *A Bill of Rights for Children*, 6 Fam. L.Q. 343 (1972); Wald, *Making Sense Out of the Rights of Youth*, 4 Human Rights 13 (1974); *In re* Gault, 387 U.S. 1 (1967). *But see* Hafen, *Children's Liberation and the New Egalitarianism: Some Reservations About Abandoning Youth to Their "Rights,"* 1976 B.Y.U.L.Rev. 605.

2. L. Tribe, American Constitutional Law § 10–7 (1978).
3. *Id.* § 11–1, § 11–4.
4. Joint Anti-Fascist Refugee Committee v. McGrath, 341 U.S. 123, 168 (1951) (Frankfurter, J., concurring).
5. Cafeteria & Restaurant Workers Union v. McElroy, 367 U.S. 886, 895 (1961).
6. *See* Goss v. Lopez, 419 U.S. 565, 584 (1975).
7. *Compare id.* (suspension) *with* Dixon v. Alabama State Board of Education, 294 F.2d 150 (5th Cir. 1961) *cert. denied,* 368 U.S. 930 (1961) (expulsion).
8. L. Tribe, *supra,* note 3, § 10–7.
9. *Id.* at 503 (quoting 367 U.S. at 171–72).
10. *Id.* at 503 (quoting Fuentes v. Shevin, 407 U.S. 67, 97 (1972)).
11. *Id.* at 503.
12. *Id.* at 505–6.
13. *See* P. Smith, The Constitution: A Documentary and Narrative History 466 (1978).
14. *Id.* at 447–64. *See also* the Slaughter-House Cases, 83 U.S. (16 Wall.) 36 (1873).
15. U.S. Const. amend. XIV, § 1.
16. *See generally* L. Tribe, *supra* note 3, § 11–2.
17. *See, e.g.,* Chicago, B. & Q. R. Co. v. Chicago, 166 U.S. 226 (1897).
18. *See, e.g.,* Fiske v. Kansas, 274 U.S. 380 (1927).
19. *See, e.g.,* Near v. Minnesota, 283 U.S. 697 (1931).
20. *See, e.g.,* DeJonge v. Oregon, 299 U.S. 353 (1937).
21. *See, e.g.,* Hague v. CIO, 307 U.S. 496 (1939).
22. *See, e.g.,* Cantwell v. Connecticut, 310 U.S. 296 (1940).
23. *See, e.g.,* Everson v. Board of Education, 330 U.S. 1, 15–16 (1947).
24. *See* Wolf v. Colorado, 338 U.S. 25 (1949).
25. *See* Mapp v. Ohio, 367 U.S. 643 (1961).
26. *See* Malloy v. Hogan, 378 U.S. 1 (1964).
27. *See* Benton v. Maryland, 395 U.S. 784 (1969).
28. *See, e.g.,* Gideon v. Wainwright, 372 U.S. 335 (1963).
29. *See, e.g.,* Klopfer v. North Carolina, 386 U.S. 213 (1967).
30. *See In re* Oliver, 333 U.S. 257 (1948).
31. *See* Duncan v. Louisiana, 391 U.S. 145 (1968).
32. *See, e.g.,* Pointer v. Texas, 380 U.S. 400 (1965).
33. *See* Washington v. Texas, 388 U.S. 14 (1967).
34. *See* Robinson v. California, 370 U.S. 660 (1962).
35. *See* Palko v. Connecticut, 302 U.S. 319, 325 (1937).
36. *See* Adamson v. California, 332 U.S. 46, 69–72, 77–78, 83–85, 89–90, (1947) (Black, J., dissenting).
37. *Id.* at 123–25 (Murphy, J., dissenting).
38. *See* Poe v. Ullman, 367 U.S. 497, 543 (1961) (Harlan, J., dissenting).
39. Meyer v. Nebraska, 262 U.S. 390 (1923).
40. Pierce v. Society of Sisters, 268 U.S. 510 (1925).
41. Skinner v. Oklahoma, 316 U.S. 535 (1942).
42. Rochin v. California, 342 U.S. 165 (1952).
43. Aptheker v. Secretary of State, 378 U.S. 500 (1964).
44. Griswold v. Connecticut, 381 U.S. 479 (1965).
45. *See* pp. 35–38, *supra.*
46. *Compare* Pierce v. Society of Sisters, 268 U.S. 510 (1925) *and* Wisconsin v. Yoder, 406 U.S. 205 (1972) *with* Brown v. Board of Education, 347 U. S. 483 (1954).
47. *See* S. Goldstein, Law and Public Education 13–15 (1974).
48. *See, e.g.,* N. Y. Educ. Law § 3202 (McKinney 1970) ("A person over five and under twenty-one years of age is entitled to attend the public schools main-

tained in the district of city in which such person resides without the payment of tuition").

49. 48 Cal. 36, 50, 17 Am. R. 405, 410 (1874).
50. 347 U.S. 483 (1954).
51. *Id.* at 493.
52. 411 U.S. 1 (1973).
53. *Id.* at 37.
54. *See generally* L. Tribe, *supra,* note 3, §§ 11–1, 11–2.
55. 411 U.S. at 35.
56. The broad view of *Brown* has been that the Court meant to remedy racial segregation and discrimination wherever it occurs. In other words, *de facto* (actual) segregation is sufficient evidence of past *de jure* (embodied in law) discrimination. Thus the *Brown* mandate applies to all cases of de facto discrimination. The narrow view posits that there must be a specific showing of past *de jure* discrimination. This would limit the application of *Brown* and its principles to the states that actually had legislation at one time that discriminated between the races—predominantly the southern states.
57. L. Tribe, *supra* note 3, §§ 10–9, 10–10.
58. See pp. 74–80 *infra.*
59. *See generally* C. Wright, Handbook of the Law of Federal Courts §§ 17–19 (1976). The recurrent federal questions that are considered in this chapter are violations of students' constitutional rights.
60. U.S. Const. art. 3, § 2.
61. There are some matters over which federal courts have exclusive jurisdiction. For example, federal district courts have exclusive jurisdiction over cases in admiralty, in condemnation of property taken as a prize, and in bankruptcy. 28 U.S.C. §§ 1333–34 (1976).
62. 28 U.S.C. § 1257 (1) (1976). *Cf.* 28 U.S.C. § 1254 (1976) where Supreme Court appellate jurisdiction is described in cases coming through the federal appellate courts.
63. 28 U.S.C. § 1257 (2) (1976).
64. 28 U.S.C. § 1331 (1976).
65. 42 U.S.C. § 1981 *et sec.* (1976).
66. 28 U.S.C. § 1343 (1976). Because student cases deal with rights and immunities secured by the Constitution, they fit within this exception, and the $10,000 amount in controversy requirement does not deprive the federal courts of jurisdiction.
67. *See* pp. 38–51 *supra.* This includes the traditional tort and criminal remedies available for disciplinary abuses.
68. *See* commentaries cited at note 1 *supra.*
69. *See* pp. 15–16, *supra.*
70. 393 U.S. 503 (1969).
71. *Id.* at 506.
72. *Id.* at 511.
73. *Id.* at 504.
74. *Id.* at 512.
75. *Id.* at 508.
76. *Id.* at 512–13.
77. *See* S. Goldstein, *supra* note 48, at 304–5.
78. 393 U.S. at 511.
79. *Id.* at 509.
80. 431 F.2d 594 (6th Cir. 1970), *cert. denied,* 401 U.S. 948 (1971).
81. 432 F.2d 1259 (7th Cir. 1970).
82. 431 F.2d at 596.

83. *Id*. at 597.
84. *Id*. at 598.
85. *Id*.
86. 432 F.2d at 1263–64.
87. *Id*. at 1263 (quoting Griswold v. Connecticut, 381 U.S. 479, 488 (1965) (Goldberg, J., concurring)).
88. *Id*. at 1265–66.
89. *Id*. at 1265 (quoting Z. Chafee, Free Speech in the United States 151–52 (1941).
90. Hatter v. Los Angeles City High School Dist., 310 F. Supp. 1309, 1312 (C.D. Cal. 1970).
91. Hatter v. Los Angeles City High School Dist., 452 F.2d 673, 675 (9th Cir. 1971).
92. This does not mean that the application of *Tinker* is exhausted here; this writing only means to highlight areas of recurring importance. For example, *Tinker* has been applied to protect the First Amendment right to not participate in flag ceremonies. *See* Frain v. Baron, 307 F. Supp. 27 (E.D.N.Y. 1969); Goetz v. Ansell, 477 F.2d 636 (2d Cir. 1973). *Cf.* Tate v. Board of Educ., 453 F.2d 975 (8th Cir. 1972), where students were justifiably disciplined for silent protest at an assembly, the subject matter of which was announced beforehand, and the attendance of which was voluntary. *Tinker* has also resulted in an inquiry of whether the teacher and student may exercise First Amendment rights in the choice of material and topics in the classroom. *See* Note, *Academic Freedom in the High School Classroom*, 15 J. Fam. L. 706 (1976–1977).
93. Katz v. McAulay, 438 F.2d 1058 (2d Cir. 1971), *cert. denied*, 405 U.S. 933 (1972). *But see* Rowe v. Campbell Union High School Dist. (N.D. Cal. 1971) (unpublished).
94. Scoville v. Board of Educ. of Joliet Township High School Dist., 425 F.2d 10 (7th Cir. 1970), *cert. denied*, 400 U.S. 826 (1970).
95. Thomas v. Board of Ed., Granville Central School Dist., 607 F.2d 1043 (2d Cir. 1979).
96. *See* 425 F.2d at 14. *Cf.* Papish v. Board of Curators of the Univ. of Mo., 410 U.S. 667 (1973) (college publication). There is some disagreement between circuits on whether school authorities may review student materials before distribution in schools. *See* Shanley v. Northeast Independent School Dist., 462 F.2d 960 (5th Cir. 1972); Quarterman v. Byrd, 453 F.2d 54 (4th Cir. 1971); Eisner v. Stamford Board of Educ., 440 F.2d 803 (2d Cir. 1971) which holds that prior review requirements are constitutional if adequate safeguards exist such as standards to guide administrators in making decisions and adequate time periods in which the decision is to be made. *But cf.* Fujishima v. Board of Educ., 460 F.2d 1355 (7th Cir. 1972) which holds that prior review requirements are per se unconstitutional. Seizure of a student publication has been allowed where it contained libelous, disruptive, or potentially disruptive material. *See* Frasca v. Andrews, 463 F. Supp. 1043 (E.D.N.Y. 1979). This was so even though there was not a pre-existing rule for review of the publication before distribution. Of course, it is clear that school authorities need not wait for potential harm to occur before taking protective action. Trachtman v. Anker, 563 F.2d 512 (2d Cir. 1977).
97. Healy v. James, 408 U.S. 169 (1972) (college students sought official recognition for SDS organization in order to use campus facilities for meetings and campus bulletin boards for announcements).
98. *Id*. at 193.
99. 61 App. Div. 2d 204, 401 N.Y.S.2d 544 (1978).

100. *Id.* at 545.
101. 393 U.S. at 507.
102. 546 N.Y.S.2d at 545–46.
103. The court rejected Ronald's argument that the search by school officials be equated to a search by police officers, and be based upon probable cause. The court found that school officials were not held to the same standards as police officers, but noted that police officers, upon a reasonable suspicion that an individual carries a gun, may "stop and frisk." Thus, even if the school officials were held to the same standard as police officers, they would have been justified in a nonconsensual search of Ronald based upon their suspicion that he carried a gun. *Id.* at 546.
104. *Id.* at 545. (quoting People v. D., 34 N.Y.2d 483, 486–87, 315 N.E.2d 466, 468, 358 N.Y.S.2d 403, 406 (1974)).
105. *Id.* at 546.
106. People v. Overton, 20 N.Y.2d 360, 229 N.E.2d 596, 283 N.Y.S.2d 22 (1967), *vacated,* 393 U.S. 85 (1968), *reinstated,* 24 N.Y.2d 522, 249 N.E.2d 366, 301 N.Y.S.2d 479 (1969).
107. *Id.*
108. Moore v. The Student Affairs Comm. of Troy State Univ., 284 F. Supp. 725 (M.D. Ala. 1968).
109. *Id.* at 730.
110. Piazzola v. Watkins, 316 F. Supp. 624 (M.D. Ala. 1970), *affirmed* 442 F.2d 284 (5th Cir. 1971).
111. Note that this uncertainty (or certainty) will probably depend upon the nature of the suspected danger and the actual procedure of the search. *In re Ronald* involved a search by school officials which revealed an extreme danger of a gun. The gun was turned over to police officials and made the basis for a juvenile proceeding. Similarly, a benign administrative search of student lockers by school officials may result in evidence that could be the basis of criminal proceedings. *Compare* Wyman v. James, 400 U.S. 309 (1971) *with* Camara v. Municipal Court, 387 U.S. 523 (1967). However, where police officers themselves seek to conduct a search of the student or his locker, or where the search is conducted "at the elbow" of a school official, independent police grounds for the search may be required before the police-seized evidence may be used in criminal proceedings.
112. 418 F.2d 163 (7th Cir. 1969).
113. 415 F.2d 1077 (8th Cir. 1969), *cert. denied,* 398 U.S. 965 (1970).
114. 418 F.2d at 167.
115. *Id.* (citing Tinker v. Des Moines School Dist., 393 U.S. at 513–14).
116. *Id.*
117. *Id.*
118. *Id.* at 168.
119. 415 F.2d at 1089.
120. *Id.* at 1082.
121. *Id.* at 1088.
122. *Id.*
123. *Id.*
124. 318 F. Supp. 1183 (D. Mass. 1970).
125. *Id.* at 1187.
126. *Id.* at 1188–89.
127. *Id.* at 1188 & n.8.
128. *Id.* at 1188.
129. *Id.* at 1187–88.
130. 585 P.2d 197 (Wyo. 1978).

131. *Id.* at 199 (citing Wyo. Stat. § 21–4–306(a)(iii) (1977)).
132. *Id.* at 204.
133. *Id.* (citing Goss v. Lopez, 419 U.S. 565 (1975).
134. *Id.*
135. 419 U.S. 565 (1975).
136. *See, e.g.,* Comment, *Procedural Due Process in Public Schools: The "Thicket"* of Goss v. Lopez, 1976 Wisc. L. Rev. 934.
137. *See, e.g.,* D. Kirp, *Proceduralism & Bureaucracy: Due Process in the School Setting,* 28 Stan. L. Rev. 841 (1976); M. Nolte, *The Supreme Court's New Rules for Due Process and How (Somehow) Schools Must Make Them Work,* 162 American School Bd. J. 47–49 (March, 1975).
138. 294 F.2d 150 (5th Cir. 1961), *cert. denied,* 368 U.S. 930 (1961).
139. Goss v. Lopez, 419 U.S. at 576 n.8.
140. 367 U.S. 886 (1961).
141. 294 F.2d at 157.
142. *Id.* at 159.
143. *Id.*
144. One student demonstrated with a group of other students in the school auditorium while a class was being held there. He was ordered to leave by the principal but refused. As a policeman attempted to remove that student from the auditorium, another student attacked the policeman in the presence of the principal. Other students were suspended for similar behavior. Lopez himself was suspended for involvement in a lunchroom disturbance that resulted in damage to school property. 419 U.S. at 569–71.
145. *Id.* at 568–69.
146. *Id.* at 572–73.
147. *Id.* at 573.
148. *Id.* at 574.
149. *Id.* at 574–75.
150. *Id.* at 576. *De minimis* is the abbreviation of *de minimis non curat lex,* which means: "The law does not care for, or take notice of very small or trifling matters." Black's Law Dictionary 482 (4th ed. 1968).
151. 419 U.S. at 579 (quoting Grannis v. Ordean, 234 U.S. 385, 394 (1914)).
152. *Id.* at 578 (quoting Cafeteria Workers v. McElroy, 367 U.S. 886, 895 (1961)).
153. *Id.* (quoting Epperson v. Ark., 393 U.S. 97, 104 (1968)).
154. *Id.* at 580.
155. *Id.* at 581.
156. *Id.* at 582–83.
157. *Id.* at 584.
158. *Id.* at 583.
159. *Id.* at 583–84.
160. *Id.* at 584.
161. Sweet v. Childs, 507 F.2d 675, *rehearing denied in light of* Goss v. Lopez, 518 F.2d 320 (5th Cir. 1975).
162. 518 F.2d at 321.
163. *Id.* (quoting Goss v. Lopez, 419 U.S. at 582).
164. *Id.*
165. *Id.* at 321.
166. 583 F.2d 91 (3rd Cir. 1978).
167. *Id.* at 97. The court recognized that requiring notice and a hearing prior to the removal of a disruptive student from the classroom actually exceeded the requirements of *Goss.* But this case involved the modification of a consent decree negotiated between the representatives of a class of parents and students and a teachers' association. Therefore, this holding was only meant to

insure against the removal of innocent students, even though the negotiated modification of the decree specifically provided due process to disruptive students.

168. 426 F. Supp. 397 (E.D. Pa. 1977).
169. *Id.* at 400 (employing language from Goss v. Lopez, 419 U.S. at 576).
170. This was a Philadelphia school district. *Id.* at 399.
171. This more formal requirement of appointment of an impartial hearing officer may not necessarily mean that the individual interests of this case exceed those involved in *Goss*. However, no reason is given to explain why a principal could not assume the role of the hearing officer in these kinds of cases. The only apparent reason why the principal could not is that he or she may be biased by an interest in the administrative necessities of the school. There seems no reason why any other appointee of the school district would be any less biased. In fact, it is possible that another school district official may be more biased.
172. 423 F. Supp. 767 (W.D. Pa. 1976).
173. Sports arguably represent a more significant interest than other extracurricular activities. Most courts, however, have refused to extend property status to participation in interscholastic sports. *See, e.g.,* Colorado Seminary v. N.C.A.A. 570 F.2d 320 (10th Cir. 1978); Dallam v. Cumberland Valley School Dist., 391 F. Supp. 358 (M.D. Pa. 1975). *But see* Denis J. O'Connell High School v. Virginia High School League, 581 F.2d 81, 84 (4th Cir. 1978).
174. 469 F. Supp. 1134 (M.D.N.C. 1979).
175. The court noted, however, that if education is viewed as composed of a range of components that include participation in extracurricular activities, it could be argued that due process protection should extend to extracurricular activities. "However," the court wrote, "*Goss* should not be read to establish a property interest subject to constitutional protection in each of these separate components." 469 F. Supp. at 1139. *See also* Albach v. Odle, 531 F.2d 983, 985 (10th Cir. 1976).
176. *See* Madera v. Bd. of Educ., 386 F.2d 778 (2d Cir. 1967), *cert. denied*, 390 U.S. 1058 (1968).
177. *Id.* at 788–89.
178. 435 F. Supp. 460 (C.D. Cal. 1977).
179. *Id.* at 464–66.
180. *Id.* at 469.
181. *Id.* at 470–71.
182. *Id.* at 471.
183. 82 F.R.D. 186 (N.D. Ill. 1979).
184. *Id.* at 192. *See also* Hillman v. Elliott, 436 F. Supp. 812, 816 (W.D. Va. 1977).
185. *See, e.g.,* Graham v. Knutzen, 351 F. Supp. 642, 666 (D. Neb. 1972).
186. 468 F. Supp. 54 (E.D. Ark. 1978).
187. *Id.* at 58.
188. *See, e.g.,* Dorsey v. Bale, 521 S.W.2d 76 (Ky. App. 1975); Minorics v. Bd. of Educ., N.J. Comm'n. of Educ. Dec. (March 24, 1972).
189. 435 U.S. 78 (1978).
190. *Id.* at 86.
191. *Id.* at 88.
192. *Id.* at 89–90. The Court also said that "courts are particularly ill-equipped to evaluate academic performance," *Id.* at 92.
193. Id. at 90 (quoting Barnard v. Inhabitants of Sherburne, 216 Mass. 19, 22, 102 N.E. 1095, 1097 (1913)). *Cf.* Navato v. Sletten, 560 F.2d 340 (8th Cir. 1977) (participant in psychiatry residency program academically dismissed, but

found to have property interest in contract with public agency incidental to his academic program that required due process protection). For further commentary on the Horowitz case, see Note, Academic Dismissals: *A Due Process Anomaly*, 58 Neb. L. Rev. 519 (1979); Pavela, *Judicial Review of Academic Decision-making After Horowitz*, 8 Nolpe School L. J. 55 (1978).

194. 20 U.S.C. §§ 1230, 1232 (g)–(i) (1976).
195. *See also* E. Gee and D. Sperry, Education and the Public Schools, R–3 to R–7 (1978).
196. Goss v. Lopez, 419 U.S. at 575 (quoting Wisc. v. Constantineau, 400 U.S. 433, 437 (1971)).
197. 430 U.S. 651 (1977).
198. *Id.* at 653–57.
199. *Id.* at 664.
200. These states are Massachusetts and New Jersey. *Id.* at 663.
201. *Id.* at 662.
202. *Id.* at 662–63.
203. *Id.* at 663.
204. *Id.* at 668–71.
205. *Id.* at 679–80.
206. *Id.* at 680.
207. *Id.* at 681.
208. *Id.* at 682.
209. *See* Rosenberg, Ingraham v. Wright: *The Supreme Court's Whipping Boy*, 78 Colum. L. Rev. 75 (1978). *See also* Piele, *Neither Punishment Cruel or Due Process Due: The United States Supreme Court's Decision in* Ingraham v. Wright, 7 J. of L. and Educ. 1 (1978).
210. *See* Englander, *The Court's Corporal Punishment Mandate to Parents, Local Authorities, and the Profession*, 59 Phi Delta Kappan 529 (April, 1978). The alternatives to corporal punishment suggested are:

Stimulus Control: Pinpoint the immediate antecedents to misbehavior and eliminate the stimulation that arouses the misbehavior.

Reward: Immediately reward desired behavior, particularly that behavior that is incongruent with the behavior one wants to eliminate.

Extinction: Misbehavior is frequently perpetuated by the attention it gets. It disappears if ignored.

Contract: An agreement is established whereby the individual receives a valued payoff for desirable behavior over an agreed-to period of time. Contracts can have a penalty clause. For example, a black girl on amphetamines put up $500 with the stipulation that $50 would be donated to the Klu Klux Klan for each violation.

Desensitization: Some misbehavior is aroused out of fear of a given activity, person, or object. The fear, and subsequent misbehavior, can be eliminated by pairing the feared event with a positive or pleasant condition.

Time Out: The alert teacher can sense when problem students are losing their cool or otherwise would profit from a brief (three- to five-minute) period of isolation. Time out is not for punishment or reward; it is for getting away to catch one's breath and get control of oneself.

Self-Control: Student are given the task of monitoring their own behavior and rewarding themselves for agreed-to responsible behavior.

Modeling: Peers have a significant impact on students. If a respected peer is rewarded for a given type of behavior, the others will tend to follow suit.

Id. at 532.

211. *See, e.g.,* Streeter v. Hundley, 580 S.W.2d (Mo. 1979).
212. 395 F. Supp. 294 (M.D.N.C.), *affirmed mem.* 423 U.S. 907 (1975). *See also* Sims v. Waln, 536 F.2d 686 (6th Cir. 1976).
213. 395 F. Supp. at 300–301.
214. Where school officials did not have sufficient basis for the reasonable belief, or suspicion, to justify a search, and they carried the search too far in the absence of any immediate danger, a federal district court has held that the school officials were liable for violation of the student's constitutional rights to privacy and freedom from unreasonable searches, the amount of damages to depend on the degree of mental distress the student could prove. In this case, a high school student was discovered alone in a classroom during a fire drill and was ordered to the dean's office to be searched despite the fact that nothing had been reported stolen. The student was then required to strip to the underwear, after which the school officials conducted an unproductive search. M.M. v. Anker, 477 F. Supp. 837 (E.D.N.Y.) *affirmed,* 607 F.2d 588 (2d Cir. 1979).
215. 420 U.S. 308 (1975).
216. Every person who, under color of any statute, ordinance, regulation, custom, or usage, of any State or Territory, subjects, or causes to be subjected, any citizen . . . to the deprivation of any rights, privileges, or immunities secured by the Constitution and laws, shall be liable to the party injured in an action at at law, suit in equity, or other proper proceeding for redress.

42 U.S.C. § 1983 (1976).

217. 420 U.S. at 312–14 & nn.3–5.
218. *Id.* at 310.
219. *Id.*
220. *Id.* at 319 (quoting Pierson v. Ray, 386 U.S. 547, 554 (1967)).
221. *Id.* at 321.
222. *Id.* at 322.
223. *Id.*
224. 435 U.S. 247 (1978).
225. Compensatory damages are meant to respond to actual damages sustained as opposed to punitive or exemplary damages, which are meant to punish the wrongdoer.
226. *Id.* at 260.
227. *Id.* at 263.
228. Nominal damages are rewarded only as a symbol of wrongdoing in the absence of actual damages or the malice required for punitive damages. They are usually given in a minimal amount—something between one and ten dollars.
229. *Id.* at 266.
230. 420 U.S. at 327–29 (Powell, J., dissenting).
231. *See, e.g.,* Yudof, *Liability for Constitutional Torts and the Risk-Averse Public School Official,* 49 So. Cal. L. Rev. 1322. 1331–32 (1976).
232. A particularly appropriate journal is the Journal of Law and Education. *See also* S. Goldstein, *supra* note 48, and E. Gee, *supra* note 196.
233. *See* R. Anson, *The Educator's Response to* Goss *and* Wood, 57 Phi Delta Kappan 16 (Sept., 1975); R. Von Brock, *Coping with Suspension and the Supreme Court,* 61 N.A.A.S.P. Bulletin 68 (March, 1977).

234. *See, e.g.*, M. Nolte, *The Supreme Court's New Rules for Due Process,* 162 American School Bd. J. 47 (March, 1975).

235. *See* D. Kirp, *Proceduralism and Bureaucracy: Due Process in the School Setting,* 28 Stan. L. Rev. 841 (1976).

236. *See* D. Robinson, *Is This the Right Approach to Student Rights?* 56 Phi Delta Kappan 234 (December, 1974).

237. *See* J. DeCecco and A. Richards, *Using Negotiation for Teaching Civil Liberties and Avoiding Liability,* 57 Phi Delta Kappan 23 (September 1975).

238. *See* M. Nolte, *Why You Need a Student Grievance Plan and How You Can Have a Reasonable One,* 162 American School Bd. J. 38 (August 1975).

CHAPTER FOUR

The Phenomenon of Violence in Schools

INTRODUCTION

Educators have always been concerned about discipline problems. Perhaps the greatest concern is shown by young teachers entering the profession. Historically they worried about controlling the class and about minor student disruptions such as talking to friends, shooting spit wads and hiding erasers. In recent times concerns about classroom discipline are no longer the exclusive province of student teachers approaching their first lesson and beginning teachers arriving at their first school. Now school personnel in general are worried about discipline, and for many educators these concerns have actually become fears. Over the past decade school violence and vandalism in the United States have increased to the highest level in our history. These problems have erupted in colleges as well as in secondary and elementary schools, incorporating a wide latitude of socioeconomic groups and increasing in intensity. Crime and violence in schools have gained enough publicity now to be classified as a major concern of the American public. And, violence and disruption in American education is very real; it is directly perceptible at some level to most teachers, administrators, and, of course, students. The extent and intensity of school and classroom disruption—"discipline problems"—are unprecedented in American education and perhaps in the history of education. Whether we can explain the occurrence of violence and disruption is one matter; its existence is another. There is in fact a phenomenon of violence in American schools.

The overall purpose of this chapter is the development of a position pertaining to the causes and growth of school-related discipline problems. In order to achieve this purpose we approach the problem in the following manner. The first section is an examination of violence as an emerging problem in education. The greatest emphasis is placed on the Safe Schools Study—*Violent Schools—Safe Schools*[1]—which is the most recent and extensive survey of the extent and nature in violence in schools. The aim of this section is to describe the phenomenon of violence in schools. The second section of the chapter discusses possible causes of school violence. The purpose here is to identify the unique contributions of the society, the home, the television, the school, and the students to the problem of violence. Our argument is that all of these factors contribute in varying degrees to a network of causal relationships. A discussion follows of the sequence of stages preceding the actual violence. This section will present a model of behaviors that may be termed "discipline problems." The model includes behaviors that are of the overt, acting-out type and of the inward, withdrawn type. The stages represent a continuum starting with mildly disruptive and ending in violence. By applying this model, school personnel could be assisted in the early identification of disruptive students. The model should also help educators realize that violence is the last step in a sequence of behaviors that are identifiable and, it is assumed, preventable. Throughout the latter section suggested ideas and programs that may help correct problems during earlier, less intense stages are made. An identification of these different levels of violent behavior will act as guides for school personnel who must work with these violations of rules and policies.

SCHOOL VIOLENCE

Violence As an Emerging Problem

In any discussion of school violence the first question that must be answered is—how serious is school violence? This is a difficult question since there are no standards by which one can assess "seriousness." At the extremes, some would argue that any violence in a school is serious, while others believe adolescents are expected to fight and violate rules, and therefore the majority of problems can be classified as "normal" and not very serious. The issue of seriousness will not be resolved here. The approach we have selected is to present some of the recent statistics on violence and disruption in American schools. From there we proceed on the assumption that these data indicate that violence in schools is serious enough to warrant attention.

The American public has been concerned with "lack of discipline" in schools for at least a decade. Since 1969 George Gallup has polled the American public's attitudes toward education. The results show the importance the public places on discipline; it was ranked as the most significant problem nine out of the past ten years.[2] There is good reason to suspect this trend will continue for the next several years. And, for researchers and others, the very fact that the public does consistently rank school discipline as a problem should suggest at least some element of truth to the assertion that the problem is serious. At the same time, this public perception presents a challenge and a goal: can educators reduce disciplinary problems so they no longer are ranked first on Gallup polls? This certainly is an educational goal worth pursuing.

A recent Gallup Poll of attitudes toward education[2] reveals many problems associated with violence, vandalism, and lack of discipline. For example "use of dope/drugs" was the second most serious problem perceived by American adults. Other items ranking as top problems include "poor curriculum," "large schools," "pupil's lack of interest," and "drinking/ alcoholism." All of these problems are factors contributing to the phenomenon of violence faced by school personnel. In fairness, it must be noted that many of today's problems have been developing for some time as a review of earlier statistical data will show.

Unfortunately, statistics on violence and disruption in schools have not been consistently maintained. We can, however, gain a sense of the problem by reviewing several different sources of data. A 1949 review of behavior problems by Carol Hennings[3] indicated that lying and disrespect were the most serious discipline problems encountered by 225 high school principals. The survey also reported the most frequent problems as impertinence and running in corridors. These problems are a concern for educators, but they involve neither physical violence toward teachers and students nor destruction of school property.

A 1956 National Education Association study,[4] however, gave indication that violence might be emerging as a problem. One part of the study showed that 28 percent of the teachers in larger cities were aware of an act of physical violence against a teacher within the past twelve months. There also was indication that the problems were more serious in "slum" areas. While this report hinted at the problem, the tone was still not that of urgency; the majority of youth was not delinquent and the violence seemed isolated in urban areas.

In the late 1950s there was a general increase in crime by youth. For example, FBI reports indicate that the arrest rates of fifteen-to-eighteen year-olds increased from approximately 85 per 100,000 in 1953 to 295 per 100,000 in 1974 for crimes against persons, e.g., homicide, rape, robbery, and assault. The arrest rate increased from 160 per 100,000 in 1953 to 520 per 100,000 in 1974 for crimes against property, e.g., burglary, theft, vandalism, and arson.[5] The schools were not to escape the inevitable; slowly the problem of juvenile crime invaded school corridors.

A best estimate is that school crime had escalated enough during the late 1950s and early 1960s and that it was clearly a problem by 1965. By this time National Education Association reports[6] were confronting the problem directly, and Arthur Stinchcombe had completed his important book, *Rebellion in a High School*,[7] which asserted that school-related crime and violence were taking on major proportions. The phenomenon of school violence continued to escalate into the early 1970s until it became a significant enough public issue to mandate Congressional investigation.

The Bayh Reports

A Senate Subcommittee to Investigate Juvenile Delinquency chaired by Senator Birch Bayh of Indiana initiated an inquiry into school violence and vandalism during the period 1971–1975. The results were reported in several volumes,[8, 9] the most influential of which was *Our Nation's Schools— A Report Card: "A" in School Violence and Vandalism*.[10] The Subcommittee reported a nationwide survey of 759 school districts for the period 1970–73. The alarming results were:

Homicides increased by 18.5 percent;

Rapes and attempted rapes increased by 40.1 percent;

Robberies increased by 36.7 percent;

Assaults on students increased by 85.3 percent;

Assaults on teachers increased by 77.4 percent;

Burglaries of school buildings increased by 11.8 percent;

Drug and alcohol offenses on school property increased by 37.5 percent;

Droputs increased by 11.7 percent; and

Weapons confiscated increased by 54.4 percent. (10, p. 4)

It was this report that first attempted to confirm the cost of vandalism each year. At the time of the report an estimated $600 million was being spent annually on repair and replacement of vandalized property. This is more than $10.00 per year for every student in school, more than is spent on textbooks each year, and enough to hire 50,000 additional classroom teachers. Although this estimate has recently been revised downward to just over $200 million a year, it still represents an astonishing figure. The Bayh Subcommittee's final report, *Challenge for the Third Century: Education in a Safe Environment*[11] continues to be especially helpful in identifying models and strategies for preventing school violence and vandalism.

Safe Schools Study

The problem of violence in American schools finally led to the Safe Schools Study Act of 1974, introduced in the House of Representatives by Congressmen Bingham of New York and Bell of California. The bill directed the National Institute of Education (NIE) to undertake a survey of the frequency, types, and seriousness of crime in schools; the number and location of schools affected; the cost of replacement or repair of objects destroyed, damaged, or stolen; prevention and control measures used by schools; and the individual attitudes and experiences concerning risk and victimization among students and teachers.

Survey data were collected in three phases. During Phase I, principals in 4,014 public elementary and secondary schools completed reports on known offenses during a one-month period and answered a questionnaire on preventive methods. Phase II consisted of on-site data collection at 642 junior and senior high schools. During this phase 23,895 teachers and 31,373 students completed questionnaires. Interviews also were conducted with 6,283 students who had been victims of assault, theft, or robbery. In Phase III, ten secondary schools were selected for case studies to examine the factors affecting the success of school personnel in reducing violence and disruption. The results of the survey have been published in the National Institute of Education report, *Violent Schools—Safe Schools*.[1] The next sections of this chapter summarize the important results of the Safe Schools Study.

Seriousness of Violence in Schools

The Safe Schools Study explored the question of "seriousness" in three ways: first, a time trend analysis; second, the risk of violence to youth in schools; third, principals' perceptions of the seriousness of the problem. So how serious is the problem? First, as described earlier, the problem of violence has gradually escalated over the past three decades. Data do indicate that the growth rate of violence and and vandalism has actually leveled off in the 1970s. Second, the risk of violence to youth is greater in schools than elsewhere when the amount of time spent in school is taken into account. This finding seems to be particularly compelling concerning the seriousness question. One can certainly argue that a cause for immediate action is mandated by this finding alone. Third, school principals from 6,700 (or about 8 percent of American schools) report that violence and disruption are serious problems. Higher proportions of secondary schools have serious crime problems. These problems are greater during the early secondary years, and taper off in later secondary years. Such data seem to show that the question of seriousness is answerable by more than subjective views. The problem of violence in American education certainly is serious enough to warrant the attention of policy makers, particularly when the additional element of public concern, as measured by polls, is taken into account.

Extent of Violence in Schools

The percentage of schools affected by violence increases with community size. In rural areas 4 to 6 percent of schools are affected; in urban areas this increases to 15 percent. There is another way to view this problem: while the probability of a school's having a serious crime problem is higher in urban areas, the majority of schools with serious crime problems are in suburban and rural areas. Therefore, the problem includes all schools, not just those large schools in urban centers.

Presently, there are 157,000 cases of crime and disruption in a typical school month. Of these cases only 50,000 are reported to the police. Across the nation school personnel resolve within the school structures more than 100,000 serious conflicts each month.

Violence Against Students

Eleven percent (2.4 million) of American secondary school students have something worth more than one dollar stolen from them in a typical month. Personal theft is the most widespread offense against persons in schools. In a typical month 1.3 percent (282,000) of secondary school students are attacked at school and .5 percent (112,000) are robbed. Most attacks are not serious; only 4 percent require medical attention. The robberies usually involve small amounts of money and injury is rare.

These statistics portray the more violent end of the continuum of student violence. What about other problems? There are indications that disorder and hostility are common in schools in less intense forms. For example, about 16 percent (3 million) of students avoid at least three places at school (such as restrooms or cafeterias) due to fear, and about 3 percent (500,000) students are afraid at school most of the time.

Violence Against Teachers

Twelve percent (128,000) of teachers in secondary schools have something worth more than one dollar stolen from them in an average month. One half of one percent of secondary teachers (5,200) are physically attacked at school in a typical month. Attacks on teachers are more serious than on students. For teachers, 19 percent of the attacks require medical attention. Approximately 6,000 secondary teachers (.5 percent) are robbed in a typical month.

It is also important to consider the less intense encounters teachers have because these, too, have an effect on teaching. About 12 percent (125,000) of secondary teachers are threatened with physical harm in a school month, and equal numbers hesitate to confront disruptive students for fear of physical harm. Verbal abuse of teachers is common; one half of all surveyed teachers reported that this happened to them in a typical month.

Violence Toward the School

The most frequent of all offenses committed against schools is the destruction of property. There are 42,000 incidents a month affecting one out of every four school facilities. The average cost is $481.00. There are 11,000 incidents of breaking and entering each month. The risk of burglary to schools is five times as high as it is for stores. The average cost of a school burglary is $183.00. There are 13,000 incidents of theft of school property each month; the average cost is $150.00. The annual cost of replacing and repairing school property lost or damaged due to criminal activity is over $200 million. A disproportionally large share of this cost is borne by suburban schools.

This growing phenomenon of violence in schools has received a great deal of publicity in the past several years. Many media presentations have focused on some aspect of problems in schools. While this public airing is important, and an especially powerful way to bring attention to the problem, the often sensational media approach does have the effect of leaving the viewer confused concerning the nature and extent of the problem. Further, there is often some attempt to analyze the origins of the problem in simplistic terms such as "the home" or "television." A clear and concise analysis of the phenomenon of school violence and vandalism shows that it is a highly complex problem that cannot be laid at any particular doorstep. The only clear conclusions that can be drawn from the evidence are: 1) the phenomenon has increased over three decades and has now leveled off and may be declining; 2) the phenomenon includes urban, suburban, and rural schools (that is, it is a national problem); 3) the phenomenon seems to involve youth in general rather than only those with problems such as being poor or being a minority, though these problems may contribute to the phenomenon.

SEARCHING FOR THE CAUSES

What are the causes of violence in schools? Admittedly this is a large and difficult question, one which can partially be answered by reviewing the causes suggested in the literature written by those who are interested in reducing the problem. We commonly hear that violence permeates our society and therefore the schools, since they are a part of society. Predictably, there is the familiar litany of blame. Some feel that school violence results from larger societal factors over which the school system has no control. Social conditions that depress the poor, oppress the minorities and regulate the young are thought to be the causes of violence. There is another line of thought that claims that the schools sow the seeds of crime themselves. School conditions that are outdated, repetitive, unpleasant, and irrelevant, and classrooms described as boring, dull, and inadequate can produce student disruption. Finally there are those who suggest that the problem lies with the individual. Fundamental to this position are the ideas that either aggressiveness is innate or that individuals responsible for the problems are mentally disturbed. Within these broad categories we have elected to discuss those presumed causes that dominate discussions, namely: society, television, home, schools, and students themselves.

Society

One place to start the search for the causes of large-scale violence is with the collective violence of civil disorders. Over America's two-hundred-year history there have been a number of civil uprisings. As early as 1784 Daniel Shay and a small group of farmers in dire economic stress rebelled against the state of Massachusetts. In 1863 the Civil War draft riots were caused by the exemption clause of the Conscription Act which gave advantage to the rich. Other examples are disruptions in the history of organized labor movement, Protestant attacks against Irish Catholics, and anti-Negro riots during World War I. These and other examples show the common themes of protest, perceived injustices, and collective violence of one group against another.

The civil disorder of the blacks during the 1960s provides a more recent illustration and one about which there is some evidence concerning possible causes. In one study, T. M. Tomlinson examined the development of a riot ideology among blacks participating in the 1965 Watts riot in Los Angeles. The ideological origin is suggested by a nexus of perceptions:

> Negroes express far higher rates of perceived political disenfranchisement and impotence to bring about change. At the same time, however, they appear to be deeply committed to bringing about change. The picture therefore is one of intense political concern combined with felt impotence to exert influence on the political structure, and that is a cornerstone of social unrest. (12, p. 29)

A second study by E. H. Ransford reported similar findings. Isolation, powerlessness, and dissatisfaction with treatment by those in authority were found to be the important factors contributing to participation in the Watts riots. [13]

An analysis of surveys made after the 1967 riots in Detroit and Newark supported neither a "riffraff" nor a "relative deprivation" theory to explain participation in the riots. Rather, prolonged exclusion from American economic and social life was the identified primary cause of the riots. [14] Exclusion of blacks from the mainstream of American life was the result of artificial barriers resting on a foundation of racial prejudice. The conception of a better life and greater opportunities emerged for blacks; the old stereotype of passivity was renounced in favor of a new awareness of black pride. However, their actual life situation remained one of impotence and subordination. As Ralph Ellison clearly protrayed, they were still "invisible men."

John Spiegel of the Lemberg Center for the Study of Violence has presented a collective theory of violence. [15] Spiegel analyzed the history of civil disorders in America. He found that riots originated in a strained interaction between democratic ideals and authoritarian practices and that the social structure of the United States has been maintained by the exclusion of some social groups from the decision-making process and by the bureaucratic pyramid with power concentrated at the top of the structure. In order to have access to power and decision making one has had to be: 1) white; 2) Anglo-Saxon; 3) middleclass; 4) Protestant; 5) adult; and 6) male. All of the civil disorders and recent liberation movements in this country can be correlated with an excluded group attempting to penetrate a perceived elitist barrier in order to gain power.

It seems clear that one cause for violence in certain segments of society can be found in a group's sense of isolation, subordination, insignificance, impotence, dissatisfaction, and general alienation from the dominant social structure. And, as Rollo May has pointed out,[16] when one loses a sense of individual significance there is an accompanying decrease in one's sense of human responsibility. Note that one of the categories Spiegel identified would include a potential conflict between adults and youth.

Television

Televised violence is probably the cause most frequently attributed to the increase in school-related crime. A systematic review of the available research on the impact of televised violence was undertaken by the Surgeon General.[17] The report concluded:

First, violence depicted on television can immediately or shortly thereafter induce mimicking or copying by children. Second, under certain circumstances television violence can instigate an increase in aggressive acts. The accumulated evidence, however, does not warrant the conclusion that televised violence has a uniformly adverse effect nor the conclusion that it has an adverse effect on the majority of children (17, p. 7)

Evidence suggests that there is some relationship between viewing violence and aggression, especially if the individual already has a predisposition toward aggressiveness.

The Surgeon General's report showed an even weaker effect of televised violence on older children. This result could be explained by the adolescent's higher levels of moral and ethical development as suggested by Jean Piaget[18] and Lawrence Kohlberg.[19] Adolescents would thus tend to mediate the causes and consequences of the violence viewed and their own tendencies toward aggressiveness. Studies have also indicated that preadolescent children recall only aggressive acts while adolescents recall motives and consequences of aggressive acts they viewed. And, other children apply discriminatory rules concerning the intentionality of aggressiveness and the justifiability of retribution.[20, 21] These results must be balanced with the facts of school violence and vandalism discussed earlier; that is, older children, mainly adolescents, are committing most of the school-related crime. The direct causal relationship between television violence and school crime is certainly weakened by this evidence. However, television could still be a contributing factor.

Most studies have investigated the short-term effects of televised violence on aggressiveness. Yet, common sense leads one to the conclusion that viewing televised violence over the long term must have some effect on an individual. Could it be otherwise when an individual between the ages of four and fourteen conservatively watches three hours of television per day for those ten years? The result is 10,000 hours of television with an estimated five to eight violent acts per hour. We think the effect of this long-term exposure to televised violence is at the conceptual level. In effect it teaches the growing child the concept that conflicts are resolved through aggression.

At the conclusion of the section on adolescents, the Surgeon General's report stated:

> The evidence reviewed here is consonant both with the interpretation that violence viewing leads to aggression to a limited degree and among a limited number of young people, and with the interpretation that both the viewing and the aggression are products of an as yet unidentified third variable. (17, p. 110)

The position advocated in this section is similar to suggesting a "third variable." There are many interconnected variables, however, which contribute to violent and aggressive acts by youth.

Home

The home and family are frequently blamed for students' disruptive behavior. What do educators mean when they say the problem is at home? Usually they mean discipline is either too lax or too strict; the home consists either of a single-parent family or one where the parents are together and dysfunctional; the parents either have too little influence on the children, or they have too much control; the parents either neglect the children's education, or they insist on the children studying and the children rebel. Obviously messages are mixed concerning the home's influence. There is little question but that the home environment does have an influence on youth; the problem is determining the kind and extent of the influences. An analysis of all the family variables that may influence the development of youth is beyond the scope of this book, but there does appear to be one directly related to violence at school; that problem is violence in the home.

Child abuse and neglect have recently escalated from a sole concern of physicians and social workers to a concern of school personnel. All states presently have statutes requiring school personnel to report suspected cases of child abuse and neglect. The effect on youth of having been abused or neglected at home and the relationship of this abuse to violence in the schools need further discussion. But the following are significant points for consideration by school personnel. Research indicates that abused children of preschool age may have speech and language problems,[22] learning and intelligence problems,[23] arrested or frozen developmental processes[24] and other physical, neurological, and intellectual outcomes.[25] These are exactly the types of problems that will contribute to the students' having problems in school. They could be the problems that contribute to that small percentage of students who consistently have problems, fail, and eventually drop out or cause disruption in school. Evidence for this assertion exists at the other end of the continuum. Abuse and neglect have been noted as contributing factors in adolescent suicide attempts,[26] juvenile delinquency,[27] adolescent runaways,[28] and truancy.[29] We realize that the interpolation to school violence is less than direct and that correlation is not causation, but we believe there is sufficient evidence to suggest a connection and to recommend that the problem be researched.

To summarize, violence in the home can contribute to other problems that in time can cause a slow alienation of the individual from the educational system. Second, there is the very influential role model of violence as a means of conflict resolution.

Schools

Over the past decade there have been numerous critical accounts of schools and the public education systems. What was identified as a crisis in the classroom in 1970 is now described by some as terror in the schools. We hear that schools are like prisons,[30] that they are in civil war,[31] and that life in classrooms is generally oppressive.[32] With such criticism, one must query to what degree are schools a reflection of society? Could the school generally, and classrooms specifically, be contributing directly to the problems of violence and vandalism? These questions sound like a variation of "blaming the victim," but education and educators certainly may be contributing to the violence phenomenon in the classroom; the possibility must be examined.

James McPartland and Edward McDill of the Center for Social Organization of Schools have discussed the unique role of schools in the causes of youthful crime in their book, *Violence in Schools*.[33] These authors conclude that school factors do play a role. This role, however, is not as great as nonschool factors. Three ways schools as a system respond to individuals were investigated: report card grades, security systems and access to decision-making processes. Report card grades were consistently and chronically low for self-reported offenders. In short, the reward system has mitigated against some and, over the long term, has contributed to students' estrangement from the school system. This finding has also been supported by the research of Daniel Duke of Stanford University.[34] As to the second response, security systems, the current literature on costs expended for security and reduction of school crime does not give a clear picture of the results of such expenditures. Finally, there appears to be little or no access to the decision-making process by students for some academic matters such as course offerings and staff selection, and for some nonacademic issues such as discipline rules and policies and extracurricular programs. Evidence indicates that giving students access to decision making can increase student commitment and decrease offenses against the staff and school.

The Safe Schools Study generally supported the findings of McPartland and McDill. Students need to feel their courses are relevant, and that they have some control over what happens to them at school. The question of grades revealed interesting answers: academic competition for grades decreases the risk of violence and increases the risk of vandalism. This is not as contradictory as it seems. As McPartland and McDill found, violent students have almost invariably given up on school and feel no commitment; courses, tests and grades are meaningless to them. Since many of these students are still in school, but clearly alienated from the school system, they are likely to commit aggressive acts toward teachers and other students, to use drugs, and to become truant.

The Safe Schools Study also reported that vandalism tends to be higher in schools where grades, achievement, and leadership positions are important. How can student competitiveness contribute to vandalism? Perhaps some students accept the school's reward system but, for various reasons, feel left out, denied, or cheated in the competition. One frequently cited example was the use of grades for disciplinary reasons. Feeling denied by the school system and yet still a part of that system, they take out their anger on school property in acts of vandalism.

Studies completed by O. J. Harvey on teachers' belief systems and behavior point out that they are influential factors on students' behavior. Results showed that teachers' resourcefulness correlated significantly and positively while teachers' dictatorialness and punitiveness correlated significantly and negatively with student performance.[35, 36] It is important to note that Harvey has found that approximately 55 percent of teachers have belief systems and behaviors generally characterized as authoritarian.[37] The impact of authoritarian teachers on classroom behavior is now an issue of intensive discussion.[38]

Of equal importance to this inquiry is the question, how do teachers respond to disruptive students? Criticism is found to be the most common response.[39] After second grade, teacher approval drops and punishment is used more than positive reinforcement.[40] Seventy-five percent of teachers respond to students with either authoritarian or coercive behaviors; these are followed by manipulation and persuasion.[41] The practices were shown to reduce self-esteem and often resulted in the persistence of disruptive behaviors by the students.

Corporal punishment is also used extensively in our schools. According to Safe Schools Study data, 36 percent of all secondary schools paddle students in a typical month, and 61 percent of rural junior high schools reported paddling students in a month's time.

What student responses can be expected from the teacher's excessive use of power? When teachers consistently exert their power, students tend to overvalue their freedom, become concerned about their rights, subtly and indirectly counteract the teacher's control, or resign themselves and become obedient to the teacher's authority.[42] Another study suggested a correlation between the structure of public schools and student disruption. The fact that students are sorted into groups and must be obedient to authority, and that there are an echelon of control and a disparity of goals between the controller and the controlled, all contribute to student unrest and violence.[43] Finally, while there is more serious disruptive behavior in urban schools, this behavior has been shown to increase or decrease depending on the social situation within the school.[44]

At this point it is worth reviewing the factors reported in *Violent Schools—Safe Schools*[1] as they relate to school crime. These factors are suggested here as a means to give direction to school personnel attempting to reduce disruption. These findings are consistent with the research reported above and show strong correlation with social science theories of crime and juvenile delinquency. Likewise they show agreement with earlier research on school discipline problems such as Stinchcombe's *Rebellion in a High School*.[7]

First, the size and impersonality of the school are important factors that differentiate violent schools from safe schools. Three findings support this difference: 1) large schools have greater violence toward property and slightly more personal violence; 2) the more students a teacher has, the greater the amount of violence; 3) the less value students have in teacher's opinions of them, the greater the property loss.

One of the most important identified factors relating to school crime is the school's discipline policies. Generally, the problem arises when there is weak rule enforcement. Strict enforcement of rules and tight classroom control and coordination among school personnel appear important in safe schools. This finding is different from what many would have predicted. Many educators would likely have said that rules should be relaxed. Our interpretation of this finding is that rules must be clear and that the consequences of rule violation must be consistently enforced. This is not the "get tough" position many advocate. It is a "get consistent" position. The point of rule enforcement is fairness and consistency, not harshness and punishment.

These interpretations are consistent with another factor—that of arbitrariness and punitiveness of rule enforcement. Schools where students perceive the disciplinary practices as unfairly administered have higher rates of violence. Likewise, where teachers express authoritarian and punitive attitudes toward students, the schools experience greater amounts of property loss.

Another important factor, previously noted, is the importance of the school's reward structure. Emphasis on good grades reduces violence but apparently increases vandalism. This seems also to be related to the fairness and consistency of the reward structure.

The next factor is one consistently identified in the literature as important—the relevance of the curriculum. Here it was found that student violence was higher in schools where the students felt the teachers were not teaching what they wanted to learn.

The final theme that emerges from the study of violent schools and safe schools is that of alienation. There is simply a breakdown of the bond between the individual and society, or the institutions in society, such as the school. Melvin Seeman[45] has pointed out that the process of alienation can occur in several different ways. Not knowing what social, or school, rules are or should be is the problem of normlessness. Lax or inconsistently enforced school rules could certainly contribute to this process of alienation. Another factor is powerlessness. Here the student would simply feel unable to cope with the school structure. Being unable to earn good grades, participate in leadership roles, athletics, school governance, and, as mentioned earlier, being subordinate to authority, could all contribute to a sense of failure and helplessness in the face of the school's power. Related to the sense of powerlessness is the problem of self-estrangement. Here the individual comes to depend on external rewards rather than intrinsic awards. Alienation can also derive from isolation. This is often a problem in large and impersonal schools. Individuals can slowly come to dispute the value system of the school and develop their own value system, often "antisocial" and possibly aligned with another social system such as a youth gang. A final alienating factor is meaninglessness. This is the individual's lack of clear value system by which to interpret behavior outcomes. In other words, life must make sense to the individual. More specifically, school must make sense to the individual. If the rules are not clear and are inconsistently and arbitrarily enforced, or if the curriculum is irrelevant, with obscure assignments and grades capriciously given, the student may develop an alienated view; namely that school is meaningless. It is then easy to understand that individuals will turn to other value systems that give them meaning. Unfortunately some of these value systems condone violent and disruptive behavior.

In brief, the evidence seems to indicate quite clearly that students' behavior is affected by the school, and this behavior can be disruptive, depending on their perceptions of the school and teachers. Of particular importance seem to be the ways students perceive their freedom; power; the process of educational decision making; and the teacher's authority, control, and punitiveness.

Students

Each individual has a need for a long-term, firmly established, positive view of self. This concept has been referred to as personal adequacy by Arthur Combs *et al.*[46] and self-esteem by Abraham Maslow.[47] Self-esteem includes a sense of control over one's own destiny and power to regulate the environment.

The opinion one has of oneself is an important influence on behaviors directly related to classroom discipline. This general conclusion and the ways self-esteem influences behavior have been reported by Stanley Coppersmith.[48] Low self-esteem in individuals results in feelings of isolation, lack of community, weakness against others, and personal deficiencies. Students who evidence low self-esteem generally are fearful of others, and in social groups, such as classrooms, remain isolated, shy, passive, sensitive to criticism, and preoccupied with inner problems. Characteristics such as these contribute to a downward spiral resulting in even lower feelings of self-esteem. Exploration of factors that develop high self-esteem produced the following results: high personal regard by parents, demand for high standards of behavior, and consistent and fair enforcement of rules. In contrast to low self-esteem, individual discipline was not harsh and punitive. Rewards were used much more than punishment.

What happens when individuals are continually confronted by alienating environments not fostering personal identity? An answer to this question has been proposed by Philip Zimbardo.[49] Individuals can undergo a process of deindividuation. Zimbardo defines deindividuation as a "process in which a series of antecedent social conditions lead to changes in perception of self and others and thereby to a lowered threshold of normally restrained behavior." (49, p. 251) Deindividuated behavior is emotional, impulsive, irrational, regressive and atypical for the person in the given situation. Conditions of deindividuation reduce self consciousness, personal distinction and feelings of self-esteem. Under such conditions antisocial behavior characterized by greed, powerseeking, and destruction may occur.

What are the conditions that affect deindividuated behavior? Anonymity, lack of responsibility, group size, and arousal seem to be the primary causes.[50] Zimbardo also suggests that drugs, novel situations, and sensory overload may also contribute to the process. When social conditions are such that personal identity is diminished, deindividuated behaviors such as aggression toward others and vandalism of traditional forms toward institutional structures can follow. The rioting in New York City during the blackout is an example of deindividuated behavior. School situations in which youth might undergo deindividuation are: anonymity; a large, impersonal school; peer group pressure; drugs and alcohol; or a novel situation, such as a substitute teacher.

The strength of an individual's self-esteem would certainly contribute to the degree to which deindividuating forces would influence personal choices toward or away from antisocial behavior. It is also clear that deindividuation could result in violence and vandalism specifically directed toward the school, since it can be a contributing factor in the deindividuation process. Perhaps more importantly, individuals spend a significant amount of time in school. Over a period of seven or eight years there can be an interaction of factors contributing to the process of deindividuation, but there is a simultaneous process of reindividuation into behaviors that generally could be described as antisocial.

To summarize, there are several explanations commonly heard concerning causes of crime in school. Blocked opportunity, subcultures of violence, psychological illness, and self-fulfilling prophecy are some of the terms used to describe these contributing factors. While there is some evidence supporting these ideas there is also evidence contradicting them. Proposed here is a variation on the restricted-opportunity theory. The idea of blocked opportunity is generally attributed to individuals who are economically disadvantaged, who are of minority background, and who live in an urban environment. These criteria fall quite short of the reported range of school-related crime, for such acts cut across economic class, racial groups, and living environments.

The oppression we suggest here is against youth in general. It is not necessarily group-specific, but when the youth is also a member of a particular nonwhite race, is female, and from lower economic status, the effects may be multiplied.

Powerlessness—incorporating lack of decision-making power, submission to authority, anonymity, isolation, and insignificance—seems to be a wellspring of violence and vandalism in American schools. When personal perceptions of powerlessness are combined with learned concepts that conflicts are resolved by aggression and environmental conditions that contribute to the restructuring of values, then all of the ingredients for violence and vandalism are present.

Thus far we have identified what we believe to be the important causes of violence in the schools. Granted, there are factors beyond the school walls that contribute to the problem, but schools and teachers have not responded to the needs and rights of youth, thus forcing other governmental entities, such as the courts, to do what educators have been neglecting. For example, the courts have made it clear that a student's constitutional rights are not left at the schoolhouse door, thus creating certain rights and responsibilities for students. Over the past few years several national commissions also have proposed various reforms of secondary education in order to better meet the needs of youth. During the same period these reforms were suggested, however, a small, but increasing, percentage of youth terrified other students, teachers, administrators, and parents to the point of creating a national crisis in the schools.

The available data seem to indicate that the progression of increasingly violent behaviors originates in the individual's need to maintain and develop a sense of personal esteem, dignity, and integrity. Apathy toward or suppression of these needs can result in a process that reduces the importance of social values, which in turn restricts the use of violence against self, others, or society.

THE DEVELOPMENT OF VIOLENT BEHAVIORS

Violent behavior does not emerge spontaneously and capriciously from normal behavior. The causes of violent behavior are many; the progression to violence is often slow. Violence is the last stage of a sequence that includes the outward behaviors of affirmation, assertion, and aggression and the inward behaviors of alienation, withdrawal, and depression. In the following sections we describe patterns of classroom behaviors based on our observations of various stages similar to those proposed by Rollo May in *Power and Innocence*,[51] Karl Menninger in *The Vital Balance*,[52] and Rudolf Driekurs and Pearl Cassel in *Discipline Without Tears*.[53] We propose this model as a method of analyzing the seriousness of specific disruptive behaviors. By analogy, misdeameanors are not felonies, but they are both violations of criminal codes and require some form of consequence. The levels of disruptiveness can also be defined in two ways, either of which should be helpful to school personnel. One approach is to describe the behaviors associated with the different levels of disruption; the other approach is to define the disruptive behavior as it relates to school rules, policies, or expectations of behavior. In later chapters we apply these levels of disruption to practical situations.

Affirmation and Alienation

The first behaviors that can be perceived as disruptive are those that individuals use when seeking affirmation. Attention from the teacher is one way students have of feeling personally adequate and of gaining esteem in the eyes of their peers. There are numerous examples of these behaviors, such as asking others about new clothes, hairdos, and athletic performances. It is true that behaviors at this stage can be socially acceptable and thus ignored by the teachers. This level of social acceptance has been shown to be related to disruptive behavior of fifth and sixth graders. Specifically, low social acceptance is related to resentment of group control, attention seeking, lack of self-control, temper tantrums, and difficulty in getting along with others.[54]

In the classroom, students at this level may talk excessively, move out of their seats, clown, ask questions, have "pseudo" problems, make requests of the teacher, show off and be mildly mischievous. Classroom behaviors at this stage are subtle and often overlooked by the teacher simply because they are so common.

There is also the possibility that an individual can turn inward and become detached and slightly withdrawn. Alienation is used here in the same sense it was discussed earlier in this chapter. The emphasis here is on the first perceptible behaviors that may indicate an individual's sense of self-estrangement, powerlessness, normlessness, isolation, and meaninglessness. The student is unfriendly, indifferent, dissociated, and estranged from the teacher and from most other students. Teachers describe these individuals as shy, sad, "turned off," isolated, or unmotivated. Because most teachers respond more to noise and activity the alienated student is cause for concern since this student can go unrecognized until the problem is truly serious.

The majority of behaviors at this level are within the parameters of school rules and policies. Violations are rare and not consistent. Generally, the violations that do occur are within a realm described as "expectations of behavior." Teachers have many things they expect that are not necessarily written rules. Sitting quietly, listening to others, and being ready to work are common examples of expected behaviors.

What can the teacher do? Each student has a unique background, needs, and perceptions of the situation. It is only logical to find out the student's perceptions of self, others, and the school. Listening to comments and observing behaviors over a week and developing the techniques of marginal[55] or life-space interviewing[56] are good first steps in solving the problem. These are techniques that will give the teacher information about his or her students. Students at this stage can have the experience of leadership, receive praise, make decisions, exercise rights, and have attention, all in educationally constructive ways.

The subtlety and pervasiveness of this stage make it very difficult for the classroom teacher. It is subtle because the behaviors are within a range of normal classroom behaviors and pervasive because most students engage in some of the behaviors some of the time. If the student's need for attention is continually met with apathy or repression over a period of time, a new, more intense behavior pattern will emerge.

Assertion and Withdrawal

When teachers speak of pupils who are discipline problems they are usually referring to this stage. This is the stage where problems come to their attention. Assertive behaviors are attempts to express oneself clearly, forcefully, and often boldly. Individuals who actively maintain positions or defend their rights are asserting themselves. Assert comes from the Latin *asserere* meaning "to join one's self." There is an important point here; assertive individuals are behaving positively and still wish to be recognized as working within the system or with the teacher.

The withdrawn student is moving away from others but is still partially associated with students and teachers. Withdrawn pupils will be detached from emotional involvement with school or teachers. They will be occasionally truant; that is, they physically withdraw from school, and communication is no longer easy for the teacher because the student is remote, isolated, and often unresponsive.

This stage is differentiated from affirmation and alienation by the intensity, duration, and consistency of behaviors. Students' behaviors will be sufficiently intense that teachers and other students cannot help but notice them. Disruption will be longer and occur consistently. There will be violations of school rules and policies, and consistent violations of classroom rules.

Assertion and withdrawal are differentiated from aggression and depression, the next level, by the fact that lines of communication are moderately open; there is some respect for teachers and schools even if great doubt is shown outwardly toward those in positions of authority.

In the classroom students at the assertion stage may show anger, defy authority, talk back, show off, be tardy, refuse to work, scapegoat, or have tantrums. The more withdrawn student may be stubborn, sullen, and embarrassed and avoid eye contact, talking, and responding. There is some evidence to indicate more girls than boys will withdraw.[57]

Traditionally the reaction of teachers to disruptive behavior at this stage has been punishment through the removal of privileges and rights, and/or infliction either verbally or physically of something aversive. Punishment should be avoided as it may exacerbate the teacher-student conflict and have negative results on students not directly involved. As discussed earlier and in another study, it has been shown that a disruptive effect is partly related to a struggle for power.[58]

Solutions available to the teacher are many. Varieties of behavior modification have been found effective.[59, 60, 61, 62] Also effective is positive peer pressure,[63] direct intervention,[64] various forms of individual and group therapy,[65] and a "logical consequences" approach to discipline problems.[66]

Students reaching this stage are at a crucial junction. Here is where they can turn toward improvement or further deterioration. At this stage students will decide to fail, consider dropping out, be suspended, experiment with drugs, become truant and delinquent, and join gangs. Their capacity to make choices and have power within the system has become so diminished that they start deciding against the system and forming different values that maintain their esteem, power, and individuality through antisocial activities.

Aggression and Depression

Student behaviors demonstrating aggression have the immediate aim of taking over and controlling the situation. Open and malicious disobedience or regression and disassociation characterize the two aspects of this stage. There is consistent violation of school rules and policies to the point of suspension, expulsion, and detention. Some criminal codes also are occasionally violated at this level. Use of drugs, alcohol, status offenses such as running away, truancy, and minor vandalism characterize the offenses in which these individuals may engage.

Aggressive students physically or verbally move in and attempt to dominate the classroom. For these individuals the line has been drawn between themselves and the teacher. Moving across the line, starting the disruptive behavior, and continuing the hostility all achieve a sense of power for the students.

Depression, in the sense it is used here, is a turn inward, an escape from reality. Depression literally means to "press down," and this is exactly what these individuals have done with the social values that influence the behaviors of most other students. These students, too, control the situation and have power, but it is a power personally constructed and maintained. Some of the overt signs of this stage are chronic despondency, sullenness, and dejection.

The probability of students at this level being in class is small. They are the ones who are consistently tardy, truant, suspended, or delinquent or who have dropped out. For a variety of reasons they spend more time in the streets than in school, and more time in the principal's or counselor's office than in the classroom. But if the student is in class, it is difficult for the teacher, because communication is marginal, personal relationships are tenuous, and group dynamics are delicate.

Much social psychological research has been done on human aggression. While there is still no consensus among these researchers, there are some notable results for those concerned with school aggression. There are a number of studies reporting that exposure of children to aggression tends to facilitate aggression.[67-73] It has also been found that some childhood conditions such as punishment, lack of acceptance, lack of parental identification, violent television, and transience all contribute to aggression in later childhood.[74] Greater physical punishment results in greater aggression and less identification with the punisher.[75] Turning to the specific school situation Kounin and Gump[76] found that children who have punitive teachers show more aggression in their misconduct, are more unsettled and less concerned with learning, and are more ambivalent over unique school values. Students who have been exposed to aggressive models and then experienced failure in competitive situations also tend to be more aggressive than those who succeed.[77] All of these findings appear to be consistent with those of the *Safe Schools Study*.

While several of these studies and a Surgeon General's report indicate that televised violence does have an impact on aggression, particularly if the individual is predisposed towards violence in the first place, it does little good to place the blame solely on television and ignore the fact that aggressive behaviors can be imitated from and/or instigated by classroom teachers. The impact of an aggressive, punitive teacher on an individual who is on the thin edge between assertiveness and aggression, or aggression and violence, could certainly have greater force than the one-step-removed world of television make-believe. Classroom punishment by teachers and corporal punishment by administrators is real and involving and has personal meaning for the student. Further, the adversary is clearly identifiable in fact or in symbol.

Referral to counselors and therapists, both in the school and community, is important for students at this level. When in school a combined and coordinated effort by all the teachers who interact with the student is essential. If the student has been out of school due to dropping out or suspension, special efforts should be made by the staff to help the student readjust to the school situation[78] and avoid some of the cues that evoked hostility in a prior situation.[79] In addition to these suggestions some have found role playing[80] and varieties of behavioral management and contingency reinforcement, video feedback of behavior,[81] and forms of isolation[82] effective. Working with aggressive students is serious, difficult, and trying for the teacher because of the adversary relationship. One thing appears crucial: aggressive conflict should be avoided because violence is the next stage

Violence Toward Society, School, and Self

Violence is the immoderate use of physical force exerted with the purpose of abusing, damaging, or violating another person, property, or oneself. Here is the final stage; all remnants of communication and rationality are gone. The prolonged alienation preceding this stage now takes its toll, for the individual attempts to achieve an ultimate sense of control by totally dominating the environment. For each person there is a final breaking point where the physiological, physical, or psychological needs can no longer be repressed by social values. The small percentage of students who reach this point are the statistics we hear about. They assault, murder, and rape other individuals; they steal, vandalize, and burn schools; and they have complete psychotic breaks, becoming chemically dependent or commiting suicide.

The question "Why?" is often heard as individuals try to make sense out of vandalism. In many cases the vandalism of schools is apparently senseless, meaningless, and aimless. Property is destroyed rather than stolen, and there is no ideological goal or vindictive motive. Vandalism is not the mindless destruction of just any property. Vandalism is largely the result of individuals' frustration toward the people and the institution who have been unconcerned about their rights, apathetic toward their needs, and unresponsive to requests for inclusion. The message of vandalism is clear: individuals see little hope or meaning in the school. It is the territory of the adversary, and a way to express one's anger over impotence is to destroy school property willfully. In case after case when students have been involved in the school in a meaningful way the rate and intensity of vandalism are reduced.

In closing, we have located foci of school violence and vandalism and suggested a sequence of behaviors, identifiable in classrooms, that precede violence. Precautions must be taken against the small percentage of students who are responsible for the problems. Certainly, teachers must protect themselves and their students from violent individuals. Schools also must be kept safe and secure from their vandalism. It is also true that other students, teachers, administrators, and the community can respond to the needs of youth and prevent their travel through the stages discussed in this chapter. The steps toward school violence and vandalism are taken one at a time, and we are all in a position to help prevent the journey.

SUMMARY

The recent history and related statistics on school-related violence were reviewed. Analysis of the statistics shows that the phenomenon of violence in schools has increased over the past three decades and has now leveled off and is perhaps declining. The problem is national in that it includes all communities and is not localized geographically or economically. The problem seems to center on youth in general rather than on specific subgroups of youth.

A review of commonly attributed causes—violence in society, violence on television, violence in the home, school factors, and adolescent problems—showed that a multiplicity of factors contribute to the development of youth violence in schools. There is, in effect, an ecology that slowly contributes to the restructuring of values away from a prosocial to an antisocial orientation.

Different behaviors representing levels of intensity and frequency of school conflicts include affirmation and alienation; assertion and withdrawal; aggression and depression; and finally violence toward self, others, or society. These levels can be used by school personnel to judge the seriousness of student disruption and to respond appropriately to the problems of students.

REFERENCES

1. National Institute of Education, *Violent Schools—Safe Schools*, Vols. I & II (Washington, D. C.: U. S. Government Printing Office, 1978).
2. Stanley Elam, ed., *The Gallup Polls of Attitudes Toward Education 1969–1973*

(Bloomington, Indiana: Phi Delta Kappa, 1973). See also: George H. Gallup, "Sixth Annual Gallup Poll of the Public's Attitudes Toward Education," *Phi Delta Kappan* 56, no. 1 (1974): 20–32. George H. Gallup, "Seventh Annual Gallup Poll of the Public's Attitudes Toward Education," *Phi Delta Kappan* 57, no. 4 (1975):227–41. George H. Gallup, "Eighth Annual Gallup Poll of the Public's Attitudes Toward the Public Schools," *Phi Delta Kappan* 58, no. 2 (1976): 187–200. George H. Gallup, "Ninth Annual Gallup Poll of the Public's Attitudes Toward the Public Schools," *Phi Delta Kappan* 59, no. 1 (1977):33–48. George H. Gallup, "Tenth Annual Gallup Poll of the Public's Attitudes Toward the Public Schools," *Phi Delta Kappan* 60, no. 1 (1978): 33–45.

3. Carol Hennings, "Discipline: Are School Practices Changing?" *The Clearing House* XIII (January 1949): 267, 270.
4. National Education Association, "Teacher Opinion on Pupil Behavior 1955–56," *National Education Association Research Bulletin* XXXIV (April 1956).
5. Statistics Branch, Uniform Crime Reporting Division, U. S. Department of Justice. Reported in Robert Rubel, *The Unruly School* (Lexington, Massachusetts: Lexington Books, 1977), pp. 146–49.
6. National Education Association, "Student Violence and Rebellion—How Big a Problem?" *NEA Journal* (September 1960): 60.
7. Arthur Stinchcombe, *Rebellion in a High School* (Chicago: Quadrangle Books, 1964).
8. Committee on the Judiciary, United States Senate, *School Violence and Vandalism: The Nature, Extent, and Cost of Violence and Vandalism in Our Nation's Schools* (Washington, D. C.: U. S. Government Printing Office, 1976).
9. _____. *School Violence and Vandalism: Models and Strategies for Change* (Washington, D. C.: U. S. Government Printing Office, 1976).
10. _____. *Our Nation's Schools—A Report Card: "A" In School Violence and Vandalism* (Washington, D. C.: U. S. Government Printing Office, 1975).
11. Report of the Subcommittee to Investigate Juvenile Delinquency, *Challenge for the Third Century: Education in a Safe Environment—Final Report on the Nature and Prevention of School Violence and Vandalism* (Washington, D. C.: U. S. Government Printing Office, 1977).
12. T. M. Tomlinson, "The Development of a Riot Ideology among Urban Negroes," *American Behavioral Scientist* 11 (March–April 1968): 27–31.
13. H. E. Ransford, "Isolation, Powerlessness and Violence: A Study of Attitudes and Participation in the Watts Riot," *The American Journal of Sociology* 73 (July 1968): 581–91.
14. N. S. Caplin and J. M. Paige, "A Study of Ghetto Rioters," *Scientific American* 219 (August 1968): 15–21.
15. John Spiegel, "Toward a Theory of Collective Violence," paper delivered at the American Psychological Association, Chicago, November 1968.
16. Rollo May, *Psychology and the Human Dilemma* (New York: Van Nostrand Reinhold, 1967).
17. Surgeon General's Scientific Advisory Committee on Television and Social Behavior, *Television and Growing Up: The Impact of Televised Violence* (Washington, D. C.: U. S. Department of Health, Education and Welfare, 1971).
18. Jean Piaget, *The Moral Judgement of the Child* (New York: The Free Press, 1965).
19. Lawrence Kohlberg, "Stage and Sequence: The Cognitive Developmental Approach to Socialization," in D. Goslin, *Handbook of Socialization Theory and Research* (Chicago: Rand McNally, 1967).
20. W. A. Collins, et al., "Observational Learning of Motives and Consequences for Television Aggression: A Developmental Study," *Child Development* 40 (September 1970): 799–802.

21. D. W. Shantz and T. Pentz, "Situational Effects on Justifiableness of Aggression at Three Age Levels," *Child Development* 43 (December 1972): 274–79, and D. W. Shantz and D. A. Voydanoff, "Situational Effects on Retaliatory Aggression at Three Age Levels," *Child Development* 44 (September 1973): 149–53.

22. Florence Blager and Harold Martin, "Speech and Language of Abused Children," in Harold Martin, ed., *The Abused Child: A Multi-disciplinary Approach to Developmental Issues and Treatment* (Cambridge, Massachusetts: Ballinger Co., 1976).

23. Harold Martin and Martha Rodeheffer, "Learning and Intelligence," in Harold Martin, ed., *The Abused Child: A Multidisciplinary Approach to Developmental Issues and Treatment* (Cambridge, Massachusetts: Ballinger Co., 1976).

24. Ray Helfer, John McKinney, and Ruth Kempe, "Arresting or Freezing the Developmental Process," in Ray Helfer and Henry Kempe, *Child Abuse and Neglect: The Family and the Community* (Cambridge, Massachusetts: Ballinger Co., 1976).

25. Harold Martin, et al., "The Development of Abused Children," in Irving Schulman, ed., *Advances in Pediatrics*, Vol. 21 (New York: Yearbook Medical Publishers, 1974).

26. Jerry Jacobs, *Adolescent Suicide* (New York: John Wiley and Sons, 1971).

27. Brandt Steele and Joan Hopkins, National Center for Prevention and Treatment of Child Abuse and Neglect, Denver, Colorado, personal communication.

28. Ira Lurie, National Institute of Mental Health, personal communication.

29. Rodger Bybee and Patricia Libbey, "Potential Dropouts' Perceptions of School Rules," unpublished manuscript.

30. Phillip Zimbardo and C. Honey, "The Blackboard Penitentiary—It's Tough to Tell a High School from a Prison," *Psychology Today* 9 (June 1975): 26, 29, 106.

31. John P. DeCeeco and Arlene Richards, "Civil War in the High Schools," *Psychology Today* 9 (November 1975): 51, 56, 120.

32. Phillip Jackson, *Life in Classrooms* (New York: Holt, Rinehart and Winston, 1968).

33. John M. McPartland and Edward M. McDill, *Violence in Schools* (Lexington, Massachusetts: Lexington Books (D. C. Heath, 1977).

34. Daniel L. Duke, "Who Misbehaves?—A High School Studies Its Discipline Problems," *Educational Administration Quarterly* 12, no. 3 (1976): 65–85.

35. O. J. Harvey, et al., "Teachers' Belief Systems and Preschool Atmospheres," *Journal of Educational Psychology* 57 (1965): 373–81.

36. ———, "Teachers' Beliefs, Classroom Atmosphere and Student Behavior," *American Educational Research Journal* 5 (March 1968): 151–56.

37. O. J. Harvey, "Beliefs and Behavior: Some Implications for Education," *The Science Teacher* 37 (December 1970): 10–73.

38. M. L. Crow and M. E. Bonney, "Recognizing the Authoritarian Personality Syndrome in Educators," *Phi Delta Kappan* 57 (September 1975): 40–44.

39. B. Rosenshine and N. Furst, "Research in Teacher Performance Criteria," in B. O. Smith, ed., *Research in Teacher Education* (Englewood Cliffs: Prentice-Hall, 1971).

40. Mary White, "Natural Rates of Teacher Approval and Disapproval in the Classroom," *Journal of Applied Behavior Analysis* 8, no. 4 (1975): 367–72.

41. J. DeFlaminis, "Teacher Responses to Classroom Misbehavior: Influence Methods in a Perilous Equilibrium " (paper presented at the American Educational Research Association Convention, San Francisco, April 1976).

42. D. Tjosvald, "The Issue of Student Control: A Critical Refiew of the Litera-

ture" (paper presented at the American Educational Research Association Convention, San Francisco, April 1976).

43. N. Fink and B. Cullers, "Student Unrest: Structure of the Public Schools a Major Factor?" *The Clearing House* 44 (March 1970): 415–19.

44. G. A. Rogeness, et al., "The Social System and Children's Behavior Problems," *American Journal of Orthopsychiatry* 44 (July 1974): 497–502.

45. Melvin Seeman, "On the Meaning of Alienation," *American Sociological Review* 24 (December 1959): 783–91.

46. Arthur Combs, et al., *Perceptual Psychology* (New York: Harper & Row, 1976).

47. Abraham Maslow, *Motivation and Personality* (New York: Harper & Row, 1970).

48. Stanley Coopersmith, "Studies in Self Esteem," *Scientific American* 218 (February 1968): 96–106.

49. Phillip Zimbardo, "The Human Choice: Individuation, Reason, and Order Versus Deindividuation, Impulse and Chaos," in W. Arnold and D. Levine, eds., *Nebraska Symposium on Motivation—1969* (Lincoln, Nebraska: University of Nebraska Press, 1969).

50. E. Diener, et al., "Effects of Deindividuation Variables on Stealing among Halloween Trick or Treaters," *Journal of Personality and Social Psychology* 33 (1976): 178–83.

51. Rollo May, *Power and Innocence* (New York: W. W. Norton, 1972).

52. Karl Menninger, *The Vital Balance* (New York: Viking Press, 1975).

53. Rudolf Dreikurs and P. Cassel, *Discipline Without Tears* (New York: Hawthorn Books, 1972).

54. N. M. Lorber, "Inadequate Social Acceptance and Disruptive Classroom Behavior," *Journal of Educational Research* 59 (April 1966): 360–62.

55. Bruno Bettleheim, *Love Is Not Enough* (New York: Avon, 1971).

56. W. Morse, "Training Teachers in Life Space Interviewing," *American Journal of Orthopsychiatry* 33 (July 1963): 727–30.

57. H. M. Lahaderne and P. W. Jackson, "Withdrawal in the Classroom: A Note on Some Educational Correlates of Social Desirability Among School Children," *Journal of Educational Psychology* 61 (1970): 97–101.

58. W. J. Gnagery, "Effects on Classmates of a Deviant Student's Power and Response to a Teacher-Exerted Control Technique," *Journal of Educational Psychology* 51 (1960): 1–10.

59. B. F. Skinner, "Contingency Management in the Classroom," *Education* 90 (November 1969): 10–15.

60. H. Porterfield et al., "Contingent Observation: An Effective and Acceptable Procedure for Reducing Disruptive Behavior of Young Children in a Group Setting," *Journal of Behavioral Analysis* 9 (1976): 55–64.

61. T. McLaughlin and J. Malsby, "Reducing and Measuring Inappropriate Verbalizations in a Token Classroom," *Journal of Applied Behavior Analysis* 5 (Fall 1972): 329–33.

62. H. Walker et al., "Deviant Classroom Behavior as a Function of Combinations of Social and Token Reinforcements and Cost Contingency," *Behavior Therapy* 7 (January 1976): 76–88.

63. M. Scapo, "Peer Models Reverse the 'One Bad Apple Spoils the Barrel' Theory," *Teaching Exceptional Children* 5 (1972): 20–24.

64. F. G. Winnigred and K. C. Hoedt, "Classroom-Related Behavior Problems: Counsel Parents, Teachers or Children?" *Journal of Counseling Psychology* 22 (1974): 38.

65. H. Rosenstock and D. Hansen, "Toward Better School Adaptibility: An Early

Adolescent Group Therapy Experiment," *The American Journal of Psychiatry* 131 (December 1974): 50–61.

66. D. Dinkmeyer and D. Dinkmeyer, Jr., "Logical Consequences: A Key to the Reduction of Disciplinary Problems," *Phi Delta Kappan* 57 (June 1976): 664–66.

67. Albert Bandura et al., "Transmission of Aggression Through Imitation of Aggressive Models," *Journal of Abnormal and Social Psychology* 63 (1961): 575–82.

68. L. Berkowitz, "Some Aspects of Observed Agression," *Journal of Personality and Social Psychology* 2 (1965): 359–69.

69. L. D. Eron, "Relationship of T. V. Viewing Habits and Aggressive Behavior in Children," *Journal of Abnormal and Social Psychology* 67 (1963): 193–96.

70. R. Green et al., "The Facilitation of Aggression by Aggression: Evidence against the Catharsis Hypothesis," *Journal of Personality and Social Psychology* 31 (April 1975): 721–26.

71. P. Kuhn et al., "Effects of Exposure to an Aggressive Model and Frustration on Children's Aggressive Behavior," *Child Development* 38 (1967): 739–46.

72. R. Walters and O. Willows, "Imitation Behavior of Disturbed Children Following Exposure to Aggressive and Non-Aggressive Models," *Child Development* 19 (1968): 81–82.

73. R. G. Green and L. Berkowitz, "Some Conditions Facilitating the Occurrence of Aggression after the Observance of Violence," *Journal of Personality* 35 (1967): 666–76.

74. L. Eron et al., "How Learning Conditions in Early Childhood—Including Mass Media—Relate to Aggression in Late Adolescence," *American Journal of Orthopsychiatry* 44 (April 1974): 412–23.

75. M. Lefkowitz et al., "Punishment, Identification and Aggression," *Merrill Palmer Quarterly* 9 (1963): 159–74.

76. Jacob Kounin and P. Gump, "The Comparative Influence of Punitive and Non-Punitive Teachers upon Children's Concepts of School Misconduct," *Journal of Educational Psychology* 52 (1961): 44–49.

77. J. D. Nelson et al., "Children's Aggression Following Competition and Exposure to an Aggressive Model," *Child Development* 40 (December 1969): 1085–97.

78. D. Mayer, "Aggressive and Delinquent Adolescent Behavior Patterns: Effective Curriculum Adjustments in the Middle School," *Clearing House* 49 (January 1976): 203–209.

79. L. Berkowitz, "Aggressive Cues in Aggressive Behavior and Hostility Catharsis," *Psychological Review* (1964): 104–22.

80. J. Gumaer et al. "Affective Education through Role Playing: The Feeling Class," *The Personnel and Guidance Journal* 53 (April 1975): 604.

81. K. C. Esveldt et al., "Effects of Videotape Feedback on Children's Classroom Behavior," *Journal of Educational Research* 67 (July-August 1974): 453–56.

82. R. Drobman and R. Spitalnik, "Social Isolation as a Punishment Procedure: A Controlled Study," *Journal of Experimental Child Psychology* 16 (October 1973): 236–49.

CHAPTER FIVE

Ethical Development and Education

INTRODUCTION

In education ethical development occurs in the interaction between students and school personnel. Of primary concern here is the context of the interaction, in particular, school-related discipline problems. Discussions of ethical development usually are directed toward youth with the goal of encouraging their moral development or clarifying their values. There is a tacit assumption that the ethical level of teachers and administrators is unimportant or of marginal importance, or that they are at advanced levels of ethical development and so need not be considered. Our point is not to debate the differences in ethical development between students and school personnel; it is to point out that in the interaction between students and school personnel the ethical positions of all individuals must be considered.

Disruptive behavior is the basis of ethical interactions in many school situations. These conflicts can be real or imagined, intrapersonal or interpersonal, verbal or physical. The themes of this chapter are: school conflicts involve rules; the resolution of school conflicts should facilitate ethical development; and justice should be a goal in conflict resolution and subsequently in ethical development.

Rules are essential for social order. Yet, rules are paradoxical. On the one hand they allow freedom, and on the other they restrict and control. There are consequences for both obeying and disobeying rules. Rules give power to some persons and render other persons powerless. Rules limit reality for some, and they free others. Sometimes we are neither aware of nor rewarded for following rules; yet we do. Rule violations, however, often are noticed and thus we have conflicts with others that must be resolved. In schools rule violations can be the occasions for learning and development just as much as lessons in other academic areas. With some care and direction the resolution of discipline problems can contribute to the ethical development of both students and school personnel. In the long term, a goal such as this can contribute to just schools and ultimately to a more just society.

In this chapter we first present examples of classroom interaction among students and teachers. Many subtle classroom conflicts and clues to their resolutions are visible within these examples. Rather than presenting extreme cases we have elected to describe students and teachers interacting within a normal range of teaching situations. Next we present a comparison of rules and responses to rule violations by teachers perceived as "favorites" and those teachers that students "didn't particularly like." After this introduction we examine several theories that may provide insights about classroom behavior and ethical development.

CLASSROOM OBSERVATIONS

The following are natural observations of students and teachers interacting. The situations are not fictional dilemmas; they are not special interviews. They are actual vignettes from instruction in classrooms. Observations of several students over a short period form the basis of this section. While such observations are often not spectacular, they are very close to the reality of interactions as they occur daily in schools. We have changed the names and italicized situations we think potential ethical (rule) conflicts. As a start it would be interesting to ask yourself: "How would I have resolved this conflict?"

OBSERVATIONS OF DON

Day 1

Don was observed today. In his homeroom he was very quiet for most of the period. He appeared to be reading. He also talked quietly with two other boys. He sat alone. Don spent a lot of the time watching the teacher. When the teacher went to the back of the room, Don opened the book he had closed, jumped up, and followed her, presumably to ask her something. She spoke to him briefly, and he returned to his desk. The next class was math. *Don was late.* The teacher said nothing.

The class is divided into two sections. Don is in the slow section. There is a ninth grade student, Andre, who is a teacher's helper. In working with the slow group Andre seems frustrated that they are not learning the concepts that are simple to him. He continues using tactics for helping the students to understand even after the tactics have failed several times. *Don sits idly while he is supposed to be working on a review assignment.* After a time he asks a question but does not pay close attention to Andre's explanations. Andre is short with Don. The teacher has the slow group go to the board to work problems. *Don pays little attention to the problems and devotes most of his time to watching the other students. When the teacher insists that he complete a problem, he works it very slowly and carelessly.* He asks for confirmation of each step, many of which were wrong due to carelessness. However, when Don did work a problem through to completion he beamed at the praise he received.

Don is late to English class. He is quiet through most of the class which is spent listening to a tape of *Tom Sawyer.* At the end of class, the teacher gives the students some free time. Don jumps up, retrieves a notebook he turned in at the beginning of class, and goes to the teacher. The teacher is busy with other things and Don's request for attention is ignored. In music *Don again pays no attention to the lesson.* In piano group he seems oblivious to the taped lesson. In the guitar group he is the focus of the group because he is having trouble. Rather than paying attention to the other members of the group who are trying to show him what to do, he asks whether his guitar is tuned or not.

Day 2

Don was observed in math and English today. In math Don worked on problems at the board. He worked very slowly. "I'm tired, I'm tired," he claimed. "I'm going to have a heart attack." He wrote his numbers more slowly and sloppily as he went; however, he was doing the calculations more quickly and required less and less prompting. *After finishing the problems Don was to work at the board, he was told to sit down and begin working on a review. Instead, he kept getting up for various reasons. He exaggerated his gestures and stomped rather than walked around the room.*

Day 3

In math class Andre, the teacher's assistant, was helping Don. Observations were made from the opposite side of the room in order to record the interaction without getting involved. Andre was still helping Don with factoring. *Andre became more and more agitated and his voice became louder and louder. Don's voice got louder too. He kept insisting that he couldn't do it, couldn't remember, etc.* Finally, Don finished his work with Andre and turned it in. The teacher immediately gave Don a test to take. *Don stomped back to his seat with exaggerated gestures indicating he was tired or under some heavy burden. Don got up to sharpen his pencil. The sharpener is two steps from his seat. He stomped those steps. When he sat down he began pounding his chest. Finally, the teacher told him to be quiet.* He was quiet for a while but did not work on his test. *He began pounding his chest again.*

Day 4

Don and Andre went through the same scene today that they went through on Day 3. Andre got very frustrated with Don's slowness and apparent carelessness. Andre probably feels helpless in the situation. If Don wanted to understand, Andre could explain it to him. Don is more interested in other things. The teacher called Don to his desk and worked with him for a while. He got almost as upset with Don as Andre was. He finally sent Don back to his desk to work on his own. *Don paid no attention to his assignment; he watched the teacher very closely.*

Day 5

Today was very quiet. *In math Don was quiet and listless. He paid no attention to the instruction that was going on, but he also was not as disruptive as usual. In English class he was even more removed.* The class was listening to the end of the *Tom Sawyer* tape and *Don did not seem to be listening.*

Day 6

Don was in the slow-learner–behavior-problem room where *he was complaining about schedule changes to the teacher.* He wants to take Home Economics, and it won't fit into his schedule. The teacher explains to him how hard it is to make schedules, and Don responds that he will go talk to the counselor. In math Don receives individual attention from both Andre and the teacher. This is interesting. The school personnel are trying to get Don back into the mainstream and less dependent on special services. Don gets individual attention almost continually in math class. He is not independent. Today *Don displayed the exaggerated gestures and noise that seem to be his means of getting attention.* He is not sullen but looks to the class and the teacher smiling and hopeful when he behaves this way. In English class the students are presenting skits. *Don is late to class and makes a point of sitting alone by separating a desk from the cluster at the back of the room and moving it to a conspicuous corner in the front.* During the presentations he leaves for a long while. *When it is his group's turn, he forgets his lines and stands grinning.* There are comments from the audience about his fatness.

Day 7

Don goes through an elaborate pencil sharpening routine. He sharpened his pencil, emptied the sharpener even though it was clean, and sharpened his pencil again. He sharpens other students' pencils. Don sharpens his again. He goes to the teacher and asks him for help. He then asks if he has done a problem correctly. The problem is correct. *He goes back to his desk and then goes through the pencil-sharpening routine again with much stomping and kicking of the trash can. Don gets into a verbal joust with some other boys in the class. The teacher tells them he will give them extra work if they do not shut up. Don scratches his fingers across the board. Extra work is assigned to Don.*

Day 8

Don has a black eye this morning. The slow group is taking a quiz and *Don spends a lot of time looking around. The teacher scolds him for not starting the quiz. He tells Don he will have to come in and finish it after school if he doesn't finish it right now.* "The whole page?" Don complains. *He starts the quiz and then starts talking to another student. The teacher tells him to do his own work.* Don gets up and goes through his pencil-sharpening routine, followed by much stretching and sighing. Don goes out to get a drink and comes in feigning a limp. Another student pounds his chest and coughs the way Don does. *This student gets his quiz back.* "I only got two wrong," *he boasts.* Be quiet or I'll reduce your grade," *replies the teacher.*

Day 9

The science teacher is threatening extra assignments. Don is working too slowly on a quiz and the teacher threatens to make him come in and do extra work for the questions he gets wrong. This all goes on in front of the whole class. *Don responds to these threats by making faces at the teacher when her back is turned and then turning to the class to see their response.*

Day 10

Don is struggling with a quiz. Instead of scolding him the teacher says, "Do the best you can, hang in there." His tone is different from the usual harsh scolding. It is gentle and sincere. Andre begins explaining how to turn improper fractions into mixed numbers. He is explaining more clearly and more confidently than usual. When he begins involving the students in the problems, *some of them start needling others who aren't getting the right answers. The teacher gets very angry.* "Look, none of you are too bright in math so you shouldn't make fun of other people." Don continues working on the math problems.

OBSERVATIONS OF KAREN

Day 1

Karen is an interesting contrast to Don. Her expression is angry and tight. She earnestly tries to do her work and does not ask for help or attention. She seems to resent it. Karen was one of the better performers in English class. She spoke her lines clearly and with feeling. When everyone was sitting in the back of the room, *the teacher made some threat about sending kids out of class if they put their feet up on the chairs. Karen immediately propped her feet up on the two chairs in front of her and stared at the teacher.* The teacher did not notice her. A classmate seated next to Karen tentatively placed one foot on the edge of the chair in front of him but didn't leave it there long. Karen kept her feet up on the chair.

Day 2

There is a substitute teacher today. Some of the students are making noise. Others are trying to get everyone to be quiet. Karen appears to be having trouble with her assignment. *She asks the student behind her for help, but the student can't help her.* "Forget it," Karen says. "Just forget it." Help is offered to her a few minutes later, but she says she's already figured it out. Later she comes and asks for help. She is attentive and a little impatient. She is pleasant and makes a point of saying thank you. Later Karen is combing her hair and looking around. *She makes more and more noise. She stomps up to the teacher's desk for a tissue, stomps back, kicks the trash can.* Karen joins in the general noise in the room. *She is smiling and talking to the other students.* The teacher finally tells her to be quiet again. She responds, "I don't feel like it." "You must be quiet so the others can work," he replied. "Make me." The teacher asked Karen to leave the room, and she did. The teacher followed her out of the room and apparently talked to her in the hall. They both returned about five minutes later.

Day 3

Andre is alone in the room and the students are hassling him. They do not seem to be aware that their taunts have any effect on him. They aren't watching him, gauging the effects. It is as if they were engaging in a contest to see who can throw the most darts at an impersonal target. Andre looks irritated and frustrated. He finally shouts at them. They shout back. He pushed Karen into her seat. Karen glares back at him defiantly. The teacher comes in and tells everyone to shut up. "The next time it happens, I am going to do more than talk." Karen says something to Andre under her breath, and Andre tells her to shut up. The teacher says loudly, "Oh Andre, be quiet!" Karen essentially got Andre in trouble. Now she is grinning at Andre and saying things under her breath. Andre has lost power or the illusion of power. The teacher has done this.

The teacher works problems on the board for the slow students. He asks Karen to tell him how to work a problem on the board, and Karen tells him in reverse order. The teacher does not acknowledge the significance of this response. Karen enjoys learning about zero. She is enthusiastic, smiling, excited. Karen correctly answers fifteen out of twenty questions the teacher asks about zero. Later, Karen is not able to give the answer to a problem on the board until the teacher asks it out loud. He checks over someone's written work and comments, "You did them right for a change." *Andre reprimands Karen for not numbering her problems and for her messy work. Karen tells him to* "go to hell." *He turns and walks away.*

Day 4

It is apparent that Karen has a visual perceptual problem. She came and asked for help on some division problems. She was multiplying 120×7. She did it this way: $120 \times 7 = 810$. When asked to look again, she realized that she had reversed the one and four after multiplying 7×2, so she wrote 810 instead of 840. "I always do that," she said. The messiness of Karen's work also seems to be an indication of this problem. She also has a hard time writing columns of numbers.

Day 5

Today is game day for the fast students. The slow students are required to keep working. The slow students seem to resign themselves to this situation. The teacher reprimands Karen because her work isn't neat. The problems aren't numbered correctly. *Some of the problems* "aren't even in the book." It is obvious that Karen has simply copied them wrong. Karen looks bewildered and hurt. She doesn't seem to understand what is wrong with the paper. *"I'm doing the best I can,"* she said. *"I don't care; you do it better."* Karen sits *quietly. It is clear that she is angry, in fact furious. She says nothing.*

Day 6

The English teacher comes in and there is a lot of noise. Karen is talking to Susan. *The teacher says, "You girls stop talking,"* Karen *retorts that she is not talking. "You looked like you were,"* snaps the *teacher. Then the teacher threatens the rest of the class with an assignment if they don't shut up. He also tells them to pay attention to a particular point because it is going to be on the next quiz.* The class continues quietly.

There is nothing uncommon or extreme in the observations just described. In fact, many teachers and administrators probably responded with comments such as "What's new?" "I have students like that in all of my classes;" or "Situations like these occur all the time." Likewise, recalling when we were students, there are identifiable comments and responses of our past teachers in these observations. Responses such as these make our point. Everyday interactions with teachers and school personnel form the substance of ethical development in school.

The interactions between school personnel and students can be summarized as a dilemma:

In schools the school personnel have responsibility to both individual students and to groups of students. There are occasions when the behavior of individual students is such that it disrupts the group. What should school personnel do? Paying attention to either the individual or the group necessarily ignores the needs of the other.

We will leave this as a summary/question. There will be more about rules and dilemmas in the rest of the chapter. Now let us look at the interaction between students and teachers from the student's point of view.

STUDENTS' PERCEPTIONS OF CLASSROOM RULES AND RULE VIOLATIONS

Some understanding of students' perceptions of school-related ethical interactions can be gained by evaluating the classroom rules and teacher behavior concerning rule violations. Over the past several years we have asked some simple questions of college students and high school students.

The questions have to do with teachers they liked and disliked; the rules these teachers had in their classrooms; and what the teachers did when the rules were broken. The questions were:

1. I would like you to think of your favorite teacher in either elementary, junior, or senior high school. What rules were there in this teacher's classroom?
2. When a rule was broken, how did this teacher respond? What did he or she do about the violation?
3. Think of a teacher you didn't particularly like or get along with. What rules were in this teacher's classroom?
4. What did this teacher do about violations of rules?

We should stress the informal and open-ended nature of these questions. This was not a formal research study. Our discussion is an attempt to present as accurately as possible both qualitative and quantitative responses to these questions. First, we shall discuss the rules of teachers, then the responses to rule violations. Finally, we present conclusions based on reading the responses and listening to students discuss these questions.

The majority of rules reported for both favorite and least favorite teachers are *prescriptive*. Examples of these rules include: be in class on time; finish your work; and participate in class discussions. The next major category of rules for teachers is *prohibitive*. Don't talk; don't chew gum; don't get out of your seat; and don't question the teacher. These are all examples of prohibitive rules that were reported. One finding was of real interest concerning rules. There is a category of rules we have labeled *principles*. Rules that were reported in this category include: respect others; treat others as you would have yourself treated; and treat everyone equally and fairly. The finding of note here is that not one principled rule was reported for a teacher that students didn't particularly like or get along with. There were also many more prohibitive rules in these least favorite teachers' classrooms.

How do teachers respond to rule violations? We used these categories—mutual resolution, coercive response, threatening response, and punishment. The dominant pattern of response for teachers was coercion. The range of responses in this category was wide and included: sarcasm, humor, verbal reprimand, insults, promised reward, public ridicule, and nonverbal messages of disappointment. Threatening responses were the next largest number of responses for both teacher groups. Threats included: lowered grades, physical harm, peer disapproval, detentions, extra work, isolation, and removal from class. Punishing responses were used most often by teachers the students didn't particularly get along with or like, and least often by teachers they liked. In the punishment category were included: pushing, grabbing and shoving, hitting (with an object or one's hand), angry and emotional yelling, losing one's temper, and expulsion from the class or school.

Students only reported mutual responses from teachers they liked. Included in the category of mutual response were: discussing the problem calmly; trying to see what could be done to help meet it; treating students as concerned equals; talking privately; and explaining the situation.

Even though this was an informal survey there are several conclusions we would like to report. For the most part, classroom rules themselves do not distinguish favorite from least-liked teachers. The old myth that favorite teachers have few rules and are not strict is just not supported. Just as many favorite as least-liked teachers had a rule such as "no gum chewing," so it does not seem to be a matter of specific rules that differentiates students' perceptions of teachers.

We did find that about favorite teachers many students would say something like "They didn't seem to have specific rules; you just respected them and knew how you should behave in class." On the other hand it seems that "least-liked" teachers had numerous rules. Students would recall long lists of "dos and don'ts." This, of course, leads to some bias in the strict quantification of responses to our questions. With this noted, we still think that the effect of a lack of principled rules and an emphasis on prescriptive and prohibitive rules is worth consideration by school personnel.

There is another myth concerning favorite teachers that is weakened by our questions on rules and responses. The myth that favorite teachers are lenient; they let students get away with misbehavior. Not so. We found that not only did favorite teachers have rules, they had consequences for breaking the rules. There seemed to be a fundamental equity that students expressed concerning the consequences.

There are some subtle and more qualitative differences worth mentioning. Teachers who were liked had fewer rules, and students were often vague about specific rules. However, they reported that they "knew" how to act and what was to be done in class, and they did so out of respect for the teacher. Teachers students didn't particularly like had more rules. The rules were specific, and there was usually a negative tone to the students' discussion of the teachers' responses to rule violation. Large numbers of least-liked teachers used ridicule, humiliation, insults, and detentions and induced fear as means of coercion. Many students perceived a basic inequity between the rule violation and its consequences in regard to the teachers they didn't particularly like—being paddled for chewing gum or having the teacher go into a rage when work is late. We are not excusing the students' violation of rules; we are questioning the response of teachers to the violation. This point should be clear.

Perhaps the difference in classroom atmosphere that we are trying to describe is best expressed by the students themselves. Here are some of their comments about the responses to violations of rules by favorite teachers and teachers they didn't particularly like or get along with (least-liked).

Favorite	Least Liked
stated that it was time to work	denounced our level of morality
verbal reprimand	yelled at students
looked at you and you knew what to do	locked students out of classroom
talked about respect for others	humiliating and degrading statements
admonished students for not using good judgement	kicked students out
he would just say the individual's name	lost temper and shouted
she became sullen and serious	always made fun of the student
talked to student privately	awarded points that were later translated to swats given by other students! (Points could be reduced by catching flies, which the teacher abhorred.)
sat down and talked to the student	
responded with a quiet request that the student alter his behavior	the teacher made people look foolish
asked the offender to see him after class	he made the student admit he had broken a rule and would pay the consequences
asked the person to shape up	
took the student aside	put gum in the student's shirt pocket and smashed it into the shirt
spoke with firm words, asking why the student had done something	

The relationship between rules and responses is crucial in classroom management. Respect and regard for the teacher are also important in the educational environment. As we have pointed out in this chapter, the interaction between students and school personnel is the focus of our attention. We do not intend to say that either students or teachers are right or wrong. We would like to show that their interaction can be improved. The next sections on human motivation and values and theories of ethical development should bring some understanding to the teacher-student interactions we have described so far.

HUMAN MOTIVATION AND VALUES

Understanding human motivation is fundamental to clarifying the interaction between students and teachers. When we ask questions such as "Why is this student so restless?" or "What causes teachers to respond to students with threats?" we are in large part asking a more basic question:

"What motivated these individuals?" All of us have needs that influence our behavior. The ability to recognize motivational factors is essential to facilitating ethical development and resolving discipline problems in schools. There are basic biological drives that influence our behavior, but there are also physical, psychological, and social needs that are unique to human beings. Both Don and Karen, the students in our opening observations, had adequate diets. Yet it was clear from many of their behaviours that they were motivated by needs for recognition, identity, and other more social-psychological needs. The motivational theory of Abraham H. Maslow meets the criteria we have specified; it includes physiological, physical, and social-psychological needs and relates to our theme of ethical development as well.

In *Motivation and Personality*[1] Abraham Maslow theorized a hierarchy of human needs, the most basic of which were physiological and the highest of which were needs for continued growth and development.

The most basic needs are physiological and include food, water, air, sleep, and sex. These needs have the greatest motivational force in the hierarchy. They are clearest to the person motivated by them, and they are essential to the biological survival of the individual and the species. The influence these needs can have on behavior, specifically disruptive behavior, is fairly clear. For example, students who are hungry may be restless; those who are sleepy may be inattentive. Since physiological needs are the strongest motivators in the hierarchy it is worth using them as clarifying examples for several points. When a person is dominated by a particular need, let us say hunger, it is accurate to say the whole of that person's consciousness is focused on satisfying that need. All capacities are used to fulfill the need for food. This is also to say that the person's value system, his or her personal ethical principles, will be dominated by the need for food. This is the connection between motivation and personal values that is important for school personnel to understand. The example is clearest at lower levels, yet this does not deny the existence and influence of higher-level motivations on the value system and ethical development of the individual.

The need for safety and security is the next motivational level. The constellation of these needs is described as a need for order, structure, stability, dependency, and freedom from chaos and fear in the physical environment. School personnel (and all parents) have observed the fears and unusual behaviors of children placed in new environments. It takes time for us to feel safe and secure in new situations. If an environment, be it school or home, is perceived as dangerous or frightening, individual motivations are thus aligned to insure personal well-being and, in extreme situations such as physical abuse, to insure survival.

Next in Maslow's hierarchy are love and belongingness needs. The previous level was primarily associated with the physical environment; at this level motivation is primarily social and psychological. The specific needs at this level are to give and receive affection, to have friends, to belong to groups, and to have a place in the community and society. Frustration of needs at this level is characterized by words such as alienation, loneliness, and rejection.

Think for a moment of the "problem students" in your school. How many of them don't seem to fit into the system? By this we mean they do not belong to recognized clubs or activities such as band, drama, athletics, the newspaper, or the student council. These students seem to be outcasts; they do not have friends and do not belong to school groups. Yet they still have these needs, and they will fulfill them somehow. These students are often associated with other groups—namely gangs—and they often find each other as friends. They achieve a sense of friendship, belongingness, and even love in others and groups not perceived to be socially acceptable. To belong to these groups they must accept the values of the group, thus forming a value position that often stands in opposition to the rest of the school (and social) system.

Self-esteem is the fourth set of needs in Maslow's hierarchy. Motivation at this level is toward a stable, firmly based, positive perception of one's self. Self-esteem needs are divided into mastery and prestige. Mastery is the personal knowledge that one can, in fact, do certain things. School-specific examples might include reading, writing, and computing. Other examples are numerous: mastery in athletics, music, academics, and so on. We want to point out that this is real mastery, not ungrounded statements of achievement. These in fact are often indications of unfulfilled needs of self-esteem. One implication for school personnel is for accurate and clear feedback to the individual concerning mastery and achievement. Prestige, the other aspect of self-esteem, is the public recognition of the individual. Respected others, such as peers, teachers, and parents give recognition of the individual's accomplishment and achievements.

School personnel often mention the low or negative self-concept of students such as Don and Karen. Individuals will strive to maintain their sense of integrity and adequacy as best they can in their environment. School personnel are often central influences in the lives of students, and it is incumbent on them to help students develop self-esteem in educationally constructive ways.

Throughout this discussion of Maslow's hierarchy our examples have placed the student at center stage. Teachers and administrators have the same motivational needs. Ignoring this reality is failing to give recognition to important factors involved in the interactions between students and school personnel.

The hierarchy of motivational needs ranges from the physiological to the physical and through the social-psychological. The needs of an individual have a direct influence on his or her immediate perceptions and values. In addition, fulfillment of motivational needs requires us to extend ourselves to the physical and human environments. This initiates the interaction that can result in further ethical development of the individual. In some cases the behaviors associated with this extension to the surrounding environment are defined as disruptive because they violate rules. These conflicts are the opportunity for ethical development as described by Jean Piaget, Lawrence Kohlberg, and June Tapp, whose theories we review in the next sections.

THEORIES OF ETHICAL DEVELOPMENT

Three theories of ethical development are discussed in this section. These theories were selected because their orientations relate directly to the position we have assumed in this book. It is clearly not possible to explore all of the individual theories. We have presented a general view of the theory and then described the themes of rules and justice.

Ethical Development—Jean Piaget

In the early 1930s Jean Piaget conducted research in ethical development. His studies were published in *The Moral Judgment of the Child*.[2] Piaget's work involved children up to the age of adolescence. For this reason, his findings seem particularly important for elementary teachers and administrators.

Piaget first observed and questioned children about the rules of playing marbles. In these naturalistic observations Piaget was trying to answer a fundamental question—what was the child's point of view concerning respect for rules? Here he observed the ways different-aged children applied rules and the ways children viewed the character of the rules. That is, he studied the children's practice of rules and their consciousness of rules.

Piaget also presented children with pairs of similar stories. Differences in the stories were relevant to the moral judgments that were elicited from the children. For example, one story is about a boy who accidently knocked over and broke fifteen cups on his way to dinner. A second story is about another boy who, against his mother's orders, tried to get some jam out of the cupboard. While doing this he knocked down one cup. The cup fell and was broken. Piaget would ask two questions. "Are these children equally guilty?" "Which of the two was naughtier and why?"

Development of the idea of justice was Piaget's next area of inquiry. Again using stories he studied children's conception of punishments, collective responsibility, and finally, retributive and distributive justice.

Based on his observations Piaget theorized two major stages in the ethical development of children. The first stage he called *heteronomous;* "hetero" meaning "from others." Moral rules at this stage come from others like parents or teachers and the rules are perceived to be "laws of the universe." They are not changeable and must be accepted as givens. Constraint is the primary orientation of heteronomous mortality. Piaget's second stage is *autonomous* morality. According to Piaget this stage originates chiefly due to the interactions among children. With time children come to understand the positions of others. Obligations at this stage are not unilateral; they are reciprocal. We shall look more closely at some of Piaget's ideas, particularly those related to rules and justice.

Young children, below two years of age, have no sense of rules; their play is purely motor activity. If the child appears to follow rules, it is mere physical repetition with no consciousness of the rule.

The second level, age two to six, is one of imitation. There is consciousness about rules and the practice of rules is egocentric, a simple imitation of what other children have done. Children are not aware of the social nature of the game. This is heteronomous obedience. The children know there are rules. They are obligatory, but there is no application of the rules except by copying.

By ages seven to ten rules are recognized as regulatory and important for social interaction. Children's awareness of rules is still heteronomous.

Sometime around eleven or twelve autonomy emerges over heteronomy in the child's approach to rules. Cooperative play and cognitive maturity both contribute to this development. Rules are matters of mutual consent; they are not laws presented by authorities. Evidence for the emergence of autonomy and mutual consent is seen in the preadolescent's own legislating of rules for games and their cooperative agreement on various aspects of games.

Piaget has stated: "All morality consists in a system of rules, and the essence of all morality is to be sought for in the respect which the individual acquires for these rules." (2, p. 13) We have seen how understanding and respect for rules develops over the years. First there was a morality of constraint or heteronomy, and this developed into a morality of cooperation or autonomy. Development of the idea of justice is similar to the child's consciousness and practice of rules.

For young children justice is obedience to authority. Justice is the rule. Obeying the law, or command, is the just action even if it is not fair or equitable. At the next stage the child appeals to the principle of equality. Because the child is in between a heteronomous and autonomous position the rendering of justice must be by strict equality. Finally, in the third stage, children clearly recognize injustices and consider the situation and weigh circumstances before acting.

There are several important observations that should be made concerning the child's understanding and development of rules and justice. Cooperative interaction with peers seems to be the key to ethical development according to Piaget.

The sense of justice, though naturally capable of being reinforced by percepts and the practical example of the adult, is largely independent of these influences, and requires nothing more for its development than the mutual respect and solidarity which holds among children themselves. (2, p. 198)

This observation is very important for educators. Certainly Piaget has overstated his point. Mutual respect can be established between students and adults, and some educational efforts can be directed toward advancing students' understanding of rules and justice. This, however, requires an interaction between adults and youth that is not grounded on a unilateral respect given only because of the adult's size, power, and authority. There is not a way around some facts of the student-adult relationship in classrooms. Teachers are often larger; they have power; by definition they are authorities; and there must be order.

But just as educators make allowances for different levels of reading and mathematics development, so they can give recognition to the increasing autonomy of students. Group projects, activities, and work in classroom are other ways that teachers can encourage ethical development based on an understanding of Piaget's ideas.

Ethical Development—Lawrence Kohlberg

Educators are generally aware of Lawrence Kohlberg's theory[3, 4] of moral development and his use of dilemmas to determine individual levels of moral reasoning. We shall start with a school-related moral dilemma that can later be used as an example of different developmental stages.

THE TEACHER ASSAULT DILEMMA

A youth has been accused of assaulting a teacher. The evidence is unclear as to the innocence or guilt of this student. The student has, however, been in trouble with the authorities and has recently violated rules of probation. The probation officer has decided that unless the school will support the student, he shall be sent to reform school. There is a teacher in the school who believes in the student's innocence in the assault case and thinks the school should not allow him to go to reform school. When this teacher approached the administration and other teachers, they refused to write a letter in support of the student. The administration and teachers claimed it was their right not to write a letter on the grounds that: 1) the student had been in trouble before and probably assaulted the teacher; 2) reform school may be a good experience for the youth; and 3) whether this youth is guilty or not it would be a good example for any other youth who might assault a teacher. On the other hand the teacher argues for the student on the grounds that 1) we do not know whether he is innocent or guilty so we should assume innocence; 2) reform school may, in fact, be bad for the individual, not good as is claimed; and 3) there are better ways to deter future assaults than to send this student to reform school. The teacher tried to persuade the administration and teachers, but they will not change their position. Having exhausted all avenues, in final desperation the teacher steals school stationery, writes a letter, forges administrative signatures, and submits supportive documents. Should the teacher have done this?

Pause and consider your response to this dilemma. Go beyond a simple yes or no. Once you have decided, try to justify your answer. Why should the teacher have done or not done what he did?

The studies of Lawrence Kohlberg extended and clarified many of Jean Piaget's ideas that were discussed earlier. Importantly, Kohlberg used a greater age-range than Piaget. He interviewed individuals well beyond early adolescence. In addition, Kohlberg interviewed individuals over a number of years to see if they changed their levels of moral reasoning. Kohlberg's studies generally confirmed Piaget's early theory. He also found there was moral reasoning beyond the heteronomous and autonomous levels originally posited by Piaget. We shall not go into Kohlberg's validation of his theory here; he has done so psychologically[5-7] and philosophically.[8, 9] Likewise, we shall not detail criticisms of his theory; others have done so.[10-13]

Table 5–1 is Kohlberg's summary of his stages of development. Since we are later going to discuss the dilemma presented at the beginning of this section, and since it relates to the judgments of teachers and administrators, here we shall briefly discuss Kohlberg's stages in terms of students' classroom behavior. Table 5–1 gives an understanding of Kohlberg's general orientation.

At Stage 1 the orientation is toward avoiding punishment from powerful individuals. Students would make moral decisions based on the possible consequences from teachers and/or administrators. "We had better not do that because the principal will spank us." This is simple and straightforward obedience to authority.

Stage 2 is an orientation toward personal, material reward. What is right is what satisfies one's own needs; it is "taking care of number one." Trading of goods and favors is done with a "you scratch my back, I'll scratch yours" type of reciprocity. Successful ends justify sometimes suspicious means. So, small misdemeanors are permissible as long as you don't get caught. Changing report card grades, cheating on tests, and telling small lies to achieve some personal reward are acceptable to the individual at this developmental level.

Individuals at Stage 3 have an orientation toward social approval. Judg-

TABLE 5-1. Lawrence Kohlberg's Stages of Ethical Development*

At the *preconventional level (I)*, the cultural labels of "good" and "bad" are interpreted in terms of physical consequences (e.g., punishment, reward, exchange of favors) or in terms of the physical power of those who enunciate the rules and labels. The Physical Power stage (1) characteristically orients toward punishment, unquestioning deference to superior power and prestige, and avoidance of "bad" acts. Regardless of value, physical consequences determine goodness or badness. The Instrumental Relativism stage (2) is basically hedonistic. Right action consists of that which instrumentally satisfies one's own needs and occasionally the needs of others. Elements of fairness, equality, and reciprocity are present, but interpreted pragmatically, not as a matter of loyalty, gratitude, or justice.

The *conventional level (II)* is characterized by active support of the fixed rules or authority in a society. Maintaining the expectations and rules of the family, group, or nation is valued in its own right. The Interpersonal Concordance or good-boy/good-girl stage (3) orients toward pleasing others and gaining approval. There is conformity to stereotypical images of majority behavior. Also behavior is frequently judged by intention: "He means well" becomes important for the first time. The Law and Order stage (4) is typified by doing one's duty (obeying fixed rules), showing respect for authority, and maintaining the given social order. Respect is earned by performing dutifully.

The *postconventional level (III)* is characterized by a clear effort toward autonomous moral principles with validity apart from the authority of the groups or persons who hold them and apart from individual identifications. The Social Contract stage (5) has legalistic and utilitarian overtones; strong constitutionalism pervades. Right action is defined in terms of individual rights, critically agreed upon by the whole society. Awareness of the relativism of personal values is attended by an emphasis upon procedural rules for reaching consensus. The stress is on the legal point of view, but with the possibility of changing law in terms of rational, social utility rather than freezing it in terms of law and order. The Universal Ethic stage (6) moves toward conscientious decisions of right based on principles that appeal to logical comprehensiveness, universality, and consistency. These principles are abstract and ethical; they include justice, the reciprocity and equality of human rights, and respect for individuals.

*Reproduced with permission from: June L. Tapp and Lawrence Kohlberg, "Developing Senses of Law and Legal Justice," *Journal of Social Issues* 27, no. 2 (1971): 69.

ments concerning moral action are based on what is "nice" or "pleasing" to others. Students will determine right from wrong by their perception of what immediate peers and teachers will accept; they are "other directed." Thus, conformity is what they imagine to be the desires of the majority. These are the students who will go along with the group or respond that "everyone was doing it" when asked about their behavior. Right and wrong are defined by group desires.

Stage 4 is a law-and-order orientation. Somewhat similarly to Stage 3, individuals at Stage 4 look to others for social conventions, rules, and laws. These individuals have a slightly larger social perception than at Stage 3;

they do not look to the immediate group for sanctions. Rather they appeal to conventions within the larger society. Social authorities, e.g., principals, presidents, rules, and laws, must be obeyed for the maintaining of social order. Further, the rules and laws are viewed as static and unchanging.

Stage 5 is a social contract orientation. There are individual rights and there are social laws, and both must be respected. Such a position requires procedural rules for resolving conflicts. There is a possibility of individuals changing their position through cooperative negotiation.

Finally, Stage 6 is an orientation toward universal principles. Decisions at this level consider all the complexities of a situation and are made on the grounds of ethical principles, such as the golden rule or the categorical imperative. Comprehensive and universal ethical principles, such as justice, are the grounds for moral choice.

The heart of understanding an individual's stage of moral development is not in the answer given to a moral dilemma but in the justification for the answer. To what do individuals appeal when justifying their response? We can go back to the dilemma at the beginning of this section and use it as an example of *pro* and *con* justification at the different stages.

Stage 1

Pro: It wasn't bad to write the letter. The teacher did try to convince the administration, but they would not listen. It isn't a bad crime, and the teacher didn't do much damage to school property.

Con: The teacher did not have permission to write the letter. The administration (backed by the teachers) had made a decision and this teacher should abide by that decision.

Both answers disregard the teacher's intentions. Instead they focus on the consequences of the act. In the pro statement the "crime" is minimized while the con statement makes it clear that an authority has made a decision and the teacher should be obedient. Because of the punishment and obedience orientation of this stage, the pro statement was harder to write, and the tendency is for individuals at this stage to present the con argument.

Stage 2

Pro: The teacher isn't really doing any harm to the administration or the school. If the teacher works hard, the school will surely be repaid. Since all avenues had been attempted, there was nothing left for the teacher to do or face losing the student's friendship. Besides, someday the student might do something for the teacher.

Con: The administration is acting on their own behalf and on behalf of the teachers. They must support one another if the school is to run smoothly. If the administration supports the teachers, they will support the administration. So, the teacher should have gone along with their decision.

Individual intentions are now considered. In the pro statement the teacher will "repay" the school, the teacher may lose a friendship, and the student may do something for the teacher. The con argument is clearly a "you scratch my back and I'll scratch yours" orientation between the teachers and administrators.

Stage 3

Pro: Stealing is generally not a good idea. However, this situation is extreme. The teacher isn't doing that much wrong when you consider that he may help the student without really hurting the school staff. The teacher's actions were natural for any good professional—a good professional tries to help those who need it.

Con: The teacher really cannot be blamed if the student goes to reform school. It would really be inappropriate to condemn the teacher for not breaking the law. Surely others would have judged the school administrators negatively. Others would judge the teacher positively because he did everything possible to help the student. But, he did break the law and that is wrong.

The emphasis in both justifications center on an appeal to interpersonal agreement among those associated with the problem. While rules and laws are mentioned it is clear that the focus of both answers is on who will accept or reject the persons involved. This exemplifies Stage 3, the social approval orientation.

Stage 4

Pro: The administration is wrong if they let a student who they do not know is guilty go to reform school. You can't send somebody to reform school as an example. It was the teacher's duty to steal the stationery and write the letter. But, the teacher broke the law too and must take the punishment.

Con: Supporting students is a natural thing for teachers to do. But what this teacher did was against the law. All people, including teachers, have to follow the law. How the teacher feels or the circumstances don't make any difference. What if all teachers did what they thought best!

Here the justifications appeal to one's obligations to the law. In the pro statement there is an indication that the administration broke the law, and this is not right. At the same time, the teacher broke the law and must suffer the consequences. The con position is a straightforward law-and-order orientation. One does what the law says; no questions asked. The final comment indicates that anarchy would probably ensue if laws were not obeyed.

Stage 5

Pro: One must really consider all the circumstances before you say what the teacher did was right or wrong. The laws are clear about what the teacher did, and a teacher more than most persons should know that he or she was breaking the law. On the other hand, the situation was such that the action seemed reasonable. It seems that other means could have been used to reach the same ends.

Con: One can surely see the possible good that could come from the teacher's actions. But a partial good is often evident in wrongdoing. The same can be said for the administration's position. We must remember, however, that the ends do not justify the means in either case. The teacher was not completely wrong, but in this situation should not have acted in this way.

It is apparent that the justifications at this level become complex. Good intentions, immediate consequences, and civil obedience are not the foundations of moral actions. Both responses try to weigh either side of the situation and consider the circumstances. In both responses there is a "tone" that says neither the teacher nor the administration has acted appropriately, and it is difficult to approve or disapprove of either. Probably the best resolution would have been a cooperative agreement established through agreed-on procedures. But this is not the case; a decision had to be rendered on the evidence given. So, the individuals made the best decision given the situation.

Stage 6

Pro: If a choice must be made between following an administrative rule and keeping another human from an unjust consequence, the higher principle of justice takes clear precedence and makes it morally right to do what the teacher did.

Con: The ideal course of action is to follow one's own conscience. The teacher should act only as he or she would have all others act in this situation. In this case the teacher should not do what he or she did because of the great injustice it rendered to all school personnel and, on balance, given that the student had indeed violated his parole, there is a lesser injustice rendered to the student.

In both cases the higher moral principle of justice is the grounds for the decision. While others are mentioned (i.e., student, school personnel) the dilemma is resolved on a principle that these teachers would be willing to have others follow in similar decisions. The pro position seems a clear statement of applying justice in this situation. The con position was difficult to write. While we think it qualifies as a Stage 6 justification, the principle of justice is complicated by trying to decide who would receive the greater injustice, the school personnel or the student. We can imagine an equally powerful argument claiming the greater injustice would be rendered to the student, given the situation.

Determining someone's level of moral judgment depends on more than seeing what decision the person makes. The justification is the crucial variable, for it reveals the structure of the individual's moral reasoning. The outcome of an athletic event does not define the sport. To understand tennis is not to know who won; it is to know the rules of tennis and to be able to differentiate it from racquetball. As we have tried to show by presenting both pro and con responses to the educational dilemma at all stages, it is not the yes or no that defines one's stage of moral development. And, it is not agreement between individuals that defines a stage. One must listen closely to the reasoning, the underlying structure of the argument that is given in justification for the decision in response to the question, "Should the teacher have done this?" The reasoning behind the justification will center on a universal ethical principle such as the value of life, liberty, freedom, truth, or justice. Since justice is one of our themes we will use it as an example. At Stage 1, justice is valued because of the power it has (manifest through those in authority) to punish the person involved; at Stage 2, justice is respected for the usefulness it can have in bringing rewards to those who abide; at Stage 3, justice is respected because others will respect the individual for doing so; at Stage 4, justice is followed because it is the law. At Stages 5 and 6, justice comes to be recognized as an important principle in and of itself and decisions are made in reference to the principle, not in reference to other things that may represent the principle, i.e., punishments, rewards, social esteem, and laws.

There are several notable points concerning Kohlberg's theory. First, development through the stages in invariant. Stages are not skipped as individuals develop. One must develop through Stage 3 before reaching Stage 4. An important educational implication of this finding is to avoid "teaching" a higher stage such as 5 or 6, since all students will not understand the reasoning involved at higher stages. This brings us to a second point. Individuals can comprehend one stage higher than their own. In fact, they are attracted to higher levels of moral reasoning. They understand the arguments and often find them better resolutions to dilemmas. So how do individuals develop into a higher stage? The answer to this is our third point. Imagine a person at Stage 4 having an argument with a person at Stage 5. In many respects the Stage 4 argument will be inadequate in comparison. This situation can cause a cognitive disequilibrium in the person at Stage 4. In attempting to regain cognitive equilibrium, the Stage 4 person will attempt to reestablish a cognitive structure that is more adequate to the situation. Since arguments at a higher level are understood, elements of the higher stage are incorporated into the new cognitive structure. This last point connects very well with one made by Piaget. That is, in the natural course of argument and debate among children there is cause for disequilibrium and development.

Educators can facilitate moral development by having students express their views on issues involving moral decisions. If the atmosphere is one of open dialogue, no doubt students will be exposed to levels of reasoning higher than their own. Likewise, they will often be challenged by others with different arguments, thus causing a cognitive dissonance between their own position and that of others. We think educators can make important contributions not only by using standard "moral dilemmas" such as those Kohlberg used in his research, but also by using actual classroom situations such as rule violations to facilitate the ethical development of youth.

Ethical Development—June Tapp

So far in this chapter we have "observed" student behavior from a teacher's point of view, reviewed students' perceptions of rules and responses to rule violation, and described the theories of Jean Piaget and Lawrence Kohlberg. Through all of this, rules have been the immediate concern and justice the principal orientation of the discussion. June Tapp and her colleagues have brought the themes of this chapter together in a theory that is especially important for teachers and administrators. June Tapp has completed cross-cultural studies with different age groups from kindergarten to adults.[14, 15] She has used a rather simple, though very important, series of questions inquiring into the value and function of rules and laws, compliance with rules and laws, and the changeability and breakability of rules and laws.

An individual's sense of the law and legal justice develops through three broad levels: a preconventional level which is rule-obeying; a conventional level which is rule-maintaining; and finally a postconventional level of rule-making. Table 5–2 gives the questions June Tapp, Felice Levine, and their colleagues used in the interviews, and it details the responses found in the three levels of moral reasoning.

TABLE 5–2. Classification of Interview Categories by Moral Levels[a]*

Subject/Question	Level I Preconventional Categories	Level II Conventional Categories	Level III Postconventional Categories
1. *Value of Rules and Laws* What if there were no rules?	*Violence-crime:* laws prevent concrete physical harm, i.e., specific bad acts or crimes and secure physical necessities.	*Personal desires not principles:* Laws restrain bad, guide weak, e.g., insure personal control over greed. *Anarchy-disorder-chaos:* laws maintain social order. *Impossible to imagine:* society cannot exist without rules; accepts abstract regulation as requisite for society.	*Man as self-regulatory:* man guiding behavior via principles; distinguishes law from moral principles.
Function of Rules and Laws What is a rule? What is a law?	*Prohibitive:* functions as proscription or flat command restraining actions; serves no positive social good.	*Prescriptive:* functions as shared guide interpreted by normal actor; generality to whole system of rules as facilitating, e.g., "maintaining society" or "preventing antisocial behavior." *Enforcement:* distinguishes between badness of act and consequent punishment.	*Beneficial-rational:* functions to achieve rational purpose behind law, usually for maximizing personal and social welfare consequences; cognizant of the utility of agreed-upon standards.

Note.—Because of our differing methodologies, the *beneficial-rational* category on What is a rule? What is a law? and the *rational-beneficial-utilitarian* category on Why should people follow rules? and Why do you follow rules? seemed to have transitional qualities between levels II and III. However, the empirical criteria for coding these categories suggested they were predominantly, though not exclusively, level III.

[a]The classification schema is part of the more extensive conceptualization of legal development in Tapp and Levine (1971).

*Reproduced with permission from : June L. Tapp and Lawrence Kohlberg, "Developing Senses of Legal Justice," *Journal of Social Issues* 27, no. 2 (1971):74, 75.

TABLE 5–2. Classification of Interview Categories *(Cont.)*

Subject/Question	Level I Preconventional Categories	Level II Conventional Categories	Level III Postconventional Categories
2. Dynamics of Legal Compliance Why should people follow rules? Why do you follow rules?	*Avoid negative consequences:* punishment reason for conformity or reason why act is bad, simple compliance, not respect, for rules. *Authority:* obedience to power figures as ultimate guides; rules derived from them; badness of proscribed activity confused with badness of disobeying authority's rule.	*Personal conformity:* confuses obedience with stereotypes of socially desirable in order to be good and maintain what lawmakers think is good individual behavior. *Social conformity:* role requires compliance to be fair to other obeyers and to avoid chaos; law and order maintaning perspective.	*Rational-beneficial-utilitarian:* obedience to maintain individual and social welfare based on rational mutual decision making and utilitarian considerations; no fixed obligation, obedience from weighing consequences. *Principled:* obedience guided by principles, e.g., sense of justice independent of socity; conform only with principled rules.
3. Changeability of Rules and Laws Can rules be changed?	*No:* laws fixed, permanent, or quasiphysical things.	*Yes:* laws not for "good of all" because they permit unkindness or are made by uncharitable persons.	*Yes:* for reasons of social utility, rational purposes; lawmaking perspective; can change unprincipled laws.
Breakability of Rules and Laws Are there times when it might be right to break a rule?	*No:* no differentiation between legal and moral; badness of breaking equated with badness as such. *Yes:* simple "yes" but does not differentiate moral norm from prudential directives.	*Morality of circumstance:* extreme circumstances justify breaking, recognize sociomoral function of rules (e.g., preservation of life) to which law obedience is instrumental; conformity with personal judgment.	*Morality of rule:* justify breaking when law immoral or unjust, when law violates moral principles (e.g., fundamental individual rights).

As part of their studies Tapp and Levine asked both students[14] and teachers [15] many of the same questions. In the next paragraphs we review some of their findings concerning these two populations.

To try to understand the value individuals place on rules and laws, Tapp asked, "What if there were no rules?" The question was asked of primary and middle school students and college-age students. The findings are presented in Table 5–3. In general, young children responded at a preconventional level while young adults were at the conventional level. It was only at the college level that postconventional positions assuming humans to be self-regulatory and guided by ethical principles were found.

As part of another study on legal socialization Levine and Tapp[15, 16] asked this same question of teachers. All teachers questioned answered at the conventional level. Ninety percent of teachers could not imagine a society without rules, or they thought that anarchy, disorder, and chaos would

TABLE 5–3. Response Percentages on Legal Development Questions by Age: U. S. Developmental Study[a]

	Educational Group			Comparisons (by t test)	
		Middle			
	Primary	School	College		
Levels: categories	(1)	(2)	(3)	(1) × (2)	(2) × (3)
	What would happen if there were no rules?				
I: violence/crime	50	57	6		***
II: personal desires not principles	15	20	15		
II: anarchy/disorder/ chaos	25	57	46	**	
II: impossible to imagine	—	7	32		***
III: man as self-regulatory (nothing would happen)	—	—	8		*
	What is a rule?				
I: prohibitive	60	30	14	**	**
II: prescriptive	20	40	58	*	*
II: enforcement	—	10	5	*	
III: beneficial/rational	15	27	26		
	What is a law?				
I: prohibitive	60	43	11		***
II: prescriptive	20	43	34	**	
II: enforcement	10	23	37		*
III: beneficial/rational	—	13	29	**	**

Levels: categories	Educational Group			Comparisons (by t test)	
	Primary (1)	Middle School (2)	College (3)	(1) × (2)	(2) × (3)
Why should people follow rules?					
I: avoid negative consequences	50	13	3	***	**
I: authority	5	—	—		
II: personal conformity	35	13	9	**	
II: social conformity	10	53	25	***	***
III: rational/beneficial/ utilitarian	5	27	51	**	**
III: principled	—	—	5		
Why do you follow rules?					
I: avoid negative consequences	60	47	25		**
I: authority	10	10	3		*
II: personal conformity	20	40	34	*	
II: social conformity	—	40	12	***	***
Why do you follow rules?					
III: rational/beneficial/ utilitarian	—	7	22		**
III: principled	—	—	11		**
Can rules be changed?					
I: no	20	—	—	***	
II & III: yes	70	100	95	***	
Are there times when it might be right to break a rule?					
I: no, unqualified	55	7	3	***	
I: yes, unspecified	25	—	5	***	
II: morality of circumstance	20	73	35	***	***
III: morality of rule	—	17	54	**	***

Note.—All questions except "Can rules be changed?" and "Are there times when it might be right to break a rule?" are multiple coded; therefore, percentages may total over 100 percent. Where answers were idiosyncratic or uncodeable, the categories were omitted from the table. Level I: Preconventional; Level II: Conventional; Level III: Postconventional.

$*p < .10$
$**p < .05$
$***p < .01$

[a]Reproduced with permission from: June L. Tapp and Lawrence Kohlberg, "Developing Senses of Law and Legal Justice," *Journal of Social Issues* 27, no. 2 (1971): 76–77.

prevail. In general, they thought rules and laws exist to maintain order in the social system which, we assume, includes the school.

The function of rules and laws was investigated by asking the questions "What is a rule?" and "What is a law?" Most primary school children were preconventional, reporting only the negative, prohibitive aspects of rules and laws. At middle school and college levels most students were at the conventional level. Most students at the conventional level saw rules and laws as prescriptive. (See Table 5–3.)

Levine and Tapp did not report responses to these questions in their study of legal socialization. We do have an estimate of teachers' actual approach to rules that we discussed in this chapter. Caution should be taken in the comparison because 1) we did not ask the questions of teachers; 2) we were not replicating or trying to parallel Tapp's study. Still, we feel some parallels are worth noting. As perceived by students, the majority of teacher rules are prescriptive (conventional level). The next largest set of rules are prohibitive (preconventional level), and the smallest number of rules are principled (postconventional level). As we noted earlier in this chapter, there is a difference between the most-liked and-least liked teachers in the categories of rules. Specifically, all principled rules were reported for favorite (or most-liked) teachers while the least-liked had almost as many prohibitive rules as they had prescriptive.

Compliance with rules and laws was the next realm of study. Two questions were asked about compliance, one dealing with the ideal, "Why should people follow rules?" and one dealing with the real, "Why do you follow rules?" On the ideal question primary school children responded at a preconventional level with avoidance of punishment a major justification. Significant numbers (45 percent) of young children did respond at the conventional level. While the majority of middle school students provided conventional answers, some had progressed to the postconventional level. The majority of college students were postconventional. Sixty-six percent of teachers responded to the ideal question about legal compliance at the postconventional level, 32 percent were conventional, and 3 percent preconventional.

On the question concerning the real, "Why do you follow rules?" primary school students' responses were preconventional. Middle school students' responses were about evenly split between preconventional and conventional, and college students were conventional with some pre- and some postconventional.

Teachers were primarily conventional (64 percent) in their response to the "real" question. So, for youth and teachers alike, there is an understanding of the ideal that seems to emerge ahead of actual behavior. This discrepancy is important for teachers to understand, as they are required to interact with students in activities and conflicts that result in socialization. The ability to comprehend, and it is hoped, move toward higher levels of ethical development, is of great importance.

"Can rules be changed?" The pattern of response to this question was what one might expect. Some (20 percent) of the preschool children indicated "no." In later years all students responded "yes" to the question. It seems that the majority of youth, from kindergarten to college, understand that rule systems can be changed.

What about breaking rules? "Are there times when it might be right to break a rule?" Fifty-five percent of primary school children think that rules cannot be broken. The majority of middle school children indicate they would break a rule. Conditions under which they would break rules are extreme—"if it's a matter of life and death." The reasoning at the conventional level centered on the "morality of the situation." At the higher, postconventional level, the justification for breaking a rule amounted to the "morality of the rule." The majority of college students (54 percent) used this justification.

The majority of teachers (54 percent) used the conventional level of reasoning for breaking a rule. Thirty-four percent were postconventional when asked if there were times when it might be right to break a rule.

LAW-RELATED EDUCATION

Law-related education is a clear extension of discussions of ethical conflicts and students' understanding of law and rules. There is now substantial curriculum development in the area of law-related education. Originating in the 1960s, the development of law-related materials has the goal of increasing basic literacy concerning fundamental principles of the Constitution and Bill of Rights.

Law-related studies have established an important place in the curriculum of many schools. With the increasing need for students to understand basic concepts of law, schools have implemented law-related education programs as part of the social studies curriculum. We support the development and implementation of law-related education programs as one important means of reducing violence and disruption in schools and in society.

Law in the School Curriculum

Law-related education programs generally involve students in experiences that result in the development of concepts, skills, attitudes, and appreciations of law that are necessary for living in society. In brief, the goal is legal literacy. There is a wide range of approaches used to meet this goal. Law-related programs usually take one of three approaches. Some programs directly involve students in the criminal justice system. For example, students might work with criminal justice personnel or visit courtrooms where criminal cases are being tried. A second approach focuses on the conceptual bases of law. Here, curriculum and instruction are directed toward students' understanding concepts such as justice, equality, power, liberty, and authority of law, that affect the daily lives of citizens. For example, juvenile law, consumer law, and environmental law are central components of instruction.

While studying law in the school curriculum students acquire a common body of knowledge and values concerning the Constitution and Bill Rights, regardless of the particular program. Most law-related programs use instructional materials such as case studies, conflict-resolution techniques, readings, simulation games, field trips, and the analysis and interpretation of cases.

The themes of this book—violence, values, and justice—can readily be seen as integral to the major objectives of law-related education. In most cases it can be assumed that legal literacy contributes to a reduction of criminal violations and, indeed, of school disruptions and violations of rules and policies. This assumption is based on the idea that acquiring information about the law (and school rules) and also about the processes and consequences of violations will deter individuals from breaking the law. Inquiry into legal problems will also contribute to ethical development and higher levels of moral reasoning by students. This objective is achieved through analysis of problems and confrontation of ethical dilemmas in the context of meaningful situations for the students. Finally, justice is central to law-related education. As students are involved in readings, problems, cases, simulations, and field experiences they come to appreciate the legal system and its conceptual foundation of justice.

Curriculum Programs

Let us be clear and unequivocal about our recommendation: school systems should implement law-related education programs. Doing so will not, in and of itself, reduce violence and disruption. But it is one of many things school systems can do to help reduce violations of laws, rules, and policies. Here are some examples of national projects of law-related curriculum programs.

Institute for Political/Legal Education (IPLE)

This program consists of a year-long social studies curriculum for high school students. The curriculum provides students with practical experiences in political, governmental, and legal processes. There are three major units: voter education; state, county, and local government; and individual rights. The program is heavily oriented toward community involvement; it requires a minimum of twenty days of field work and internships in local, county, and state agencies. Address: Institute for Political/Legal Education, 207 Delsea Drive, R. D. #4 Box 209, Sewell, New Jersey 08080.

Law in Action

Law in Action is designed for middle school students, grades 5 through 8. Topics in the program include: Lawmaking, Juvenile Problems and the Law, Youth Attitudes and Police, Courts and Trials, and Problems for Young Consumers. Simulations, mock trials, and community involvement are important components of the instructional program. Address: Law in Action National Office, 393 North Euclid Avenue, Room 25, St. Louis, Missouri 63108.

Law in American Society Foundation

Curriculum materials are for both elementary and secondary schools. A series entitled *Trailmarks of Liberty* introduces constitutional concepts for elementary school and junior and senior high school levels. *Justice in America* focuses on issues such as urban problems, welfare, housing, criminal law, and the juvenile justice system. This series is appropriate for grades 7 through 12. Multimedia materials are available. Address: Law in American Society Foundation, Lyceum Building, 2235 North Sheffield Avenue, Chicago, Illinois 60614.

Law, Education and Participation (LEAP)

Law, Education and Participation is a project of the Constitutional Rights Foundation. The project disseminates law-related materials developed by the Constitutional Rights Foundation. In addition, the LEAP project provides consulting services and assistance in developing community programs; organizing resources and voluntary services of legal personnel for schools; planning inservice programs; and arranging programs, conferences, and seminars in law-related education. Address: Law, Education and Participation, 6310 San Vicente Blvd., Suite 402, Los Angeles, California 90048.

Law in a Free Society (LIFS)

Law in a Free Society is a K–12 curriculum program based on the concepts of authority, diversity, freedom, justice, participation; privacy, property, and responsibility. Instructional materials include modules, filmstrips, tape cassettes, student resource books, and teacher's guide. Preservice and inservice materials are available. Likewise, consulting services and implementation programs are a part of the LIFS project. Address: Law in a Free

Society, 606 Wilshire Boulevard, Suite 600, Santa Monica, California 90401

National Street Law Institute

The National Street Law program emphasizes areas of law common to the daily lives of all citizens. The text, *Street Law: A Course in Practical Law*, has units on criminal law, consumer law, family law, housing law, environmental law, and individual rights law. There are also materials entitled *Street Law: A Course in the Law of Corrections*. The project also provides program assistance in the development of law-related education programs. Address: National Street Law Institute, 605 G Street, N.W., Washington, D. C. 20001.

We suggest that school personnel first obtain a *Directory of Law Related Curriculum Materials, Media: An Annotated Catalogue of Law Related Audio-Visual Materials* and *Gaming: An Annotated Catalogue of Law Related Games and Simulations*. All can be obtained from: Special Committee on Youth Education for Citizenship, American Bar Association, 1155 East 60th Street, Chicago, Illinois 60637.

Every state has developed law-related education materials. In many cases information about these projects can be obtained from the bar association in your state or the state Department of Education. However, the easiest way of locating materials in your state is through the directory listed in the previous paragraph.

In closing this chapter we strongly recommend that school personnel consider the implementation of a law-related program. Doing so is a direct step toward reducing student disruption and facilitating ethical development and legal literacy through education.

SUMMARY

Understanding ethical levels of development and the resulting positions on various issues is important for school personnel. We are particularly interested in the role one's level of ethical development plays in the resolution of school conflicts. The ethical subtleties of normal classroom interaction are often overlooked by educators.

In an informal survey we found that the majority of rules for both favorite and least-favorite teachers were prescriptive. The next major category of rules was prohibitive. The category of principled rules was reported least often and never for teachers with whom students did not get along.

Individual motivation is also related to ethics and values. The hierarchy of motivational needs as described by Abraham H. Maslow ranges from the physiological to physical and through the social-psychological. The needs of an individual have a direct influence on his or her immediate perceptions and values. In addition, individuals must extend themselves and interact with the physical and human environment in order to fulfill these needs. The subsequent interaction between an individual and other individuals can facilitate positive ethical development or, on occasion, can be labeled disruptive.

The theories of Jean Piaget, Lawrence Kohlberg, and June Tapp were used as a basis for discussions of ethical development. Ethical development can be summarized in the following way. There is a preconventional level at which the orientation is to rules; this level is one of obedience. The conception of justice is based on punishment and rewards meted out by authorities. There is an unquestioned acceptance of rules and laws with little or no understanding of an underlying system of morality and justice.

At the conventional level, rules and laws exist to maintain social order. Individuals behave in terms of the law to gain approval from others or to maintain order within society. This is the level at which most adolescents function, and it seems to be the principal orientation of most teachers.

Individuals at the postconventional level have an orientation toward ethical principles and, in particular, toward justice. Rules and laws should be obeyed for rational considerations, based on the idea that they are beneficial to those in society. While rules and laws are important for the social order, they are not immutable. If they are unjust, or have no clear purpose, they can be changed; the principle of justice defines the limits of the law at this level. For individuals at lower levels, the law or those in authority define justice.

Students' preconventional reasoning decreases from kindergarten to college. The general orientation of middle school to college-age students is conventional. Postconventional reasoning by students is not evident at lower levels; it increases steadily as students reach college age.

The majority of teachers are at the conventional level of development. However, they understand the postconventional level and present this level as an ideal. This is an encouraging fact since teachers are the ones responsible for promoting ethical development in schools.

REFERENCES

1. Abraham H. Maslow, *Motivation and Personality* (New York: Harper & Row, 1970).
2. Jean Piaget, *The Moral Judgment of the Child* (New York: The Free Press, 1965).
3. Lawrence Kohlberg, "Moral Education for a Society in Moral Transition," *Educational Leadership* (October 1975): 46–54.

4. _____, "The Cognitive-Developmental Approach to Moral Education," *Phi Delta Kappan* (June 1975): 670–77.

5. _____, "The Development of Modes of Moral Thinking and Choice in the Years Ten to Sixteen," (unpublished doctoral dissertation, University of Chicago, 1958).

6. _____, "Stage and Sequence: The Cognitive-Developmental Approach to Socialization," in David Gaslin, *Handbook of Socialization Theory and Research* (Chicago: Rand McNally, 1967).

7. _____, "Moral Stages and Moralization: The Cognitive Developmental Approach," in Thomas Lickona, ed., *Moral Development and Behavior* (New York: Holt, Rinehart and Winston, 1976).

8. _____, "The Claim to Moral Adequacy of a Highest Stage of Moral Judgement," *The Journal of Philosophy* LXX, no. 18 (1973): 630–46.

9. _____, "From Is to Ought: How to Commit the Naturalistic Fallacy and Get Away With It in the Study of Moral Development," in T. Mishel, ed., *Cognitive Development and Epistemology* (New York: Academic Press, 1971).

10. William Kurtines and Esther B. Greif, "The Development of Moral Thought: A Review and Evaluation of Kohlberg's Approach," *Psychological Bulletin* 81, no. 8 (1974): 453–70.

11. Elizabeth Leonie Simpson, "Moral Development Research: A Case Study of Scientific Cultural Bias," *Human Development* 17 (1974): 81–106.

12. John C. Gibbs, "Kohlberg's Stages of Moral Judgement: A Constructive Critique," *Harvard Educational Review* 47, no. 1 (1977): 43–61.

13. Jack Fraenkel, "The Kohlberg Bandwagon: Some Reservations," *Social Education* 40, no. 4 (1976): 216–22.

14. June L. Tapp and Lawrence Kohlberg, "Developing Senses of Law and Legal Justice," in June Tapp and Felice Levine, eds., *Law, Justice and the Individual in Society: Psychological and Legal Issues* (New York: Holt, Rinehart and Winston, 1977).

15. Felice Levine and June Tapp, "The Dialectic of Legal Socialization in Community and School," in June Tapp and Felice Levine, eds., *Law, Justice and the Individual in Society: Psychological and Legal Issues* (New York: Holt, Rinehart and Winston, 1977).

CHAPTER SIX

Educational Conflicts

INTRODUCTION

Conflicts between teachers and students are inevitable. Most conflicts in schools are resolved quickly and with little difficulty, but some have unpleasant consequences. The issues of violence, discipline, and order in schools are important concerns for those entering education, those already teaching, and those administering. Conflict is central to the issues of violence and disruption. Conflict is also an everyday occurrence in schools where violence and disruption are not dominating concerns of students, parents, and school personnel. Yet, discussions and analysis of educational conflicts are a much neglected area in education. For these reasons we think understanding educational conflicts, and especially their resolution, is essential for effective education.

There are some conflicts that can be prevented, and educators should certainly try to anticipate problem situations and deter their occurrence. Still there will be conflicts. The orientation of this chapter is toward understanding the nature of educational conflicts so school personnel can avoid destructive results and facilitate constructive resolutions to conflicts.

There are two ways of viewing educational conflicts. One centers on the individual student's problems and the other considers social-psychological factors within the classroom or school, such as the development of behavioral norms that condone disruption, general messing about, and unnecessary talking within a group of students. In this situation, for instance, the class is out of control, and many otherwise good students may become discipline problems. Here the conflict is between the teacher or administrator and a group of students. Another type of discipline problem is one dominated by an individual student. Our concern in this chapter is primarily the latter type of problem, particularly how a sequence of minor disruptions can develop into a serious discipline problem.

We shall start by looking at several actual conflicts.

ELEMENTARY SCHOOL MATHEMATICS LESSON

Dave was drawing on his desk and not working on mathematics. The teacher asked him to stop drawing on the desk. He kept on drawing. She picked up the pencil and placed it on his desk saying, "This is not to be used on the desk." She walked back to the front of the class. Dave picked up the pencil and began drawing again.

What would you do next?

JUNIOR HIGH SCHOOL SCIENCE CLASS

From the beginning of class Mary had looked around to see who was paying attention to her. She was taking great care to look her best, combing her hair and checking her makeup. As the teacher started the lesson, Mary interrupted several times with subtle comments focusing attention on herself. She asked, "Can I go early?" "I'm thirsty. Can I get a drink?" Later, while students were working on an assignment Mary continually talked to girls around her. Many of her comments were designed to elicit compliments. "My hair never looks as good as yours." "I wish I had a blouse like that." On several occasions the teacher had to tell her to stop talking and get to work.

What would you do next?

JUNIOR HIGH SCHOOL ENGLISH CLASS

"I know what we are doing today. Should I tell everybody?" This was Robert's announcement as he walked through the door. The teacher and class could not help but notice since the comment was loud, and he was late. "No, I'll tell them, and you go to your seat." "O.K., but I really know what we're doing." This dialogue continued off and on for several minutes. The teacher would mention something about the day's work and Robert would make a (sometimes humorous) comment for all to hear. Finally, he was up, out of seat, pointing to, and commenting about, some students who were outside. In an angry tone the teacher said, "Robert, you just sit down and shut up." He did so for the rest of the period.

What would you do next?

HIGH SCHOOL HALL

An administrator approached a student who was acting strangely. "What are you doing? You are supposed to be in class. Are you hiding something behind you? Are you smoking?" The student responded by saying, "It's none of your fuckin' business what I'm doing. Leave me alone." As the administrator approached the boy, he turned and ran down the hall and out a door.

What would you do next?

HIGH SCHOOL COUNSELOR'S OFFICE

Jane had been referred to the counselor. Several of her teachers had reported that she simply sat in class. She did not disrupt; she sat quietly and did nothing. Jane seemed as if she was "in a trance" or "on another planet." She had no friends and barely talked when spoken to. Jane responded in a similar manner to the counselor. She mumbled answers to his questions, was sometimes incoherent, and often didn't answer. She just sat staring into space.

What would you do next?

As an educator, you no doubt had some response to these students' behavior. Can you state the rule that constituted the conflict? What about Dave? Mary? Robert? The student in the hall? Or Jane? What was your first reaction to the situation? How would you have resolved the conflict? What factors did you consider about the students? What else would you like to know about these individuals? We encourage you to reflect on these questions concerning similar conflicts or others you have had with students.

It would be presumptuous for us to attempt to answer these questions and tell school personnel how to resolve individual conflicts. There are too many variables. Students differ, educators differ, and school situations differ. When it gets to the actual conflict, school personnel have to consider all the variables and proceed on an appropriate course. We can, however, introduce you to different ways of resolving conflicts, types of school conflicts, the context of educational conflicts, the resolution of conflicts, and finally, different ideas to assist in resolving conflicts.

DEFINITIONS OF CONFLICTS

The examples in the introduction clarify a fundamental definition of conflict. *A conflict occurs when activities or behaviors are incompatible.* So, in the examples, the teacher or administrator had planned a series of activities or expected certain behaviors. The actions (or lack of action in Jane's case) of the students were in opposition, in disagreement, or in a direction that was not compatible with educational or administrative goals.

We can also define conflict in terms of school rules, or policies. *An educational conflict is any violation, challenge, or questioning of a school rule, policy, or expectation of behavior.* The rule, policy, or expectation of behavior may or may not be written, stated, or known to both of the parties to the conflict. The point of view expressed here is neutral. We have defined educational conflicts and resolutions without discussing the appropriateness or fairness of the rules or of teacher and student behaviors. The constructive or destructive outcome of a conflict, then, is not based on the rules or policies per se, but on the appropriateness of the processes used to resolve the conflict and the eventual judgment concerning the conflict's resolution.

DYNAMICS OF CONFLICTS

Everyday school occurrences such as those presented earlier suggest many questions relative to the dynamics of conflicts. How do educational conflicts start? What is the relationship between teachers and students that produces conflicts? What factors affect the course of conflict? These and other questions are answered in the next sections.

A model from the literature on child abuse is useful in clarifying educational conflicts.[1] One important reason for modifying and using this model is that conflicts are not simple victim-villain relationships. Rather, there is a broader view, one that includes many factors within the conflict system.

EDUCATOR + STUDENT + SITUATION = CONFLICT

One need only recall several recent discussions of school-related discipline problems to realize that individuals tend to emphasize different aspects of this equation. Some direct their attention to educators as the primary source of problems, others focus on students, and still others attribute the problem to situational issues such as poor home or school environments. In our view, some aspects of each factor can contribute to educational conflicts. One might also note that the equation is balanced by an equal sign. That is to say, as the weight of factors on the left side are increased, there is a corresponding increase on the right side. The increase on the right amounts to changes in the intensity, frequency, and severity of the conflicts. As we proceed through this chapter we will explore the interaction among educators, students, and situational factors, and the changes in intensity, frequency, and severity of educational conflicts.

In *The Resolution of Conflict: Constructive and Destructive Processes*[2] Morton Deutsch has synthesized the research on conflict resolution. According to Deutsch, the course of conflicts is influenced by a number of factors. Some of the factors include:

1. The characteristics of those in conflict (e.g., values, motivations, objectives, history of conflicts and means of resolving conflicts, known and available strategies for resolving conflicts).
2. The relationship between those in conflict (e.g., beliefs, attitudes, values, expectations about each other).
3. The nature of the issue of the conflict (e.g., importance, general versus specific).
4. The environment of the conflict (e.g., deterrents or encouragements for escalating or resolving the conflict).
5. The influence of others on the conflict (e.g., interest of others in the outcome, perceptions that conflicting parties have of others).
6. The means used to resolve the conflict (e.g., dominance, discussion, coercion, incentives, withdrawal).
7. The consequences of the conflict to each party (e.g., long- and short-term consequence, the future relationship between parties, gains and losses).

The variables influencing the course of a conflict are many, and they exist for both school personnel and students. What are some of the situational factors in educational conflicts?

Control is one of the main situational variables in educational conflicts. For many educators decisions concerning the classroom or school are not to be shared with students. Conflict often results when students want to assume some decision-making power.

Preferences and Expectations form a second set of situational issues. School personnel and students may have different preferences and expectations of behaviors, and different means of achieving goals and activities. Related to preferences and expectations are the values and beliefs of educators and students.

Environmental Factors within the school can be an issue in conflicts. This category includes such intangibles as school climate[3] and some very tangible things such as architecture, colors, dark spaces, time of day, and air conditioning.

While many of these factors are unique to specific individuals and schools, it may be helpful to examine some personal information concerning certain aspects of educators, students, and conflict situations. As mentioned above, one thing that influences the direction of a conflict is the means used by the parties to try to resolve the problem.

How do you typically try and resolve conflicts with others? We have modified an exercise originally developed by Lawrence and Torsch[4] and later modified by Johnson[5] that provides some insights concerning ways individuals solve conflicts. We suggest you complete the exercise.

The following sayings can be thought of as descriptions of different ways individuals resolve conflicts. Read each of the statements carefully. Using the scale of 1 through 5 given below, indicate how typical each saying is of your actions in a conflict situation.

> 5–Very typical of the way I act in a conflict
> 4–Frequently typical of the way I act in a conflict
> 3–Sometimes typical of the way I act in a conflict
> 2–Seldom typical of the way I act in a conflict
> 1–Never typical of the way I act in a conflict

_____ 1. Soft words win hard hearts.

_____ 2. Come now and let us reason together.

_____ 3. Arguments of the strongest have the most weight.

_____ 4. You scratch my back, I'll scratch yours.

_____ 5. The best way of handling conflicts is to avoid them.

_____ 6. If someone hits you with a stone, hit the person with a piece of cotton.

_____ 7. A question must be decided by knowledge and not by numbers if it is to have a right decision.

_____ 8. If you cannot make a person think as you do, make the person do as you think.

_____ 9. Better half a loaf than no bread at all.

_____10. If someone is ready to quarrel with you, that person isn't worth knowing.

_____11. Smooth words make smooth ways.

_____12. By digging and digging, the truth is discovered.

_____13. One who fights and runs away lives to run another day.

_____14. A fair exchange brings no quarrel.

_____15. There is nothing so important that you have to fight for it.

_____16. Kill your enemies with kindness.

_____17. Seek till you find, and you'll not lose your labor.

_____18. Might overcomes right.

_____19. Tit for tat is fair play.

_____20. Avoid quarrelsome people—they will only make you unhappy.

Some insights about your typical style of resolving conflicts can be gained by adding the responses to different sayings. Add your typical responses to the sayings as indicated.

Sayings	Total	Response Style
1, 6, 11, 16	= _____	Smoothing
2, 7, 12, 17	= _____	Negotiating
3, 8, 13, 18	= _____	Forcing
4, 9, 14, 19	= _____	Compromising
5, 10, 15, 20	= _____	Withdrawing

Two goals are often considered in resolving conflicts. One is personal and usually involves achieving, gaining, or maintaining something; for example, achieving an educational goal, gaining personal recognition, or maintaining one's safety and security. The second goal has to do with preserving or changing the relationship with the conflicting party. In education we assume this usually means preserving the relationship with a student. The results of typical responses to conflicts have bearing on the personal and relational goals of educators. In the following discussion we use education and schools as the point of reference.

Withdrawing

Withdrawing from a conflict fulfills neither the personal nor the relational goals. Essentially it is a lose/lose approach to conflict resolution since the educator gives up whatever educational goals he or she had and does not try to maintain the relationship with the student. In brief it is:

PERSONAL—LOSE

RELATIONAL—LOSE

Smoothing

Smoothing over the conflict gives highest priority to maintaining the relationship, often at all costs, including giving up personal goals. This is a resolution that usually results in:

PERSONAL—LOSE

RELATIONAL—WIN

Forcing

Here, personal goals are achieved at any cost. The cost is often to give up a personal relationship with the students. So we have a situation of:

PERSONAL—WIN

RELATIONAL—LOSE

Compromising

The educator gives up some personal goals, and some relational goals are modified in order to resolve the conflict. All parties to the conflict give up something and are often dissatisfied with the results. The grounds for resentment by both educators and students have been established. The amount of resentment will depend on the perceived amount of compromise by each party to the conflict. In essence this is a resolution of:

PERSONAL—TIE
RELATIONAL—TIE

Negotiating

Educators and students resolve conflicts through cooperative problem solving. Though some changes occur, essentially the goals of both educators and students are achieved and relationships are maintained. This approach is one of:

PERSONAL—WIN
RELATIONAL—WIN

Different conflict situations lend themselves to different resolutions. For instance, meeting an intruder with a weapon in the hall may require force; you are interested in self-preservation and you are not too interested in establishing an ongoing positive relationship with the individual. On the other hand, forcing a resolution for numerous minor infractions of classroom rules and policies can establish an atmosphere that eventually alienates students from you and the school. There are times when each of the different means of resolving conflicts is appropriate. Educators understand this and can make judgments concerning the situation, their personal goals, and the relational goals. Students have different conflict resolution styles, personal goals, and relational goals. Some of these goals will be discussed in the following sections.

DIMENSIONS OF CONFLICTS

Conflicts in schools range from minor infractions such as chewing gum or tapping a pencil to the use of lethal weapons or arson. Over the past several years we have recorded and analyzed more than two hundred conflicts in urban, suburban, and rural schools. In Chapter Four we proposed a typology of identifiable student behaviors that can be labeled disruptive. We return to that typology here and use it as a way of describing the dimensions of school conflicts. The previous section dealt primarily with the teacher or administrator in the equation EDUCATOR + STUDENT + SITUATION = CONFLICT. In this section we concentrate on student behaviors and the intensity, frequency, and severity of school conflicts. Since we will present examples of actual school conflicts, all factors in the equation will, however, usually be present.

The development of behaviors that end in violent conflicts can originate in a confrontation between an individual's needs and a lack of recognition, apathy toward, or required repression of those needs by others. An interaction between school personnel and students that results in a sense of powerlessness, isolation, anonymity, boredom, and insignificance within the school is one of the wellsprings of school conflicts. No doubt there are other deeper origins within some individuals, but these issues provide important school-related sources for violence, vandalism, and disruption. Loss of a sense of control or power to influence one's life, combined with a long-term socialization into aggression as the primary means to resolve conflicts, and placement in a particular situation make a volatile mixture. Like many reactions, the product can foment over time, or it can precipitate rapidly.

Generally, educators view discipline problems as discrete events and not elements in consistent patterns of behavior. Observing hundreds of classroom conflicts of varying intensity, interviewing students who represent varying types of discipline problems, and discussing conflicts with school personnel has led us to a different conclusion. We think there is an identifiable range of school conflicts. The sequence starts with mild, often acceptable, forms of behavior and ends in violence. There is also the possibility that an individual may turn inward and become alienated, withdrawn and depressed; ultimately the violence here is toward the self. The conflicts that occur at these stages are discussed in the following sections.

Affirmation

The earliest behaviors that can produce school conflicts are those that individuals use when seeking affirmation. Attention from the teacher is one way students have of feeling personally adequate and of gaining esteem in the eyes of their peers. Some students achieve acknowledgement through socially acceptable behavior such as working hard, participating in school activities and achieving. While these behaviors are often seen as "model," students may in fact be pursuing a goal of self-affirmation much more than educational goals. Other students have problems with school work, are left out of school activities, and do not achieve. Some of these students turn to other ways of gaining personal affirmation at school.

Disruptive behaviors at this level include many of the minor day-to-day classroom problems such as "showing off," "clowning," and "being lazy." Conflicts with school personnel may occur because of minor mischief, restlessness, "nuisance" behavior, and incessant questioning for recognition.

The passive quest for affirmation includes pseudo reading difficulties, shyness, inattention, and untidiness. All of these behaviors result from the student's need for recognition that can be gained from the teacher's attention. While not all of these behaviors result in conflicts they can easily develop into more serious problems.

AFFIRMATION—RURAL JUNIOR HIGH

Ron came to class totally unprepared for anything academic—no pencil, paper, or book. I gave him a pencil, found a book, and borrowed some paper from another student.

Ron did nothing for about twenty minutes. Then he started doing immature things that disturbed me and other students. I verbally reprimanded him and cautioned him to not bother others. After about three minutes he was back at it; I felt ignored, and my authority threatened. I then verbally belittled him (in front of others) and he stopped. In another three minutes he was back at it. I once again reprimanded him verbally—restricted him to his seat facing front. I ended up keeping him after school, giving the big lecture (suggesting in great disgust that this better never happen again).

AFFIRMATION—URBAN JUNIOR HIGH

I was teaching the skill of reading word problems, math problems stated in sentence form. The directions to the students were: don't jump to conclusions or try to guess the answers. Instead, think about the steps each of us must go through in order to find the answer. The first problem was simpler than the second. One student began a loud conversation with another student. She copied the problem mechanically from the board as she talked, then she called out an incorrect answer. I reminded her of my instructions, then followed the problem step by step. She continued talking and another student began talking. She was reminded again that her talking interfered with the learning process, and I went on to re-explain the problem to students who did not understand how the answer was obtained. She and the other student continued to talk and I reminded her that both would receive a failing mark for the day's classwork. She then began a long discussion with me about the other students' talking, her good work, my constant harassing of her, etc. The discussion continued for ten minutes, and I was not able to write the last problem on the board before the bell rang.

Alienation

There is also the possibility that an individual can turn inward and become detached and alienated. The student becomes unfriendly, indifferent, disassociated, and estranged from the teacher and other students. Teachers would describe these individuals as shy, sad, "turned off," isolated, or unmotivated. Because most teachers respond to noise and activity, alienated students are cause for concern since they cause few conflicts and go unrecognized until the problems are very serious.

ALIENATION—RURAL JUNIOR HIGH

John talked about hating the songs the class was singing, saying they were dumb. He also didn't like the teacher, who he thought tried to be too domineering. John was pretty bored with the whole scene. This is apparently an activity he doesn't like. He is very rarely with anyone for any length of time. He is definitely a loner.

In speech class, John sat by himself but spent most of the period trying to get the attention of a student who was obviously angry at him. His attention devices were conciliatory and almost pleading. The other student responded near the end of the period. Math class found John roaming around class, not really being able to settle on any one thing. He was reprimanded once for being noisy.

John was sitting on the radiator at the beginning of the class period by himself. He made comments to other students trying to interact with them. There was really no work for him to do. He asked other students what they were going to do for Enrichment Day. He liked roller skating and was trying to get someone to go with him.

On the whole John was relatively quiet, sitting back talking to a few students, somewhat bored. He didn't seem very outgoing from what I could gather. He didn't disrupt the class because there was no structure. He asked me what I wanted to do on Enrichment Day. He seemed as if he wanted to talk and be friendly.

John did not do any work. He had been absent for a week so the teacher asked him to write a paragraph on what he had done the past week. He fidgeted at writing when the teacher came around to him, but then just sat back, sharpening his pencil endlessly. He also kept trying to talk to the student next to him. Occasionally he would look at his paper but would return to his idle sharpening, chattering, or rocking on his chair. When the teacher came around and saw he had not written anything, she chewed him out a little. He only smiled at this, looking away. When she told him to start writing, he did make the motions to, but when she left he just reverted to not doing anything. After class was over, he quickly walked out the door.

John got a brief description of what he was supposed to do in the art exercise and then sat down. He spent a lot of time talking and fooling around trying to decide on a figure to draw. He kept asking the students around him, "What should I draw?" John looked a little uncomfortable in the setting. He just couldn't get started on his own. He wasn't being disruptive by talking because it was a loose type of activity. He didn't get up and ask for help from the teacher. He did a lot of staring out the window.

John was one of the few students the teacher had to chew out for horsing around. He and the fellow sitting next to him would get into playful slugging and joking. John would do things to entertain the class or to show them that he wasn't afraid of the teacher. While John showed some interest in sports, he appeared to be disinterested. He was more interested in getting the attention of others. At one point John was asked to read some things, which he did with deliberate care, taking it seriously.

The student demonstrates consistent patterns of behavior that can be described as affirmation-seeking or alienated. The nature of the conflicts and the situations may vary, but on analysis the behaviors consistently result in personal recognition. Most students engage in some of these behaviors some of the time. Classroom teachers and administrators should, however, be aware of the students who demonstrate these behaviors a majority of the time and in ways that exceed the range of normal adolescent behavior. For students at this level, it is important and relatively easy to be given attention in educationally and personally constructive ways. Helping students who are seeking affirmation or who are slightly alienated can be done through listening closely to students for cues concerning their needs and perceptions and giving praise and personal recognition for work.

Assertion

When educators speak of discipline problems they are usually referring to conflicts at this level. While students at the earlier stage only occasionally violate school rules and policies, students at this stage consistently violate rules and policies and may occasionally violate criminal codes.

This stage is differentiated from affirmation and alienation by the intensity and frequency of conflicts with school personnel. Here, conflicts between teachers and students will be more intense and frequent, so much so that teachers and other students cannot help but recognize the disruptive individuals for their behavior.

Assertion (and withdrawal) differs from the next stage, aggression and depression, by the fact that lines of communication are moderately open; there is some respect for the teacher and school even if great doubt is shown outwardly toward those in positions of authority.

Assertive behaviors are attempts to express oneself clearly, forcefully and boldly. Individuals who actively maintain positions or defend their rights are asserting themselves. Assertive individuals still wish to be recognized as working within the educational system or with the teacher. So, even though they will be in conflict with teachers and administrators, when they detect that they are reaching the limits of tolerance, they will relent and do what the teacher asks. The line is fine, however, because the teacher can also escalate the students' disruption to more intense behavior patterns.

ASSERTION—URBAN JUNIOR HIGH

The student came in the room at the assigned time. Within thirty seconds he demanded that I get him a Coke because it was hot. I explained that our agreement was a Coke on Friday if his work was done and that I was not going to leave the classroom today. The student sat down at my desk and started to cut attendance slips into small pieces and drop them onto the floor. I stated that he should pick them up—he disagreed. About forty-five minutes later he began to show interest in books I was working on with another student. He still refused to pick up the paper before leaving. I stated that I would turn the matter over to the assistant principal and did that the next period. Two hours later the assistant principal sent the student to the room and the mess was cleaned up.

ASSERTION—URBAN JUNIOR HIGH

I was leaving the school building via the main entrance. On the front steps leading down to the street I saw a young man playing with a large knife. I approached the young man and asked him to close the knife and to "please give it to me." The student seemed surprised, closed the knife, and gave it to me. He started telling me about the incident; he said he had been holding the knife for a friend. I asked the student his name and referred the matter to the school principal for appropriate action.

Withdrawn

The withdrawn student is moving away from others but is still partially associated with students and teachers. Withdrawn pupils will be detached from emotional involvement with school or teachers. They will occasionally cut class or be truant; that is, they physically withdraw from class or school. Communication is not easy since these individuals are remote, isolated, and often unresponsive.

WITHDRAWN—SUBURBAN JUNIOR HIGH

The student was not participating with the class in the group assignment. The student was told to participate. "You should be doing the assignment. Put your book away and work with the rest of the class. You need this information." The student refused. She said she had already passed her proficiency and review test and did not need any more information. She further stated that the teacher did not know all the right answers anyway, so why should she care.

WITHDRAWN—SUBURBAN JUNIOR HIGH

Laurie would come into art class before anyone else arrived. She would sit down, open a book (always fiction), and begin reading. If there was a lecture/discussion, Laurie only paid the slightest attention, focusing instead on her reading. If there was a demonstration, Laurie would have to be asked to join the group, which she would do reluctantly, speak to others little, and then get back to her book. When the class would be working on an assignment, Laurie would continue reading unless questioned. When asked why she was not working on the class project, if she needed help in getting started, she would say, "I can't work here. I do better at home," making it obvious that she did not want to be disturbed. She always sat at a table with other students, but she would not participate in their conversation. Laurie was absent often. When coming back to school from an absence and asked about the progress of her missed work, she always said that she had forgotten it at home or that it had been stolen from her locker. Work just never materialized. Laurie always seemed to be in another world.

Students reaching this level of interaction with school personnel are at a very crucial position. They can turn toward improvement or further deterioration. At this level students deliberately fail, consider dropping out, are sometimes suspended, experiment with drugs, become truant or delinquent, and join gangs. These students' capacity to make choices and have power within the system has become so diminished that they start deciding against the system and thus maintain their esteem, power, and individuality through antisocial behavior. Clearly, the stage is set for numerous conflicts in the school.

Traditionally the reaction of teachers to conflicts at this stage has been punishment. Punishment can expand the teacher-student conflict and have destructive results on students not directly involved. The probability is very high that verbal or physical aggression toward an assertive student will bring about an escalation of the conflict to aggression or violence.

Aggression

Aggressive students have the immediate aim of taking over and controlling the classroom. Open and malicious disobedience characterize this level of conflict. Needless to say, these students are continuously violating school rules and policies.

Aggressive students attempt to physically or verbally dominate the classroom. For these individuals the line has been drawn between themselves and the teacher. Moving across the line, starting the disruptive conflict, and continuing the hostility all help them achieve a sense of dominance.

AGGRESSION—URBAN JUNIOR HIGH

Paraprofessionals indicated that the student was extremely rude, uncooperative, and disruptive during the lesson. Paraprofessionals are strong disciplinarians, but this student's verbal behavior had them totally turned around. "If you didn't have such big ears, you wouldn't have heard me." "You can't tell me what to do." "No one was talking to you." These were some of the student's comments. The paraprofessionals dealt with him and survived the period, but felt it ended with the student in control and with them about to lose the respect of the entire class.

I told them to send the student in to my class the next day. As I began my seventh grade demonstration lesson, he walked in. I didn't know him, but assumed he must be the pupil. I asked his name in a stern tone. When he answered I remained stonefaced and said, "Oh yes! Wonderful! Just wonderful! Have a seat. I'll be with you just as soon as I get this class started." I pointed to a chair nearby and turned to address the class. As I did so, he sucked his teeth, turned on his heels saying, "I don't have to take this shit! You don't know me!" I said fiercely, "I said have a seat. We have plenty to talk about, fella, and I don't like your attitude already. Now, sit!" He walked out saying, "I don't have to take this shit and talk to you!"

AGGRESSION—RURAL JUNIOR HIGH

The student came to class two minutes late, sauntered in, and just sat down. This behavior had been going on repeatedly, and I told the student to get here on time, that I was tired of his coming late. He got up and said he didn't have to take that and that he was going up to the office to get a pass. I told him to sit down and get here on time after this. However, he then walked out of the class. I went after him and confronted him in the hall. I grabbed him by the arm. He turned as if he was going to swing at me. I told him to get back in the room and, if he wanted to swing, it would be his first and last. He then went back to the room where he did nothing for the rest of the period.

AGGRESSION—URBAN JUNIOR HIGH

I was trying to settle the class down to be dismissed. This boy continued to create a disturbance, talking out and being a bother to prolong the class's "unreadiness." When I spoke to him he said, "I'm not the only one. Why do you always blame me?" My reply was, "I'm talking to you because you are making the most noise." He began yelling at me to "shut up." My response was that "he had better get himself together or I would take some drastic measures." He didn't care. I said I would call his mother again and get her up here. He said he didn't care. She would only break my glasses. He said "shut up" again. I walked to the back of the room and pushed a chair aside and picked up one and banged it against the chair he was sitting in. He jumped and wanted to run. I told him to "cool out." I dismissed the class and went to the dean and told him of the incident. I told the dean that I didn't want the student back in my class until I had talked to his mother. I called the mother, told her the complete story, and she is to come to see me. The dean talked with the student before readmitting him, and the student has been trying since to stay out of trouble.

Depression

Depression is a turn inward, an escape from reality. Depression literally means to "press down" and this is exactly what these individuals have done with their social values. These students, too, control the situation and have power, but it is a power personally constructed and maintained. Some of the overt signs of this stage are chronic despondency, sullenness and dejection.

DEPRESSION—SUBURBAN JUNIOR HIGH

The situation described here has continued for two years. The student upon entering the school demonstrated complete withdrawal from any classroom or school activities. The student was very passive, uncooperative, and silent. She would not respond to the teacher or counselor except in a sullen, noncommittal form that is best described in statements such as "I don't care" and "you can't do anything about it." This behavior was consistent and continued for two-and-one-half months while she was in my classroom. The student never removed her coat regardless of the very high temperatures that often existed, and any effort to have her remove it led only to frustration and anxiety for both the student and teacher. Comments were of this type:

Teacher: "Ruth, why don't you take off your coat?"
Student: No response, then, "I don't want to."
Teacher: "Why not, Ruth?"
Student: "I don't want to, leave me alone."

When asked to respond in a class situation the teacher was consistently greeted with silence. Ruth attended very few classes, although she was in school every day. She was not forced to go to class, either. During this time it was observed that she never smiled and formed no friendships. She remained entirely isolated and after two months the staff could say, as a whole, that they knew nothing about her, although the student-staff ratio was 10:1.

In all the school meetings, Ruth attended but did not participate even so much as to vote on an issue.

During this time Ruth was evaluated as failing to respond in any manner academically except with an occasional completed assignment.

The probability of these students being in class is small. They are consistently tardy, truant, suspended, or delinquent or in the process of dropping out. For a variety of reasons they spend more time in the streets than in school, and more time in administrators' offices than classrooms. But it is also difficult if the student is in class, because communication is marginal, personal relationships are tenuous, and group dynamics are delicate. Conflicts will be frequent, intense, and severe. It is clear that teachers confronted with aggressive students may feel threatened or defeated or question their ability to control the student and class. These feelings can, unfortunately, result in the teacher using techniques that bring about a power struggle.

Violence

Violence is the immoderate use of physical force exerted with the purpose of abusing, damaging, or violating another person, property, or oneself. Here are the final stages of disruptive behavior and the most severe educational conflicts. All remnants of communication and rationality are gone. The prolonged problems that preceded this stage now take their toll. Each person has a final breaking point where physiological, physical, or psychological needs can be repressed by social values no longer. The small percentage of students who reach this point are the statistics we hear about daily. They assault, murder, and rape other individuals; they steal, vandalize, and burn schools; and they have complete psychotic breaks, become chemically dependent, or commit suicide.

VIOLENCE—URBAN JUNIOR HIGH

A male student entered my homeroom. My class knows the rule of no visitors; the class president informed me of the intruder. Since he had no pass and no one claimed to know him, I asked him to leave. He then started throwing over empty chairs, taunting me to catch him to put him out. I tried cornering him in the room, and when he saw he wasn't going to get away, he picked up a chair, threatening to throw it. I continued toward him, talking all the time. He finally put down the chair very hard, and I was able to escort him to the assistant principal's office. I went back to my room; the class and I picked up the chairs. Ten minutes later the assistant principal escorted the boy to my room, where he said, "Sorry."

The incident ended here; I haven't seen the boy in the halls again.

VIOLENCE—URBAN JUNIOR HIGH

James refused to take my monthly exam. He also decided that no one else in the class would take the test by going around the room tearing up everyone's paper. I asked him to stop and he refused; he continued tearing up everyone's paper. The students were getting very upset and began asking me to stop him. I tried reasoning with him, but he continued. At this point I stepped out in the hall to get some assistance. One of the male teachers was on patrol, and I asked him to assist me with removing James from the class. James refused to go and also refused to stop tearing up the students' papers. He also got very hostile and picked up the window pole to throw at the male teacher who was assisting me. Quite a struggle began and the disturbance spilled into the hall. The principal came by and tried to help out. The window pole was finally gotten away from James, and he was sent to the dean's office.

VIOLENCE—URBAN JUNIOR HIGH

Last week two girls, very suddenly, began arguing about some outside issue. Loud responses were heard, and then preparations for fighting started. I proceeded to separate them. One of the girls pushed me, saying "Get your hands off" and shouting "Leave me alone!" Looking at the other girl, she said, "Go ahead. Try it. I'll beat your fucking' ass!" The class was at that point in an uproar, trying to separate the girls. I was pushed and told by others, "Let them fight it out and get it over with." I managed to hold the girl and walk her to the hall while other students tried to calm the other girl down. The other girl broke away from them and came running out to the hall to continue. The bell rang; the girls fought again. Boys in the hall broke up the fight. I wrote referrals to the dean. I have asked the parent of the child who created the scene to come to the school. Since then the students are back working together as though nothing had happened between them. I haven't heard from the parent yet.

We will end this section with four examples of conflicts that escalated from incidents of disruptive behavior to violent episodes in the classroom. Each of the four examples has been selected for a different reason. In the first incident the violence is, by the teacher's own report, an accident. However, violent behavior is not unusual for this student, and there is some suggestion of violent attitudes in the family. The second incident is a situation where a generally nonviolent student was placed in very stressful circumstances and struck out at the teacher. The third incident is one that could have probably been prevented if the teacher had been informed of the circumstances surrounding the student's life. The final example is one that contributes a bit of humor in the midst of an unfortunate sequence of events.

VIOLENCE—SUBURBAN JUNIOR HIGH

I noticed a group of boys being unruly in the hall and I walked over to investigate the problem. Just as I arrived, a boy who was being handcuffed by a group of students broke away from them. He was swinging his fists wildly and hit me in my eye with a beautiful right. The result for me was a beautiful shiner. When the student saw who he had hit, he ran down the hall and out of the building. He remained away from school for three days. I later found out he thought I would "kill him." I laughed about the situation since I knew no malice was directed toward me. The boys who were trying to handcuff the boy to a locker said they were just goofing around. The boy who hit me could best be described as hostile. He and his brother would fight any or all comers just for kicks. They thought fighting was the only method of settling conflicts. The saying "might makes right" was their slogan. I have no idea where the student had been during his three-day truancy. I talked to his brother during that time and told him to tell his brother to return as I was not angry. His brother told me he didn't know where he was, but to go ahead and "knock the shit out of him" when he did come back. This entire family has a violent streak and only responds to violence or threats of violence. Kindness is a sign of weakness according to them.

VIOLENCE—SUBURBAN HIGH SCHOOL

This conflict involves a male student in a tenth-grade music class. The entire class had been noisy and was given a writing assignment as a punishment. The boy had not learned to read or write. He was very intelligent and had developed extensive ways to compensate for his deficiency. School authorities did not know how poor his skills really were. He could not write the assignment, so he wrote his name on the paper and turned it in. His paper ended up on top of the stack. The teacher asked why he didn't do it. Rather than admit he couldn't write, he said he didn't want to. The teacher made him go to the blackboard and told him to write on it. He refused; the teacher grabbed the boy by the neck of his shirt and accused him of defiance. The boy then struck the teacher with his fist. The boy was expelled from school for violent, uncontrolled behavior.

He is now an adult and still has minimum reading and writing skills. He was a T.V. technician but quit when they wanted to promote him. The job would have involved keeping records. He would not apply for any job where he had to write or fill out forms. Now he owns his own karate school but wants to develop writing and reading skills so he can take other jobs. His symptoms were similar to the now common problems of dyslexia, but at that time they were not recognized by the teacher.

VIOLENCE—SUBURBAN JUNIOR HIGH

Toward the end of the school year I was asked by another teacher in an adjacent room if I would mind watching a student who did not want to attend an assembly. Since I had several students who wanted to work instead of going to the assembly, I agreed to supervise the student. The student sat by himself for several minutes and then began to walk around the room. I was helping a couple of students when I heard something strike the chalkboard behind me. I looked up and saw a pinto bean on the floor just as another struck the chalkboard. I looked up and saw the student throwing the beans around the room. I hollered at him to stop it and come pick up what had been thrown. He did so grudgingly and proceeded to pull the breast pocket of my lab coat open and dump the beans in the pocket. I told him to take them back where he had found them, and he told me that I could "get fucked." I then attempted to take him to the office and succeeded only when I pinned his arms to his sides and carried him bodily to the office amid continued profanities and threats. When I got the student to the office and released him, he picked up a chair and attempted to assault me. Another teacher and I again subdued the student and turned the matter over to the assistant principal for discipline. The student continued his profanity and began also to threaten the assistant principal. The student was suspended and a parent-school conference was held where it was learned that the student was:

1. New to the school (second day);
2. Had just been released from a juvenile detention facility;
3. Had a history of attempted assaults and violent, aggressive behavior.

The staff had not been informed of these circumstances. The student was withdrawn from school within two weeks and went out of state to another school district.

VIOLENCE—SUBURBAN JUNIOR HIGH

The incident took place in a seventh-grade biology class. The teacher was known for, shall we say, eccentric behavior and strictness. He was, for most, a very difficult teacher in that he required a lot of rather complicated work and undivided attention to the material. Biology was a required class.

The student was known for being a troublemaker. He was not generally aggressive or hateful, but he was bored and probably hyperactive. He had to be doing something for his own amusement almost all the time. Also, he liked attention of any kind.

The conflict began when the teacher (Mr. B) noticed the student (Willis) floating all the erasers in the aquarium tank (which, like most of the classroom, was never cleaned, and which held, besides a toad that had been placed on one of the erasers, nothing alive that we were aware of).

Mr. B yelled at Willis.

Willis denied knowledge of his or anyone else's activities relative to the aquarium.

Mr. B continued to yell at Willis while approaching him.

Willis stood up and became increasingly defensive.

Mr. B informed Willis that he would see him after school.

Willis denied that he would come, claiming he had a prior engagement.

Mr. B threatened Willis saying he would go to his parents. He turned away and attempted to resume class.

Willis said in a loud voice that he didn't care.

Mr. B ignored this.

Willis then shot Mr. B in the ear with a squirt gun.

Mr. B turned, roared Willis's name, and pushed Willis backward over a table that spilled Willis's textbooks and laboratory materials all over the floor.

Willis leapt up and exited the classroom running.

Mr. B pursued, yelling very loudly.

The class could hear Mr. B all the way down the hall. Pandemonium broke loose in the classroom.

CONTEXT OF CONFLICTS

In our review of 225 educational conflicts we found that most occurred at the junior high level, followed by elementary and high school levels. Fifty-five percent involved women teachers. The majority involved male students.

Table 6–1 shows the percentages of reported conflicts at the levels described earlier.

TABLE 6–1. Percentage of Conflicts at Different Levels

Affirmation	47%	Alienation	11%
Assertion	37%	Withdrawn	5%
Aggression	13%	Depression	.5%
Social Violence	7%	Personal Violence	.5%

Of the cases reported 73 percent were conflicts where students had "acted out," while 17 percent were problems involving "withdrawn" behaviors. We suspect this difference is a result of the "squeaky wheel" getting attention. There are probably as many students who withdraw as who act out.

Approximately one fourth of reported conflicts (57) were identified as consistent patterns of behavior for the students involved. Forty-eight percent of the conflicts were resolved in less than three minutes. The percentages steadily decreased as the time required to resolved the conflict increased.

Table 6–2 presents the different situations in which conflicts occurred.

Independent work, free time in class, and teacher presentations are the situations in which the probability of conflicts seems highest. Recognition of this should enable teachers to anticipate problems and design lessons and assignments to reduce the probability of conflicts.

We maintained a category of "unusual circumstances" that immediately preceded the reported conflict. "Unusual circumstances" were related to educational conflicts. Here are examples of unusual circumstances: student

TABLE 6–2. Percentage of Conflicts Occurring in Different Educational Situations

Teacher Presentation	14%	Student Presentation	1.6%
Class Discussion	9%	Free Time (Class)	15.5%
Film	2.1%	Free Time (School)	15.3%
Laboratory Work	9.6%	Free Time (Outside)	2.6%
Independent Work	27.8%	Field Trip	1.6%

worried about teacher-parent conference; malfunction of audiovisual equipment; substitute teacher; student tired of being tested; parent had just left the school; heat (85–90 degrees); last hour of the day; student had been humiliated in prior class; eccentric teacher; student bored by low level of materials; new equipment in room; new arrangement of room; first class for new teacher. There is not a pattern to these except that they were "unusual circumstances." In cases such as these, teachers and administrators have to judge the situation and the circumstances. Circumstances that contributed to the conflict one day may have little influence the next.

Prescriptive rules were violated most often (40 percent). This was followed by prohibitive (33 percent) and rules that were beneficial to the group (27 percent) or individuals. Most rules were classroom rules (47 percent). Most were stated (31 percent) and known (47 percent) to the student.

Most educational conflicts:

1. Were at the junior high level;
2. Involved women teachers;
3. Involved male students;
4. Were minor "acting out" behaviors;
5. Were resolved in less than three minutes;
6. Occured during independent work, teacher presentation, or free time;
7. Often had "unusual circumstances" immediately preceding the conflict;
8. Involved prescriptive (you should) rules;
9. Were related to classroom rules;
10. Involved rules that were stated and known to the student.

RESOLUTION OF CONFLICTS

How were the observed conflicts resolved? Teachers and administrators have numerous ways of resolving educational conflicts, and several means are often used in any one conflict situation. For our discussion we have used four different categories: mutual resolution (Table 6–3); coercive resolution (Table 6–4); threatening resolution (Table 6–5); and aggressive or violent resolution (Table 6–6).

The largest percentage of conflicts was resolved using some form of mutual resolution. This result is very encouraging.

Teachers tend to warn of negative consequence, to reprimand, or command as means to resolve conflicts. Combined, these categories account for about 17.6 percent of coercive resolutions. It is not surprising to find that the predominant response of students was to sulk or leave the room. These are common responses when one has the feeling of loss.

TABLE 6–3. Mutual Resolution of Educational Conflicts

	Teacher	Student
Discussed the issue calmly with the other individual, encouraging alternative behaviors	22.2%	10.2%
Brought in a third party to settle things	2.1%	2.9%
Had a group discussion and talked about rules, policies, expectations	3.2%	.7%
Turned the situation over to the group for resolution	.8%	.7%
Turned the situation over to a higher authority for resolution	5.3%	.7%
Gave affirmation to other	1.6%	—
Ignored (gave time)	4.8%	—

While teacher threats are used rather often compared with student threats, it was interesting that most threats concern personal disapproval, isolation, and peer disapproval. Compared to these, threats related to physical punishment were fewer in number. The first course of action thus seems not to be physical aggression.

Small percentages in the category of aggressive and violent resolution are a pleasant note upon which to end. We do not know how many referrals to a higher authority (Table 6–3) ended in corporal punishment. The evidence indicates there is more corporal punishment than we observed or had reported. This result is understandable given our approach of identifying and describing actual school conflicts.

While the use of aggressive and violent means to resolve conflicts is limited, it is probably also true that these means are used on students who have the highest potential for a negative reaction. Educators cannot ignore the fact that aggressive behaviors by students can be imitated from and/or instigated by classroom teachers. The impact of an aggressive, punitive teacher on an individual who is on the thin edge between assertiveness and aggression, or aggression and violence, could certainly have greater force than the often-blamed television violence. Corporal punishment by teachers and administrators is real and involving and has personal meaning

TABLE 6–4. Coercive Resolution of Educational Conflicts

	Teacher	Student
Sulked or refused to talk	—	25.7%
Left the room or situation	.8%	12.5%
Insulted, swore at, or verbally demeaned the other	3.4%	17.6%
Warned the other of negative consequences	10.4%	3.6%
Promised reward, told of positive consequences	1.8%	—
Reprimand or command	7.2%	4.4%

TABLE 6–5. Threatening Resolution of Educational Conflicts

	Teacher	Student
Threatened isolation or removal from immediate environment	4.8%	.7%
Threatened physical punishment	.2%	5.1%
Threatened physical restraint	.5%	.7%
Threatened personal disapproval	7.2%	1.4%
Threatened peer disapproval	2.6%	.7%
Threatened parental disapproval	2.4%	.7%
Threatened poor grades, marks, detention points, etc.	2.9%	.7%
Threatened more work	.5%	—
Threatened long-term suspension	1.0%	—
Threatened loss of privilege, after-school detention	2.4%	—

for the student; and further, the adversary is clearly identifiable. Recently there was a student who, after being paddled by an assistant principal, walked home, obtained a pistol, returned to school, and announced "You are not going to whip me anymore!" and shot and wounded the assistant principal. Here we see the elements of transition from the stage of aggression to the stage of violence. Preceding the violence was a denial of control in the form of corporal punishment. This seems to have brought about the shooting. Consider the statement made by the student; it makes reference to the whipping that brought about the violence and also reveals the sense of dominance created in the student by his destructive act.

TABLE 6–6. Aggressive or Violent Resolution of Educational Conflicts

	Teacher	Student
Removed the individual from immediate environment	7.5%	—
Pushed, grabbed, or shoved the other	2.4%	2.9%
Slapped or spanked the other	.5%	—
Kicked, bit, or hit with fist	—	2.2%
Hit or tried to hit with something	.2%	5.1%
Arranged for physical punishment by another	.2%	—

DISCUSSION OF CONFLICTS

This discussion of educational conflicts is divided into two parts, prevention and intervention. More attention is directed to prevention since specific models of intervention and conflict resolution are presented in Chapter Seven.

Prevention

The strength of the stage model presented earlier is in its potential for early identification and prevention of serious conflicts. Personal problems often prevent students from seeking help. It will usually be up to the teacher to recognize the early warning signals of disruptive behavior and initiate preventive actions.

Understanding Yourself, the Student, and the Situation. Pay close attention to the disruptive student over a few days. During this time, try to identify patterns of behavior for both yourself and the student and specific situations that seem to initiate conflicts. Casual, informal conversation, or even marginal interviews about students' perceptions of themselves, others, and the school would be helpful means of gaining information. After this ask yourself, what can be changed? There is often something within the educator's control that can be changed, especially in the early stages. Some ideas that might help are: pay some attention to the student in educationally constructive ways; be sure to include the student in group activities; provide a tutor or extra time for academic problems; give the student opportunities to participate and to make some decisions with the class. Before there are serious conflicts, have a meeting with the student and talk over his or her behavior and your expectations. You can also ask colleagues for helpful ideas.

If a classroom conflict does occur, it is wise to remember that educators, too, can progress through the same stages described earlier for student. Try to stay calm and work with the student for at least two minutes. Much can be done in this crucial period. Your behavior in the conflict situation should be at a stage lower than the student's. If the student is assertive, be firm but not aggressive. This can prevent the escalation to violence. This, of course, assumes some rational communication; if the individual is already violent, you must take the appropriate action for your own protection and for that of your students. Here we think the best advice is—get help.

Cooperation Within the School. Isolation, fear, and loss of control are feelings commonly expressed by teachers discussing disruptive students and school conflicts.[6] These feelings are more real than imagined, especially when they also tell of administrative pressure on teachers to resolve conflicts—alone in the classroom. With the combined feelings of isolation and pressure, it is easy to see why teachers will often resort to any means to resolve a conflict. If teachers are forced to stand alone, they are at risk of serious problems. If teachers are part of an educational community working on their problems, then there is strength and hope. As a first preventive step, establish schoolwide cooperation—don't blame anyone for the problem; go to work at solving the problem! Far too much time has been spent establishing who or what was to blame, only to realize the problem still existed. There are several references that will help school personnel develop cooperation within the school. We particularly recommend the following references.[5,7,8]

Start by setting up professional staffings. For example, once a week teachers and support staff who interact with a particular student (or students) can meet and design a program for the student. While there is often frustration expressed at these meetings, they can also prevent some problems. Staffings, as suggested, have a twofold advantage. First, they give the teachers, administrators, and counselors a feeling of colleaguehood and cooperation that in turn helps reduce their sense of isolation and helplessness in dealing with the problems. Second, they result in a coordinated and consistent approach to disruptive students.

Avoid Using Corporal Punishment. It is time we ceased using corporal punishment. If we do not want violence in education, then we should not use violence to resolve educational conflicts. What is the lesson of an adult who, for example, hits a student and says, "You must not hit other people?" We develop concepts for resolving personal problems just as we develop concepts for solving mathematical problems, that is, through means such as experience, involvement, modeling, and reinforcement. Educators should not have any trouble understanding this idea. Corporal punishment is not the "last resort." There are many "resorts" that can be used to help youth in trouble. We can certainly design programs that treat students with dignity even though they have violated a school rule or policy. This is not to say there are no consequences for rule violation; there are and there should be, but they should be clear, consistent, reasonable, and, especially, nonaggressive or nonviolent. According to recent Supreme Court rulings corporal punishment may not be cruel and unusual, but we think its usefulness is obscure and questionable. A good review of this position is found in *Corporal Punishment in American Education.*[9]

Review the Curriculum. To what degree does the curriculum result in boredom for some students and frustration for others? Sometimes minor changes in the curriculum can improve the behavior of students. It may also be helpful to include value clarification, conflict resolution, arbitration, negotiation, and law-related curricula in the school program. Many disruptive students have literally learned that the only way to resolve a conflict is through aggression. With some effort and with proper role models these students can be taught otherwise.

Cooperation with the Community. There are many sources contributing to the conflicts in schools. Likewise, there will be many resources contributing to the resolution of the unfortunate situation existing in many schools.

In most cases the community is very interested in helping the school. Parents and other community members should be included in activities such as developing school discipline policies, providing security, tutoring, and sponsoring extracurricular activities. There are also many community agencies ready to help youth who are in trouble. They can be a valuable resource to administrators, counselors, and teachers. One example of using community resources was implemented by the New York Urban Coalition in a program designed to reduce discipline problems in a junior high school. The New York Urban Coalition sponsored a weekend retreat for parents, administrators, teachers, and community agencies. After an initial period of confronting, arguing, and blaming, a cooperative and productive group was established. The participants left the weekend with short- and long-term goals that were implemented upon their return to school. Compared to prior years, vandalism, truancy, teacher absenteeism, and assaults within the school decreased substantially.

Prevention is an important first step. Still, conflicts are inevitable, and school personnel must intervene and resolve those conflicts.

Intervention

Intervention is used here to describe the educator's action when a student has violated a school rule or policy. Intervening, in fact, defines the conflict. There are two goals to keep in mind in educational conflicts. First, you do not want the conflict to expand or escalate in personally or socially destructive ways. Second, you do want to resolve the conflict in educationally constructive ways. Some factors that might expand conflicts or produce resistance and alienation have been suggested by Deutsch.[2] They are described here in terms of educational conflicts.

1. Using *illegitimate techniques,* such as reducing academic grades because of personal behavior, tends to result in alienation.
2. Using *negative sanctions* such as coercion, threat, and punishment results in greater resistance and alienation toward the teacher and school system than does using positive sanctions.
3. Using *inappropriate sanctions,* such as giving monetary rewards when personal affirmation is needed, can result in continued disruptive behaviors.
4. Using *excessive power* or authority tends to result in resistance or escalation of the conflict.

There are recommendations for constructive resolution of educational conflicts.

1. Both students and educators should have the opportunity to *express their perceptions* of the conflict.

2. Educators should try to consider the *situation and any unusual circumstances* involved in the conflict.
3. Educators should *express sincere interest in resolving the conflict mutually*.
4. There should be *clear communication and agreement* on the issues, rules, and policies involved in the conflict.
5. *Possible solutions* should be suggested by both educators and students.
6. *Workable plans* with specific actions and changes should be developed and implemented.

Cooperative problem solving is the best means of approaching educational conflicts. Naturally, prevention and intervention are going to be most effective with students whose disruptive behavior is less intense, severe, and frequent. Because educators are adults and have more experience, they have greater responsibility for resolving educational conflicts cooperatively and constructively.

SUMMARY

There will inevitably be conflicts between students and school personnel. Even though there has been long-standing concern about educational conflicts, educators still know little about the dynamics of school disruption. A conflict occurs when activities or behaviors between two or more individuals are incompatible. Conflicts also can be defined in terms of school rules or policies. An educational conflict is any violation, challenge, or questioning of a school rule, policy, or expectation of behavior.

We have presented a systemic model of conflict dynamics. The model can be summarized as: Educator + Student + Situation = Conflict. Changes in any or all of the variables on the left side of the equation results in a corresponding change in the intensity, frequency, and severity of the conflict. Conflicts of the following types were reviewed: affirmation and alienation, assertion and withdrawal, aggression and depression, and violence.

The context of educational conflicts can be summarized as follows: occurring primarily at the junior high level; involving male students and female teachers; involving minor infractions that are resolved in less than three minutes; occurring during independent work, teacher presentation, or free time; and following "unusual circumstances."

Most conflicts studied were resolved mutually by means such as discussion. Teachers also tended to warn of negative consequences and threaten personal disapproval before other tactics were used. Aggressive actions taken by teachers tended to be the removal of disruptive students from the immediate environment.

The model of conflicts presented above has the advantage of preventing conflicts from becoming serious. Several measures can be taken to prevent serious school conflicts: understanding students; cooperation within the school; eliminating corporal punishment; reviewing the curriculum; and cooperating with the community.

When intervening in conflicts, school personnel should proceed with caution and work toward the constructive resolution of educational problems.

REFERENCES

1. Rodger Bybee, ed., "Violence Toward Youth in Families," *Journal of Social Issues* 35, no. 2 (1979).
2. Morton Deutsch, *The Resolution of Conflict: Constructive and Destructive Processes* (New Haven: Yale University Press, 1973).
3. Phi Delta Kappa, *School Climate Improvement: A Challenge to the School Administrator* (Bloomington, Indiana: Phi Delta Kappa, 1977).
4. P. Lawrence and J. Torsch, *Organization and Environment: Managing Differentiation and Integration.* (Cambridge, Mass.: Division of Research, Graduate School of Business Administration, Harvard University, 1967).
5. David W. Johnson, *Human Relations and Your Career: A Guide to Interpersonal Skills* (Englewood Cliffs, N.J.: Prentice-Hall, 1978).
6. Patricia M. Libbey, *Teachers' Conceptions of Discipline: A Cognitive-Developmental Framework,* Unpublished Dissertation for Ph.D. (Minneapolis: University of Minnesota, 1980).
7. David Johnson and Roger Johnson, *Learning Together and Alone: Cooperation, Competition and Individualization* (Englewood Cliffs, N.J.: Prentice-Hall, 1975).
8. David Johnson and Frank Johnson, *Joining Together* (Englewood Cliffs, N.J.: Prentice-Hall, 1975).
9. I. Hyman and J. Wise, *Corporal Punishment in American Education* (Philadelphia: Temple University Press, 1979).

CHAPTER SEVEN

Justice and the Resolution of School Conflicts

INTRODUCTION

"What can we do about disruptive students?" The question sets the stage for this chapter. In the first sections, we present conflict resolution models for classroom teachers and for school administrators. Then we outline our own comprehensive plan for the just resolution of school conflicts. Our overall aim is to provide help for school personnel who wish to facilitate learning and to pursue educational goals, not simply to maintain control in a classroom or a school.

The presentation of conflict resolution models seems appropriate for several important reasons. First, they cost little (or no) money. Second, teachers and administrators can implement the models with a minimum of effort. Third, they have both a short- and long-term benefit; that is, they can help resolve current problems and in the longer term can provide good nonviolent-participator models for the student. Finally, they serve the dual purpose of showing teachers how to intervene when disruption or rule violations have occurred and how to prevent some future disruption by involving students and school personnel in a cooperative problem-solving process.

Criteria for selection of the models were aligned with the justice themes discussed thus far. In addition, in earlier chapters we have presented theoretical, legal, and empirical grounds upon which we can support the approaches recommended. This is not to say we are against other methods of reducing school disruption, such as curriculum revision or security systems; indeed, we support these efforts where they are needed and appropriate. Many approaches, such as school security systems, are needed in schools where extreme violence and vandalism are pressing issues. The majority of personnel in American schools do not work in violent schools, but teachers do encounter varying degrees of disruptive behavior almost daily. Thus, we believe conflict resolution models can help the majority of school personnel, including those in violent schools, and provide a better learning environment for more students more of the time. While the models presented can contribute to the resolution of immediate problems, they also hold promise for the long-term amelioration of school violence and vandalism since they provide educationally constructive means of involving students in decision-making processes, giving them appropriate power, and showing them that they have some degree of control over decisions affecting them.

One of the most important criteria in our selection was that the models demonstrate fair and equal treatment of all parties to the conflicts. Here again is the theme of justice. Critics have long described the "hidden curriculum" of schools, and they have attributed to it any number of undesirable results. Implementing some form of the models presented in this chapter would also create a "hidden curriculum," one that would have desirable benefits for students and school personnel alike.

Why not present only one conflict resolution model? We present different models to meet different needs. The idea that one of anything would be appropriate for all schools is, on the face of it, impossible and surely would be rejected by most, if not all, educators. If we present only one model, who is it for—teachers, administrators, counselors? Is it for rural, urban, or suburban schools? By presenting several models for the classroom teachers and several other models for school administrators we hope to overcome these problems. Educators can select the model, or aspects of different models, that meet their needs. Variety and diversity have been important in American education; we believe that they also will be important in the reduction of violence and disruption.

RESOLVING CLASSROOM CONFLICTS

We start with models that teachers can use in the classroom, usually the first area in which problems are encountered. We think some of the major problems can be prevented by focusing on this fundamental level of American education.

A Ten-Step Program for Discipline

This ten-step program to effective discipline is based on the ideas of William Glasser. The model is consistent with the philosophy and psychology Glasser has presented in his books *Reality Therapy*[1] and *Schools Without Failure*.[2] The ten-step program was outlined in the spring 1976 issue of *Educare Journal*.[3]

There are two prerequisites to Glasser's program. First, the school should be a place where students feel there is at least one person who cares about them personally. This simple idea is prerequisite to anything else that may be done to alleviate discipline problems in schools. Schools simply should not be a place where students are not accepted and where they do not belong. Second, failing grades should be eliminated from the school. We have seen throughout this book that grades have had an important influence on school-related disruption, and they seem to be directly related to vandalism in some schools. In many cases, however, it seems not to be grades themselves but the way teachers use grades that is the cause for trouble in schools. Now the ten-step program:

One: Identify the Most Disruptive Student or Students in Class. Do this step at home, in a discussion with friends, after class, or at other times conducive to reflection. What do you usually do to try to change the disruptive student's behavior? What are all the disciplinary actions you can remember trying? Now ask if what you have done has worked. If the answer is no, go to step two.

Two: Stop Doing What Is Not Working. Just stop, simple as that, since whatever it is you are doing does not work anyway.

Three: Spend Five to Twenty Seconds Each Day with the Disruptive Student When the Student Is Not Being a Problem. Start with simple gestures such as meeting the student at the door: "How are you today?" or, during class, "Do you understand the activity? Can I help?" Exactly what you do will vary. The important point is to take some positive action while the student is *not* being troublesome.

Four: When the Student Is Disruptive Tell the Student to Stop. Simply, directly, and quietly say something like "I would like it if you would quit (state the behavior, e.g., talking)." If the student stops, the problem is resolved. If the student does not stop, go to step five.

Five: Tell the Student There Are Rules in the Classroom and That the Student's Behavior Is Breaking a Rule. Many students will refrain from disruptive behavior at this stage because they realize the rules are fundamental to the orderly conduct of class, and there are social pressures encouraging proper behavior. Step six follows if the student does not stop.

Six: Tell the Student That the Disruptive Behavior Is in Violation of Class Rules and That "We Will Work This Out." Using the statement consistently will reduce the student's perceptions that some rules can be violated some times. According to Glasser the teacher must not deviate from the statement, "We will work this out." The statement implies several things. There should be an understanding that the problem will be resolved between the student and teacher, that there is a neutral process where both the student and teacher will have their say, and that there is no need for harsh treatment, yelling, or physical punishment. Often the statement,

"We will work this out" settles the problem. Yet, it is very important for the teacher to develop some kind of plan with the student, to talk over the problem and see to it that something is done. Examples might include students realizing they broke a rule and stating they will try to improve; the teacher helping a disruptive student with an assignment, changing seating, or paying more attention to the student.

Seven: If Disruptive Behavior Persists, Sanctions Are Imposed. Glasser recommends that the disruptive student be isolated from class, not in an uncomfortable place, but one away from other students. He emphasizes that the teacher should always use the same sanction. Repeat step six when the student settles down.

Eight: The Student Is Removed from the Room. "We Have Not Been Able to Work This Out; You Must Leave. Perhaps Someone Else Can Help Work Out the Problem." The student is sent to a quiet room and told to sit and relax. There are only two rules for this room: 1) be quiet; and 2) do not disrupt. A counselor, a special learning-and-behavior-problems teacher, or an administrator should be in charge of this room. While in the room no work is required and no credit is given. The details for returning to the regular classroom are worked out with the person in charge of the room, the student, and the teacher.

Nine: The Student Is Sent Home. The trip home is temporary and emphasis is on the fact that efforts will be made to help the student remain in school upon return. In most cases this step is taken with the chronically disruptive and violent student. Glasser indicates there is no purpose served by having violent students in classrooms or schools.

Ten: Referral of the Disruptive Student to Appropriate Neighborhood Agencies for Help. At this final step the student is very disturbed and consistently aggressive and violent. We would also suggest that extremely withdrawn and depressed students may require professional attention.

Glasser's program is a progression for resolving increasingly difficult situations. The consistent response is important: "We will work this out." This idea and the process behind it, must be applied with "boring consistency." Every attempt is made to be fair, to recognize the student's needs, and yet to be absolutely clear about the reality of school rules and policies. While there are sanctions and consequences, they are applied consistently and without harshness, physical punishment, or malice.

A Logical Consequences Approach

The logical consequences approach to discipline has been developed by Don Dinkmeyer and Don Dinkmeyer, Jr.[4] According to the Dinkmeyers, discipline should be a part of the learning process as there is a need for students to develop the belief that they are responsible, that they can decide how to act, and that they can accept the consequences of their behavior. A logical consequences approach, as opposed to authoritarian punishment, helps students recognize that there are rules governing a social order and that there are educational consequences related to misbehavior in the classroom. The Dinkmeyer plan has two components—prevention and intervention. The four preventive methods are discussed first.

First: Avoid Provoking or Reinforcing Disruptive Behavior. The Dinkmeyers use a model developed by Rudolf Dreikurs and colleagues[5,6] to identify the motives for student behavior: getting attention, acquiring power, obtaining revenge, or displaying hopelessness and inadequacy. By understanding the purpose of the student's behavior, teachers can avoid fulfilling that purpose. Instead, teachers can encourage other, educationally constructive, behavior that fulfills the students' needs.

Second: Develop a Relationship of Mutual Respect through Kindness and Firmness. The term "mutual" expresses an underlying principle of great importance in interpersonal relationships. The interpersonal relationship is developed through kindness, which shows a respect for the student, and through firmness, which shows respect for yourself. One can maintain order without being unkind and harsh. Students will soon understand and respect the attitude of mutual respect in their teachers.

Third: Look for Assets in Students. Try to identify any talents, strengths, or skills that a student has. Personal assets can be a focus of discussion and of the development of a personal relationship.

Fourth: Show Flexibility in Your Attitudes toward Students. If you expect disruptive behavior, you will more than likely get disruptive behavior. Act as though you expect cooperation and constructive work. These, too, can be self-fulfilling expectations.

The preceding suggestions are concerned with preventing classroom conflicts. As we have stated before, conflicts will undoubtedly occur. The Dinkmeyers give five suggestions for the resolution of classroom conflicts.

First: Try to Understand the Purpose of the Student's Behavior. Is the purpose of the disruptive behavior to get attention? power? revenge? or to cover feelings of inadequacy? Active listening is the method by which you will get some indication of the student's purpose. Listen for 1) beliefs being expressed, 2) feelings being experienced, 3) nonverbal messages. Active listening will also convey the important message that you are interested in and concerned about in the student.

Second: Identify the Real Issue. The real issue is usually one of the motives described earlier—attention, power, revenge, or displayed inadequacy. Use a tentative hypothesis alluding to the motive: "It seems that . . ." or "Could it be that . . ." or "Could you possibly . . ." (a paraphrase of the motive would be added to these statements). Be sure the statement is tentative and not accusatory. Students will thus be less defensive and more open and honest in their response.

Third: The Student's Suggestion for Alternatives Should Be Considered. Once the student starts evaluating the situation and possible solutions, you might ask, "How else can we resolve this problem?" or "What else could you do that might change this situation?" Here the student has the opportunity to suggest alternatives, to choose among them, and to decide on approaches that will resolve the conflict.

Fourth: Have the Student Give a Commitment to a Specific Course of Action. Once the two of you have agreed to a plan ask the student to make a specific contract of approaches, procedures, and steps to be taken. After the commitment has been obtained, do not accept excuses for failing to act as indicated. If the student violates the contract, the student knows it and you do not have to ask for justifications. Ask when the student intends to honor the contract. With continued disruptive behavior you should try to isolate the cause—is it the plan, the student, or the student-teacher interaction that seems to be the origin of the problem?

Fifth: Use Logical Consequences—not Punishment. When rules have been broken, use the consequences that seem most logical. If work has not been done, it must be done; if a student cannot work with others, the student must work alone; and so on.

The Dinkmeyer program seeks to identify the purposes behind student behavior and then direct the student toward educationally constructive goals. There is the important combination of both preventive and interventive procedures. One of the key points of this program is to avoid punishment since it represents the authoritarian approach to conflict resolution. The democratic approach is to use logical consequences for the violation of rules.

The Teacher Effectiveness Method of Resolving Conflicts

The book *Teacher Effectiveness Training* by Thomas Gordon[7] is the basis for this model. Like Glasser and the Dinkmeyers, Gordon also approaches conflict resolution in a democratic and humane way. He argues that for too long and without effective results teachers have relied on either power and authority or the giving up of power and authority in order to maintain order in the classroom. Both approaches, the authoritarian and the permissive, have proven to be unacceptable for a variety of reasons. Gordon's approach is what he calls Method III: the no-lose method of resolving conflicts. Using this method, both parties to the conflict unite in their search for a solution that is acceptable to each.

Prerequisites for Gordon's model include active listening by the teacher. Active listening encourages students to talk about their needs and to feel accepted and understood. Teachers must also learn to state their own needs in clear, honest "I-messages." Using you-messages that involve blame setting, putting down, and utilizing power tends to make students reluctant to enter into the problem-solving process because they sense the conflict has already been "resolved." Students must understand that the teacher is using an entirely new method that is different from old (authoritarian or permissive) methods. Students will best understand the method as a process of problem solving. "We have a problem here and we are going to solve it together." Obviously there is much more required than this brief summary can reveal. Still, this should give an indication of the approach.

The teacher effectiveness training model is an application of the "scientific method" and an approach to learning suggested by John Dewey. Here are the six steps for the resolution of conflicts.

First: Define the Problem or Conflict. Some of the dos and don'ts for this step include: involve only parties to the conflict; take care that students enter discussions willingly; use "I-messages" and accurately present your needs in this situation; do not state solutions, define the problem as it is; be sure "the problem" is expressed as one of conflicting needs, not competing solutions.

Second: Generate Possible Solutions. Once the problem has been defined both teacher and student should offer possible solutions. Here are some ideas that may help: avoid evaluating solutions; ask open-ended questions; write down proposed solutions; and keep the discussion focused on the problem.

Third: Evaluate the Solutions. Now it is time to see which solutions are appropriate. Teachers should ask which solutions students prefer; cross off any solutions that receive a negative response; listen actively to be sure all opinions are expressed; state your own opinions; do not rush; try to get all parties to respond.

Fourth: Decide on a Solution. Sometimes this step is very easy because a solution has emerged from step three that is clearly superior. If all the participants agree, step four is over. What if several solutions remain? Here are some suggestions: work for consensus; see if the proposed solutions will work; have individuals give their opinions or arguments for solutions (including your own); be sure not to use power or authority to make the decision or obtain consensus.

Fifth: Determine How to Implement the Decision. This step gets down to the basics of who does what and when they will do it. Individuals should discuss how they will get started, who does what, when the plan will be in use, and what are possible standards of performance. It is always helpful to write down the procedures.

Sixth: Assess the Solution's Success. Teachers will know how effective the solution is within a short time. Has the problem disappeared? Are all parties still satisfied with the solution? Some things to watch for are unrealistic commitments; unforeseen difficulties with the solution or implementation; maintenance of a poor solution, and failure to change it in response to feedback indicating a poor solution was chosen.

The teacher effectiveness training model is a problem-solving approach to conflict resolution. The assumptions and methods of the model contribute to a democratic interaction where all parties have equal power, but in fact, neither need it nor use it.

MANAGING SCHOOL CONFLICTS

School administrators are the object of the discussions and models presented in this section. We have moved from the teacher's classroom to the administrator's office, but this is not to suggest that the conflicts are necessarily more intense or frequent, though this could certainly be the case. The conflict resolution models described below are not intended to be at cross purposes with those outlined in earlier sections.

Systematic Management Plan for School Discipline

Daniel L. Duke of Stanford University has outlined a Systematic Management Plan for School Discipline (SMPSD).[8] Duke points out several fundamental problems related to discipline. School personnel rarely meet to discuss discipline problems; they do not have accurate data on problems within the schools; they do not agree on the origins of problems; they perceive discipline problems as classroom- rather than school-related conflicts; and finally, they generally think of disruptive behavior as single incidents and not as continuing problems. These factors contribute to an uncoordinated and unsystematic approach to school-related discipline problems. This, according to Duke, can be overcome by confronting and systematizing factors within the control of school personnel. What can be done? Duke suggests six basic components.

First: Collect Accurate Data on Discipline. Before you initiate a full program to deter or resolve problems, find out some of the simple facts about discipline problems in your school. Start by keeping systematic records of referrals, teacher complaints, student complaints, reported conflicts, vandalism, and so on. Each school can develop means of collecting and organizing the data. Set aside time for this procedure, especially if discipline is a problem in your school. Analyze the data frequently and regularly. Doing this will provide information on any trends, trouble areas, and students who may need help.

Second: Develop an Awareness That the School Is a Rule-Governed Institution. To do this Duke recommends five activities: 1) rules should be developed collaboratively with school personnel, students, and parents; 2) consequences of rule violations should be developed collaboratively; 3) publicize the rules and consequences in the school and community; 4) provide for consistent application of rules and consequences; 5) include school rules and consequences in regular orientations each year and in orientations for transfer students. This last recommendation includes making the school rules a part of each student's study, testing students on the rules and giving students who achieve a high score on the tests added responsibility.

Third: Reward Students Who Obey Rules. Too often school personnel have "rewarded" students for misbehavior and ignored students who followed rules. The injunction is simple: find ways to reward students who obey school rules. The rewards will vary with schools and with age groups, but there are certainly tangible things the administration can do for students who observe the rules.

Fourth: Establish a Conflict Resolution Mechanism. Several classroom approaches to conflict resolution have been discussed earlier. And, in the next sections, conflict resolution mechanisms are described that could be adopted or adapted by school personnel to meet the requirements of this step.

Fifth: Implement a Team Approach to Managing Misbehavior. If the school-related problems are to be resolved, it will take the combined efforts of administrators, teachers, parents, neighborhood resource people, and the student. Alone an administrator will not move too far in the implementation of SMPSD; it takes the coordinated efforts of many. A first step in the implementation of a team approach is to schedule "trouble-shooting" sessions. Some guides for these sessions are: talk about specific students and specific problems; maintain in strict confidence the information discussed; make a plan of action for each student. One person should be responsible for overseeing the plan's implementation. This individual reports on the plan, and if the plan is unsuccessful, calls a case conference.

Case conferences are similar to the trouble-shooting sessions except that they involve students with chronic and ongoing behavior problems. All school personnel working with the student, an administrator, parents, and community resource people, especially any already involved with the student, are included in the conference (while Duke did not specifically include the student, we suggest the student be included at the conference). The object of the meeting is to develop and implement a plan of action to resolve the school-related problems.

Sixth: Inservice Programs on Discipline. Administrators are in a position to arrange for at least one inservice program on discipline and conflict resolution. There is a growing number of ideas and resources that would be helpful to all school personnel. Exposure to new ways and means of resolving school disruption are as vital as other programs in curriculum and instruction.

Daniel Duke's systematic management plan for school discipline is one way that administrators can confront discipline problems in a comprehensive manner. School administrators are advised to start by collecting data on discipline problems and then proceed to make rules known, reward good behavior, implement conflict resolution procedures, develop a plan of action for problem students, and conduct inservice programs on discipline.

Conflict Resolution Through Negotiation

Growing Pains: Use of School Conflict[9] and other publications[10,11] by John DeCecco and Arlene Richards are the basis for this model. The Supreme Court cases of *Tinker v. Des Moines Independent Community School Dist.*, 393 U. S. 503 (1969), *Goss v. Lopez*, 419 U. S. 565 (1975) and *Wood v. Strickland*, 420 U. S. 308 (1975) have protected the constitutional rights of students. Among the rights protected are due process, equality, dissent and participation—democratic rights granted to each of us—students and school personnel alike. In order to protect these rights and still resolve school conflicts DeCecco and Richards recommend the following procedure.

First: Parties to the Conflict Make a Statement of Issues to the Other Parties. This step may include the appropriate expression of anger by the parties to the conflict. In addition, the student should be informed of the rule infraction, have someone who can speak on his or her behalf, and be allowed to respond to the charges.

Second: Parties to the Conflict Agree to a Common Statement of the Problem. Discussion should eventually move from anger and accusation to the central issues. The third party (administrator) can see that all the issues are stated and summarized and that agreement on the problem is reached by both parties to the conflict.

Third: Parties Negotiate the Resolution. Gains and concessions will be made by both parties to the conflict and these must be equitably distributed. As a result of the bargaining process a definite plan is made and agreed upon.

Though brief, the model presented by DeCecco and Richards simultaneously contains the essentials of the democratic process and the flexibility required if the model is to apply to myriad schools throughout the country. Negotiations can be a long and tiresome ordeal; there are some things that are nonnegotiable and many that are negotiable but perceived not to be. The educational (not to mention the legal) benefits of this process are immense since it makes the democratic process real for those who are involved. Even though negotiations are hard, there is a feeling of accomplishment when the process is completed.

A Consensus Model of Conflict Reduction

Al Roark and Al Main, two counselors, developed this model of conflict reduction.[12] One important difference between this and other models we have presented is that the school counselor is the person who mediates the resolution. Prior to starting the conflict reduction process the counselor establishes the fact that each party wishes to reach an agreement that is acceptable to all parties involved. The counselor also makes it clear that this process does not result in a win-lose decision and that each party will have to concede as well as gain points in the process. Finally, the counselor clarifies his or her position as the mediator (not accusor, decider, or enforcer) who will see to it that the parties go through the conflict reduction process.

First: Parties Describe the Conflict Situation. During this stage the counselor can determine the perceptions each person has of the conflict situation. The first step requires that the descriptions be in cognitive terms; emotions and feelings will be expressed in the next step. Discussion should emphasize the present situation as each person sees it. As the discussion progresses the counselor finds some areas of agreement relative to descriptions of the conflict situation. Each party to the conflict must understand how the other party perceives the situation.

Second: Parties Describe Feelings and Meanings. While parties describe what the conflict situation means to them and express their feelings, the counselor clarifies the perceptions of each party. Before proceeding to the next step the needs of each party must be identified. If this does not occur, suggestions can be made that may continue the conflict and perhaps intensify it. As this discussion progresses a technique parallel to the first step can be used. That is, identify areas of agreement with regard to feelings and meanings.

Third: Parties Describe a Desired Situation. The actual situation has been expressed in steps one and two. Now, each party outlines a desired situation that is required if the conflict is to be resolved. The counselor determines areas of agreement. The counselor should also provide ideas concerning alternative goals. Again, the area of agreement between the conflicting parties should be increased at this stage.

Fourth: Parties Describe Necessary Changes. A discrepancy model has been produced and now the changes necessary for resolution should be pursued. The counselor will usually have to reiterate the point that this is not a win-lose model; each party cannot assume the other party will do all the changing in order to reduce the conflict. This point will be made if each party lists the changes he or she is willing to make. The counselor can also suggest changes that will contribute to a fair and practical resolution. Before going to the next stage, all parties should be clear on the changes they will make as well as the changes they expect the other party to make.

Fifth: Parties Establish an Agenda. All parties should contribute to an agenda implementing the changes to which they have agreed. Generally, this step is not hard since most of the items for the plan have been clarified. Still it is important to specify who will do what, and when it will be done. The counselor also can include checkpoints and processes to be used if the plan is not completed.

Before outlining our comprehensive plan for the resolution of school conflicts it is necessary to examine the process of conflict resolution in greater depth. Insights can be made regarding the models just presented as well as the plan we discuss later in the chapter.

UNDERSTANDING THE PROCESS OF CONFLICT RESOLUTION

A student was running down the hall. The teacher told the student to stop running. The student continued running. The teacher caught the student and pushed him against the wall saying, "I told you to stop, and if you don't I'll take you to the gym for a little 'workout.' " Later the teacher stated, "I showed the student who was boss; you have to let them know who runs the ship." The teacher continued, "Besides, the student said he wouldn't run anymore."

A student was talking to a friend. The teacher told the student to stop. The student ignored the teacher. The teacher threatened to lower the student's grade and send her to the principal if the talking did not cease; the talking stopped. Note passing started. Five minutes later the teacher said, "That's it! You have no respect for my authority; we'll see what the principal can do—get out of this room!" Defending herself, the student said, "But, you only told me to stop talking, and I did. You didn't say I couldn't pass notes."

Minor conflicts? Easily resolved? Yes, they were minor. But they were not resolved; they were ended. In spite of the assurance with which teachers often tell of incidents such as these, it is often the case that the same students are in trouble again, usually the next day.

Conflicts are learning experiences. What is learned from conflicts depends on how they are resolved. Educators are required to do many things, including handling discipline problems. Traditionally this task has been perceived as undesirable but necessary for the educational process. Taking care of discipline problems was not thought to be a part of the educational process itself. The ways school personnel resolve conflicts are all very important lessons for students. Like all lessons, any one incident may have a small impact, but the accumulation of many lessons conveys important concepts. Learning how to resolve conflicts also is an educational goal. The importance of this goal, compared to traditional educational goals, should increase as the frequency and intensity of descriptive behavior increases. In other words, disruptive behavior patterns require different educational goals and approaches.

The majority of school conflicts are easily resolved. The models presented earlier would help bring about resolutions. *We suggest, then, that the first goal for school personnel is to negotiate a just resolution to any conflict.* We recognize fully that as the disruptive behavior of students and the concern of school personnel increases, so too does the difficulty of peaceful and willing negotiation. There has been the tacit assumption underlying the earlier models that parties to the conflict are rational, reasonable, and willing to work through the conflict to a just resolution. But, these very factors decrease as the intensity of conflicts increases. If, for example, there is a violent encounter in a classroom, the very presence of fear and rage negate the possibilities of a just resolution being negotiated at that time. *This line of discussion brings us to our second goal for school personnel—regulating the conflict so the destructive consequences are minimized.* Briefly, then, the two goals are: 1) to negotiate a resolution; or 2) regulate the conflict.

In order to implement this goals, school personnel should understand some of the factors influencing the process of conflict resolution. *The Resolution of Conflict* by Morton Deutsch[15] is an important basis for discussion in this section. Many ideas from this crucial work are summarized here in the context of school-related conflicts.

Resolving Conflicts Constructively

Destructive conflicts are distinguished by their expansion and escalation. As the conflict progresses the parties to the conflict increasingly rely on power and authority, first to resolve and eventually simply to end the conflict. Harmful elements such as threats, shows of power, and coercion increasingly displace helpful elements such as open discussion, concession, and negotiation as the destructive course develops. There are the characteristics of minor classroom conflicts that escalate into assaults in which the student and teacher both use the power available to defeat the other. Also common is the case where a teacher uses authority and power to end a conflict, and a student subsequently uses power to interfere with instruction through subversive tactics or to vandalize school property.

Three interrelated processes contribute to the development of destructive conflicts: 1) the competition that results from approaching the situation as win-lose; 2) the misperceptions that result from decreased communication; 3) the commitments arising because of the need for personal and social consistency. Once sides are taken and the parties to the conflict start on a destructive course, these variables interact to the detriment of those involved. The inverse of the three processes suggests initial approaches to avoiding destructive conflicts. Avoiding destructive conflicts would be enhanced by: 1) facilitating cooperation, 2) focusing on clear communication, and 3) committing oneself to resolving the conflict peacefully if at all possible. These do not seem to be major requirements considering the importance of the problem to educators.

Conflicts will take a constructive course when there are: 1) motivations to resolve the problem, 2) conditions conducive to reformulating the problem, and 3) ideas that can be combined into patterns to solve the problem. Many will recognize these ideas as those underlying the creative or problem-solving process. It is little wonder that several of the models described earlier used a problem-solving format. It should be evident that the goal of school personnel is to resolve conflicts constructively, and that cooperative problem-solving methods should take precedence over competitive methods.

Influencing a Constructive Course

Whether conflicts take a course toward constructive or destructive ends is determined by many factors. One factor is the size of the conflict. Larger conflicts are harder to control; they tend to escalate and, thus, are likely to move in a destructive course. Time seems also to be a factor related to size in school conflicts. The longer a problem exists, the larger it is perceived to be. If at all possible, school personnel should try to define the problem as small and resolve the problem early.

As we discussed earlier in relation to Abraham Maslow's hierarchy of motivation, issues having to do with personal safety and security, social status and self-esteem are central to all of us—school personnel and students alike. When the conflict threatens these very central issues the perceived vulnerability results in an all-out effort to win. Quite easily, then, the course of the conflict can change in a destructive direction. School personnel should focus on the problem, not the person.

We return to the problem of competition as it influences the course of a conflict. When a conflict is defined as a win-lose, all-or-nothing situation, the motivation for total victory is increased until it is perceived to be the only acceptable outcome. Educators should try to isolate several different aspects of a conflict so it does not seem to be one big problem but rather several small problems. Smaller problems are easier to resolve and the idea of winning some and losing some tends to keep the resolution process on a constructive track.

Also related to the competitive theme is the tendency to magnify differences and reduce similarities. As the perceived differences increase, the possibilities of the parties to a conflict recognizing each other's needs as legitimate and meeting those needs decreases. Thus, school personnel should focus on similarities of needs.

Parties to a conflict often perceive different aspects of the conflict as crucial. Teachers may emphasize the need for students to stay in classroom, while students may emphasize their need to move around the school. Perceptions of this nature can result in an escalation because of the significance of different goals for the different parties. A consensus on the problem with all important related issues clearly evident to all parties is thus a recommendation.

Unacknowledged conflicts are clearly harder to resolve and tend to result in destructive escalation. Teachers and students can turn to passive resistence, revengeful actions, subtle coercions, and subversive manuevers while smiling and openly saying there is no problem. The party dominating the interaction, and it can be either the teacher or the student, continues to feel superior while the subordinate party continues to feel inferior. Unfortunately, unacknowledged conflicts can take a destructive course that finally results in one major conflict. Conflicts should be recognized and acknowledged, and the earlier the better.

Personality plays an important role in conflicts. This factor is, however, rather hard to regulate, change, or circumvent. As a conflict intensifies the tendency is for a greater similarity of behavior to emerge. While this observation suggests that personality differences can be nullified, it also indicates that such a situation results as conflicts move toward a destructive course. A report by Terhune[16] indicates that characteristics such as aggressiveness, dominance, authoritarianism, dogmatism, and Machiavellianism tend to result in conflicts we have described here as competitive and destructive. On the other hand, cooperative and constructive conflicts tend to result from personalities that are trusting and open, who see others as persons of dignity and integrity, and who are egalitarian and tolerant of ambiguity. Personality variables should be a consideration for all parties to school conflicts. While we cannot change personalities, we can avoid the destructive consequences of continued interactions between incompatible individuals.

A person's estimation of success in a conflict can influence the direction taken and subsequent results. Teachers who think they have sufficient power and authority for a victory may prefer a competitive approach. For the vanquished, success may come later in other forms of destruction. Doubtfulness of the outcome and/or concern for the long-term goal of conflict resolution results in a preference for the cooperative process. Educators are encouraged to use a conflict resolution process that has the possibility of some success for all parties.

The strength, insights, and clarity of an interested, but neutral, third party can have a very important and powerful effect on the course of a conflict. Third parties are usually constructive forces, especially when the person is respected by the conflicting parties and is skillful in mediating problems. When appropriate, third parties should help resolve school-related conflicts.

Discussion in these sections has been on factors influencing the constructive and destructive resolution of conflicts. This discussion is related to our first goal—negotiated resolution. The next section is a discussion of factors concerning the regulation of conflicts that, for the time, cannot be resolved.

Regulating Conflicts

When school conflicts progress beyond the point of resolution steps must be taken to regulate the conflict. Regulation sets boundaries on the interaction between conflicting parties. For the most part school conflicts should be regulated to exclude aggression and violence, as well as other forms of extreme behaviors such as depression, chemical dependency, and vandalism.

Parties to a conflict must be organized, coherent, and rational before regulation procedures can be finalized. Immediately after an intense conflict between a student and teacher is not the best time to try to set limits on future interactions. Regulation procedures should be initiated when all parties to the conflict are calm and rational.

Recognition of the legitimacy of the other party is necessary for effective regulation. Likewise, there must be an acceptance of the regulation by each party. Students must recognize the legitimacy of the school, its representatives, and its students. School personnel must recognize the legitimacy of students' needs and rights. To be effective, the regulations must be agreed to by both parties.

If conflicts have progressed to the point of needing regulation, it is almost certain that they have been recurrent. The main implication of this situation is that old approaches to resolution or regulation have not been effective. Educators are advised to try a new approach—new rules, new patterns of interaction, and perhaps new classrooms, if conflicts continue.

Regulating a conflict is easier when all parties feel as though they are part of one community. In schools this extremely important idea should have a particularly powerful effect, since the situation already should be one of community. Members of a community share many goals, values, and beliefs. Being part of a community enhances communication and increases each person's sensitivity to pressures for regulation and agreement to rules. For the most part teachers feel they are a part of the school community. There are exceptions, and administrators can certainly act on this problem. Usually it is the student, the alienated individual, who does not sense that he or she belongs in the school community. While this problem cannot be overcome immediately, the issue can certainly be confronted and acted upon. The recommendation is to see that all students feel they belong in school. If a conflict must be regulated, a part of the process should be directed toward increasing a sense of community for all parties to the conflict.

The regulation of conflicts comes about through rules defining the limits of interaction between the parties. It is especially important that the rules be known, clear, unbiased, and adhered to by all parties. There should be social approval for following the rules and disapproval for violating them. Any violations should be made known and remedied quickly.

School conflicts that must be regulated almost always require a third party. Some of the ways a third party can help include identifying and clarifying the issues of conflict, providing neutral conditions, improving communications, maintaining rational interaction, suggesting possible solutions, and facilitating an agreement between the conflicting parties. The school counselor is in the ideal position to assume the role of third party. The counselor's administrative status, skills in listening and communicating, and sense of the helping relationship are all assets that recommend counselors as third-party regulators.

This section on the resolution and regulation of conflicts can be summarized by stating specific recommendations for school personnel.

Recommendations for the Process of Resolution

1. Use cooperative rather than competitive procedures.
2. Define conflicts as small and resolve them early.
3. Focus on the problem and not on the person.
4. Reduce large conflicts to smaller components and resolve the latter in an orderly fashion.
5. Emphasize the similarities between parties.
6. Reach a consensus on the problem.
7. Recognize and acknowledge conflicts early.
8. Consider personality differences.
9. Identify the possibilities for solutions successful to both parties.
10. Use third parties when appropriate.

Recommendations for the Process of Regulation

1. Proceed when the parties are calm, rational, and organized.
2. Demonstrate the legitimacy of all parties to the conflict.
3. Reach agreement on the regulations.

4. Use new approaches to regulate interaction when old ones have failed.
5. Develop a sense of community for parties to the conflict.
6. Make sure rules are known, clear, unbiased, and adhered to by all parties.
7. Remedy rule violations quickly.
8. Use counselors as third-party regulators.

TOWARD A COMPREHENSIVE CONFLICT RESOLUTION PLAN FOR SCHOOLS

Many good models have been described and suggestions have been made, all concerning the process of conflict resolution in the school. No doubt educators are already doing some of the things recommended or perhaps using the models outlined. Still, some may be looking for another plan to adopt, or other ideas to be adapted. Our purpose is to present a simple, practical, yet comprehensive plan of conflict resolution for use in schools. The plan is a first step, an outline that must be completed by educators. The plan is comprehensive in that it starts with the establishment of class-room and school rules and incorporates a sequence of steps that can be used if disruptive behavior becomes more frequent and more intense. Likewise there is provision for isolated problems such as fights on the play-ground, disturbances on the bus, or mischief in the hall.

In developing this plan we have appealed directly to aspects of the models presented earlier, discussions of the conflict resolution process, and ideas discussed in other chapters of this book concerning the law, ethics and values, psychology, and philosophy.

A number of recommendations have been made that are related to the whole issue of improving the school climate and decreasing discipline problems. Making sure that students feel as though they belong in the classroom and school—encouraging a sense of community—has been a strong and consistent theme through many of the discussions. Other rec-ommendations are: spend brief periods with potentially disruptive students when they are not causing trouble and find the assets and special talents of these students; stop using disciplinary techniques that do not work. One recommendation we thought particularly important is to show kindness and respect for students while being firm and thus respectful of yourself. We assume many of these are standard operating procedures for school personnel; if not, they should be. We believe these recommendations can form the background for a comprehensive conflict resolution plan. Because there will always be conflicts that it is our responsibility to see are resolved in personally, educationally, and socially constructive ways, we have de-veloped the following plan.

First: Determining the Rules, Establishing Procedures, and Identifying Consequences. Other authors[8,9] have made the point that school and community efforts should be made in the development and implementation of rules. The goal is for students and school personnel to understand that the school is a rule-governed institution and that there are designated processes that will be used when problems occur. Within this program we suggest that rewards for obeying rules be used. We also recommend that data be collected concerning the prevalence of discipline problems.[8,13] If you perceive that problems are significant in your school, this step is essential. Along with this suggestion, it would certainly be encouraging and helpful for the rest of the plan if inservice training were provided for school personnel.

The aim of this step is to establish both classroom and school rules. School rules should cover conduct in the halls, in the cafeteria, on the buses, and on the playground. School personnel should be clear on any state laws, fire regulations, and so on that must be observed, as these are nonnegotiable. We think it is important that all school personnel have an opportunity to suggest rules; the secretaries, custodians, cafeteria helpers, and bus drivers may have suggestions that are unique to their situation. Probably the best approach to this recommendation is through class meetings early in the year. Each person has the opportunity to state a rule or rules that he or she thinks is important for the classroom and the school.

Initially, you should accumulate and not evaluate recommendations. After a number of rules have been suggested for both the classroom and school, go through the set and combine similar rules; eliminate rules that are beyond your authority to enact, e.g., it is probably not your prerogative to dismiss school at noon every Friday; simplify complex rules; and reduce the number of rules to a manageable number—between five and ten. We further suggest that the rules be stated as principles, not as dos or don'ts. (See Chapters Six and Eight.)

School rules should be accumulated and summarized in the manner just outlined. A committee comprised of school personnel and students could complete the task. The rules should be comprehensive, but try to avoid long lists. When the school rules have been summarized they should be distributed to school personnel, students, and parents. You may want to discuss the rules in class or at an all-school meeting, or you may wish to have a quiz on the rules. It takes time, but it is important that all participate in the process. It may be boring and detract from other educational goals, but so do fire drills, and we have many more rule violations and discipline problems than fires in our schools each year. But when a fire occurs, all should know what to do and be clear and practiced on the procedures; so too with school rules and disruptive behavior.

During the class meeting the procedures that will be followed and the consequences for rule violation also should be established. Procedures such as those we have outlined can be suggested and modified as appropriate for your school, class, or grade level. Establishing consequences should be done in the same manner as rule development. Consequences should be natural (logical) outcomes of rule violations. Avoid harsh, punitive, cruel, or unusual consequences.

Second: Offering a Request and a Reminder. All of us occasionally forget or become so involved in things that we overlook a rule or regulation. Students are no exception. The first step of intervention is a clear but gentle request that the student stop the disruptive behavior. The request would ideally be in the form of an "I-message" and describe the student's behavior: "I would like you to stop talking" or "I need more cooperation during cleanup; please put your laboratory equipment away and clean your area." At the same time as you make this request you should remind the student of the rule behind the request.

Many of the minor day-to-day problems of classroom discipline will probably be eliminated if this step is enforced consistently. Students will soon realize that you have expectations that were agreed upon by the class and that you are giving them the benefit of the doubt concerning the rule violation. You can discuss with the class how many warnings should be given before the next step is taken. We recommend no more than three. Regardless, each warning should be a request and a reminder. This procedure can be used concerning school rules as well. School personnel should use the "request and reminder" approach for problems around the school and on the buses.

Third: Describing the Disruptive Behavior and Clarifying the Consequences. If disruptive behavior persists to the point where the warnings are no longer effective, identify the student's consistent behavior patterns, and then meet with the student to define the problem. You could use the different behavior patterns described in Chapters Four and Eight and summarized here in Table 7–1 as an orientation for your observations.

At this stage the teacher informs the student of the rule violation and describes the consistent pattern of behaviors that are cause for concern. If at all possible, we recommend these procedures be taken before or after class or school. A matter-of-fact and nonaccusatory position should be stressed: "This is the rule that was broken"; "These are the behaviors that seem to have continued to cause the difficulty." Then remind the student of the consequences that have been agreed upon. Ask the student to comply with the regulation and complete whatever had been agreed to in terms of consequences. During this entire period the student should have opportunities to talk about the situation and make suggestions about future remedies for the problem. The teacher should be clear and consistent while listening very closely to what students say on their own behalf. Tell the student that when the agreed-upon consequences have occurred the situation is over as far as you are concerned, but, if there is another occurrence, "we will have to work out another plan to resolve the problem."

TABLE 7–1. A Summary of Disruptive Behavior Patterns

Behaviors Seeking Personal Affirmation or Alienation. These are the mildest behaviors that can be potentially disruptive. Behaviors seeking affirmation are subtle and often overlooked in the classroom. Examples include seeking recognition from the teacher or other students through wearing new clothes, doing outstanding work, making very mild disruptive statements, or showing off and being mischievous in ways that do not cause the teacher great alarm. Also there are those students who are detached, mildly withdrawn, and alienated.

Behaviors Showing Personal Assertion or Withdrawal. With these behaviors the student makes it very clear to a large number of individuals (including the teacher) that they must pay attention. This stage is slightly more intense than the earlier stage of affirmation. Examples from this stage are being stubborn, defying authority, being withdrawn or depressed, refusing to work, talking back. In general, this stage is differentiated from the earlier one by the fact that the teacher or other students *must* pay attention. Withdrawn behaviors at this stage are also clear enough to make other students and teachers aware of the problem.

Behaviors Demonstrating Personal Aggression or Depression. The aggressive student attempts to take over and control the immediate situation. These students are openly maliciously disobedient or have disassociated and withdrawn entirely from the classroom. The working relationship between student and teacher is extremely difficult. The student is attempting to dominate the classroom environment by actively moving forward and taking power or regressing totally into a withdrawn state either mentally or physically.

Behaviors Manifesting Violence. This is the stage of physical force, the demonstration of rage, and temper tantrums. In the withdrawn inward form, this stage shows a flight from reality through chemicals, psychological withdrawal, and attempts at self-multilation or self-destruction.

Again, this same procedure should be carried out for violations of school rules.

Fourth: Defining the Problem, Suggesting Alternatives, and Determining a Plan to Resolve the Problem. If difficulties continue, it is recommended that you have a private meeting with the student. The object of the meeting is to define the problem, generate possible solutions, and develop a plan to resolve the problem that is agreeable to both you and the student. Many of the recommendations made in earlier models apply to this stage. An attitude of "we will work this out" should prevail. This message can be conveyed by actually saying those words and in other ways such as listening, trying to understand the student's perceptions of the situation, and accepting the student's ideas and suggestions. After a period of discussion both you and the student should decide whether or not you can now work out the problem. If you or the student decide you cannot, then you will probably have to bring in a third party. (This is the sixth step and will be described later.) For the time being, let us assume that both parties agree to a goal of trying to resolve the problem. By this time the problem should be clear to both parties.

Start by outlining all the alternatives that each of you can suggest. Evaluate the different recommendations and decide on a specific course of action that may resolve the problem. This, in effect, is an individualized set of goals, rules and consequences. Make very clear who is to do what, what is to be changed, and when the changes are to occur. Be sure to establish what the consequences are for a violation. Will there be warnings? If so, how many? The next step is referral to a school administrator, probably the counselor. This point should be absolutely clear. Because of this you will want to clarify exactly what your expectations are and have the student express his or her expectations. It is strongly suggested that you write out the plan. Once you have agreed on a plan, stick to it and be consistent. At this stage you should inform your school administrator and counselor about the situation and the plan.

Fifth: Asking the Student to Leave the Room and Report to the Counselor. After the plan has been agreed to, continue doing whatever is necessary to help the student by encouraging productive behavior. Above all, do not convey an attitude of "just one mistake and you're out" or "I'll catch you and that is it." Rather, try to convey the idea that you will help, that you can be kind and show respect and that you want the student to learn. Still, you must be consistent with the plan. Don't worry; a disruptive student surely knows what the next step will be. If this step of the plan is violated, you can inform the student and ask that he or she report to the appropriate administrator.

While this approach is rather lengthy and involved, we do think it is designed so the rights of both students and teachers will be respected. Variations in procedures will occur, but the basic structure is workable. We shall continue with the next steps of the process from the administrator's view in the next section.

Our efforts here center on a conflict resolution process that is helpful for administrators and counselors. It is hoped that some steps will have been taken by classroom teachers prior to this level of intervention. In this respect, the next steps are a continuation of earlier ones. Still, there will be situations in which earlier procedures in the classroom have not been done. Conflicts in the cafeteria, in the halls, on buses, and on the playground would be examples of such situations. Even if nothing has been done prior to the student or teacher arriving in the administrator's office, the steps can be applied without reverting to earlier stages.

Sixth: Mediate a Resolution to the Conflict. It is a good idea to have a third party, preferably a counselor, attempt to mediate the conflict. This session would be similar to the two models already presented.[9,12] Counselors should clarify their position as the mediator, determine that all parties

wish to resolve the problem, and point out that the process is one of negotiating the resolution, not determining who is wrong. After this the following steps can be taken: 1) all parties describe their perceptions of the
problem, how they feel about the situation and what their position is/was
during the conflict; 2) agree on a definition of the problem; 3) describe
possible solutions to the problem; 4) determine the most reasonable solution; 5) identify what is required to reach this solution; 6) negotiate the
changes; 7) establish a plan of action with appropriate checks for successes
and processes for failures; 8) implement the plan of resolution. The counselor summarizes and records what has happened, what the plan is, and
what is expected in the future. The counselor should also inform the appropriate administrators of the situation and resolution.

Many school problems can be handled at this level. Counselors are
probably the best persons to handle the situation since they are trained in
some of the processes required such as listening, summarizing, and clarifying. They need not take sides and can see that the procedures are carried
through to everyone's benefit. What happens if there is a persistent problem or if after one or two attempts at step six there is still a problem?

Seventh: Refer the Problem to a Team of School Personnel. If students
reach this level, it should be clear that their behavior is consistently in
violation with rules and policies. The point of the meeting is to make clear
to all concerned that there is a problem and that a team approach will be
implemented in an attempt to resolve the problem. We think that the
student should be present, as well as all the student's teachers, parents,
and any other persons from the community who may be involved with the
student. Procedures described earlier should be used. The situation is
made absolutely clear to the student and all concerned. It is hard to make
specific recommendations here since each case will be unique and will
require special considerations. No doubt the individuals who are involved
at this stage will be multiproblem students. This implies a multisolution
approach. Try to identify different problems the student may be experiencing and work on plans to resolve these or to gain more information
where needed.

This problem-solving approach will have the support of school, family,
and community. Beyond the support, however, is the advantage of consistent interaction by all parties who must implement the plan to resolve the
problem. One person, perhaps the counselor, should monitor the program. The monitoring frequency would be determined by the severity of
the problem and the cooperation of the student. A part of the plan of action
should be the determination of sanctions or consequences if students do
not fulfill their part of the bargain. Such consequences can include inschool
alternatives to suspension.[14] They should not include corporal punishment
or any harsh or unusual treatment. Whatever the consequences are, they
should be applied consistently.

The person in charge of monitoring also should evaluate the plan. In some instances the plan may require modification. If this is done, the team should be called together and the modifications discussed and agreed to.

What if all of this does not work? In some cases it is possible that students will not respond to the procedures we have recommended. They will simply be too aggressive, too withdrawn, or too troubled to respond in any way to the efforts made by those who care and wish to help. What should the school do with these students? There is probably no useful purpose served by keeping these students in the mainstream of the school. On the other hand, there is little purpose served by expelling the student or transferring the student to another school since the problem will probably continue.

Eight: Assume Responsibility for Arranging Services to Help Severely Troubled Students. It may be beyond the school's responsibility to actually provide the services required for severely troubled—violent and disruptive—students. But it surely is not beyond the school's responsibility to see that such services are provided. We recommend that administration not "get rid of the problem," but that they arrange for necessary services. This is an important role of the school; it is a civic responsibility to society and a humane responsibility to the student.

We have gone as far as we can in suggesting concrete measures that can be taken by school personnel in order to resolve conflicts. The infinite variations that can be imagined, the "what if" questions, will ultimately have to be resolved by individuals in the schools and in the classrooms. While the final decisions are individual our recommendations and those of others we have presented should give some guidance in your own resolution of the question—what should we do now?

SUMMARY

How can school personnel justly resolve conflicts with disruptive students? This very practical question forms the central theme of the chapter. We present conflict resolution models as one important method of reducing violence and disruption in schools while facilitating a just school. Conflict resolution models cost little money, are easily implemented, have both short- and long-term benefits and serve the dual purpose of prevention and intervention. The models outlined are congruent with the theme of justice and the theoretical arguments presented thus far in this book.

Models that classroom teachers might use include: William Glasser's ten-step program for discipline, a logical consequences approach, and the teacher effectiveness method of resolving conflicts. Models that have a schoolwide appeal include: Daniel Duke's systematic management plan for school discipline, conflict resolution through negotiation, and a consensus model of conflict reduction.

Applying these models, or variations thereof, should be done with understanding of the basic processes of conflict resolution. The first goal of school personnel should be to negotiate a just resolution to any conflict. A second goal is to regulate conflict so destructive consequences are minimized. There are many factors that influence the course of conflicts. Size, time, safety, competition, acknowledgment of the conflict, and estimation of success are a few factors influential in directing the course of conflicts.

Among the recommendations for constructive resolutions are: use cooperative procedures, define conflicts as small, focus on the problem, reduce large conflicts to small ones, reach a consensus, identify possible solutions, and use third parties.

A comprehensive conflict resolution plan for schools was outlined:

1. Determining the rules, establishing procedures, and identifying consequences.
2. Offering a request and a reminder.
3. Describing the disruptive behavior and clarifying the consequences.
4. Defining the problem, suggesting alternatives, and determining a plan to resolve the problem.
5. Asking the student to leave the room and report to the counselor.
6. Mediating a resolution to the conflict.
7. Referring the problem to a team of school personnel.
8. Assuming responsibility for arranging services to help severely troubled students.

REFERENCES

1. William Glasser, *Reality Therapy* (New York: Harper & Row, 1965).
2. _____, *Schools without Failure* (New York: Harper & Row, 1969).
3. _____, "Discipline—A Tep Step Program," J. L. Hutchinson, (ed.), *Educare Journal* 4 (Spring 1976):18–22.
4. Don Dinkmeyer and Don Dinkmeyer, Jr., "Logical Consequences: A Key to the Reduction of Disciplinary Problems," *Phi Delta Kappan* 57, no. 10 (1976):664–66.
5. Rudolf Dreikurs and Loren Grey, *Logical Consequences: A Handbook of Discipline* (New York: Meredith Press, 1968).
6. Rudolf Dreikurs and Peral Cassel, *Discipline without Tears* (New York: Hawthorne Books, 1972).
7. Thomas Gordon, *Teacher Effectiveness Training* (New York: David McKay, 1974).
8. Daniel L. Duke, "A Systematic Management Plan for School Discipline," *National Association of Secondary School Principals Bulletin* 61 (January 1977): 1–10.

9. John P. DeCecco and Arlene K. Richards, *Growing Pains: Uses of School Conflict* (New York: Aberdeen Press, 1974).

10. _____, "Using Negotiation for Teaching Civil Liberties and Avoiding Liability," *Phi Delta Kappan* 57, no. 1 (1975):23–25.

11. _____, "Civil War in the High School," *Psychology Today* 9, no. 6 (1976): 151–56, 120.

12. Allen P. Main and Albert E. Roark, "A Consensus Method to Reduce Conflict," *The Personnel and Guidance Journal* 53 (June 1975):754–59.

13. Marvin Grantham and Clifton Harris, Jr., "A Faculty Trains Itself to Improve Student Discipline," *Phi Delta Kappan* 57, no. 10, (1976):661–64.

14. Antoine M. Garibaldi, ed., *In-School Alternatives to Suspension: Conference Report, National Institute of Education* (Washington, D. C.: U. S. Government Printing Office, April 1979).

15. Morton Deutsch, *The Resolution of Conflict* (New Haven: Yale University Press, 1973).

16. K. W. Terhune, "The Effects of Personality in Cooperation and Conflict," in P. Swingle, ed., *The Structure of Conflict* (New York: Academic Press, 1970).

CHAPTER EIGHT

Violence, Values, and Justice: Policies to Practices

INTRODUCTION

What can school personnel do to help ameliorate the problems of violence, vandalism, and disruptive behavior in schools? This question has been central to our discussion throughout the book. In the first chapter we examined the statistics on school-related discipline problems and outlined our perspective concerning violence and justice in American schools. The next chapters were concerned with various aspects of the problems and our perspective on them: a history of students' rights, a review of recent Supreme Court decisions, a discussion of the phenomenon of violence, a presentation of theories of ethical development, and a description of school conflicts and their resolution. In this final chapter we return to the theme—violence, values, and justice—and discuss policies and practices based on the foundation established in the earlier chapters.

Here our approach will be to advocate the general position we have maintained throughout the book. Namely, that justice is a viable, appropriate way of approaching the resolution of school-related problems of violence and disruption. We need to state clearly, then, that it would be a mistake to imply we are arguing either for greater leniency or greater severity in the interaction between school personnel and students. In final analysis we think the evidence and the law support what teachers have espoused in principle all along—be firm, friendly, fair, and consistent.

We also take a personal approach in this chapter. Ideas and references are presented that we believe will help school personnel. To the greatest degree possible we make practical suggestions. Because school personnel continually ask, "What does this mean for me?" the last point requires some discussion. Clearly, we do not know you, your school, your students, or your community. It is impossible to speak to school personnel about their unique educational situations. What we have done and what you will need to do is this: we have established a primary goal—that school personnel provide just treatment to students who have violated school rules and policies. This is abstract, but we are certain that school personnel sub-scribe to the idea, in principle. To be useful for teachers, counselors, ad-ministrators, and school board members, however, the goal has to be made less abstract and more practical. Through the use of examples, models, recommendations, suggestions, and implications where apppropriate in this book, we have attempted to move toward greater practicality. We con-tinue that endeavor in this chapter.

But what about the most basic question—"What can I do tomorrow?" The final, most concrete step, the step from policy to classroom practice, must be made by those directly involved in school situations. There are simply too many variables for us to make specific recommendations for each school district, much less each school, each administration, each teacher, and ultimately each student in combination with each teacher. Still, we have tried to present ideas and formulate policies that can be easily translated into practice by school personnel.

One other factor controls this discussion—the need for realism. We have identified many variables that may be contributing to violence and disruption in American education. Some possible causative factors are pov-erty, gangs, television, and violence in the family. These are all important, but realistically they are beyond the immediate power of the school system to change. We certainly support the work of other social agencies in their continuing efforts to reduce such problems. However, we think it most realistic to concentrate our time, money, and energy on those problems arising within the school from causative factors that we can exercise the power to change. It is also within the school system that we personally experience the greatest disruptions, and it is here that we have the great-est opportunity to have a positive impact on the problem.

Can educators bring about safe and peaceful schools? They probably cannot. That is, they cannot do it alone. Resolving the problems of vio-lence and vandalism, and of less intense disruptions and discipline prob-lems, will take the combined efforts of many. Educators must trust (and hope) that social workers, the courts, health care professionals, churches, parents, and many others are working on their respective tasks. But if schools are to contribute their share, to do their part, then they must not wait for others to solve the problems.

In the final analysis we all share common goals—a better education in American schools, and ultimately a better society. How can we start work-ing toward these goals? The next section in this chapter summarizes many of the ideas presented in earlier chapters that form the foundation for fur-ther discussions. Next, we discuss a reasonable approach to answering the fundamental question—what can school personnel do to help resolve the problems of violence and disruption? First, recognize the problem as it exists in your school. Second, reduce alienating factors in your school. Third, educate for democratic values and fourth, encourage appropriate behavior in your school. We feel the policies and references suggested can contribute to educational practices that hold great promise of reducing violence, vandalism, and disruption in American education.

THE PERSPECTIVE WE HAVE PRESENTED

The following list represents conclusions reached from our study. These conclusions clarify the interdisciplinary nature of our approach as they reflect a combination of philosophy, history, social psychology, law, and in many instances an important element of common sense.

Student Rights

- Students have the same constitutional rights that have long been recognized for other persons in our society. The recognition of these rights has involved social and judicial processes and has been slow in emerging.
- Judicial rulings have primarily centered on the rights of students and the responsibilities of schools vis-a-vis suspension, expulsion, and corporal punishment. The trend has been toward greater recognition of the process due students before the imposition of penalties and reduced severity in the penalties imposed.
- There is no federal constitutional right to a public education; once a state chooses to provide an educational system for its citizens, a student cannot be denied access to the system without some measure of due process.
- The Supreme Court has specifically ruled that students have First Amendment rights of free speech and associated activities, Fourth Amendment rights to be free from unreasonable search and seizure, and Fourteenth Amendment rights of due process before denial of access to education.
- The Supreme Court has made it clear that school officials are not immune from students' legal action for damages incurred at school. Students or their representatives have recourse through state and common law, or through federal civil rights legislation.
- The Supreme Court has also clearly indicated that these rights and the procedures used by school personnel are subject to the special requirements of the school environment.
- School personnel, guided by the pronouncements of the courts, must decide on the appropriate level of process due students. They should consider the interests of the school, the student, and the nature of the educational deprivations contemplated for the student being disciplined. At a minimum there ought to be an informal "give and take"

discussion between the teacher and student. Greater denial of educational rights may require that a student: 1) be notified of charges, 2) have a formal hearing, 3) be represented by an advocate or legal counsel, 4) be allowed to question witnesses, 5) be free from self-incrimination, and 6) be given an opportunity to have the decision reviewed.

– Rules governing the behavior of students should be clear and should exist a reasonable time prior to disciplinary action by school personnel. Though a specific rule need not be stated, a policy or principle from which the specific rule can be derived should exist.

Violence and Disruption in Schools

– Discipline has always been a concern of school personnel, but over the past three decades there has been an increase in violence, vandalism, and disruption in schools. Violence in the schools today appears to have leveled off and is perhaps declining.

– Violence, vandalism, and disruption in schools have occurred in all geographic settings—urban, suburban, and rural.

– The problems of violence, vandalism, and disruption involve youth in general and not exclusively specific populations of youth such as minorities or the poor.

– General factors contributing to school-related discipline problems form a complex and interrelated network. Some important factors are: the general condoning of aggression as a means of resolving conflicts, televised violence, the use of violence at home and at school, and the characteristic developmental problems of adolescents.

– Specific school factors related to student disruption include: the size and impersonality of schools; weak, inconsistent, and arbitrary enforcement of rules; use of school reward systems (mostly grades) for disciplinary purposes; relevance of the curriculum; and the alienation of students from the school system in general.

– The contrast of students' perception of their freedom, power, and decision making ability with teachers' use of authority, control, and punishment seems to be a factor of particular importance for violent versus peaceful schools.

Ethics and Values in Schools

– School rules and the enforcement of those rules represent value systems.

– Conflicts between students and school personnel are a basis for the educational development of ethics and values.

- Educators can use theories of motivation and development to: 1) help clarify the perceptions of school personnel concerning particular rules and 2) give direction concerning their interaction with students.

Educational Conflicts

- Educational conflicts occur when the activities or behaviors of students and school personnel are incompatible.
- Educational conflicts are usually related to violating, challenging, or questioning school rules, policies, or expectations of behavior.
- All school conflicts and discipline problems are not the same. There are different types of conflicts, and there is a range of intensity and frequency of conflicts. The types and levels of conflicts outlined below (Table 8–1) will help school personnel clarify these differences.
- Most conflicts reviewed were in junior high schools; were between male students and female teachers; occurred at the lower levels of Table 8–1; were resolved in less than three minutes; occurred during independent work, formal presentation, or free time; were preceded by "unusual circumstances;" and involved prescriptive rules that were known to students.
- Most conflicts between students and teachers were resolved through discussion. Teachers also tended to warn of negative consequences, and to use less coercive, threatening, and aggressive means of resolving conflicts before turning to more stringent measures.
- Many conflicts between students and teachers can be prevented through understanding the motivational and developmental needs of students; clarifying rules and policies; and being aware of environmental, educational, and situational factors that contribute to conflicts.
- Many conflicts may be prevented through cooperation with the community in the planning and organization of school programs. Cooperation by students and teachers within the school in reviewing and updating discipline policies and governance, revising of curriculum and using more personalized instruction also are recommended.
- Corporal punishment should be eliminated as a means of disciplining and educating students.

Conflict Resolution

- There are two crucial factors to consider in the resolution of school-related conflicts. First, the conflict should not escalate in personally or socially destructive ways. Second, the conflict should be resolved constructively.

TABLE 8–1. Levels of Disruptive Behavior

Affirmation or Alienation

This is the first level of behavior that can be perceived as disruptive. Behaviors seeking affirmation are subtle and often overlooked in the classroom. Examples include seeking recognition from the teacher or other students through wearing new clothes, doing outstanding work, or making very mild disruptive statements. Also there are those students who are detached and mildly withdrawn, or who show off and are mischievous in ways that do not cause the teacher great alarm.

Assertion or Withdrawal

At this level the student makes it very clear to a large number of individuals (including the teacher) that they must pay attention. This stage is slightly more intense than the earlier stage of affirmation. Examples of this stage of behavior include being stubborn, defying authority, being withdrawn or depressed, refusing to work, talking back. In general, this stage is differentiated from the earlier one by the fact that the teacher or other students *must* pay attention.

Aggression or Depression

The aggressive student attempts to take over and control the immediate situation. These students are openly and maliciously disobedient or have disassociated and withdrawn entirely from the classroom. There is no longer any working relationship between student and teacher. The student is attempting to dominate the classroom environment by actively moving forward and taking power or regressing totally into a withdrawn state either mentally or physically.

Violence

This is the stage of physical force, the demonstration of rage, and temper tantrums. In the withdrawn inward form, this stage shows a flight from reality through chemicals, psychological withdrawal, and attempts at self-mutilation or self-destruction.

— These factors lead to the goals of first attempting to negotiate a just and constructive resolution of school conflicts and, second, regulating conflicts so as to avoid destructive consequences.

— Constructive resolution of conflicts is facilitated by having all parties to the conflict express their perceptions of the conflict, giving consideration to the circumstances, expressing a sincere interest in resolving the conflict, facilitating clear communication and offering solutions and plans of action.

— Escalation of conflicts can be avoided or reduced by not using inappropriate coercion, negative sanctions, excessive power, authoritarian dominance, or alienating techniques to resolve the problem.

– There are many conflict resolution models that can be used by school personnel in different settings.

– Implementing conflict resolution models in schools has several advantages: there is little cost and effort; they have short- and long-term benefits; their recommendation is supported by psychological, social, and legal evidence; and they have the combined purpose of preventing conflicts and directing intervention.

– The course of a conflict can be influenced by many factors including size, time, perceived threat, definition, communication, acknowledgment, personality, estimation of success, sense of community, rationality, recognized legitimacy, unique aspects of the situation, and use of third parties.

– A comprehensive conflict resolution plan for schools might include:

1. Determining the rules, establishing procedures, and identifying consequences.
2. Offering a request and a reminder.
3. Describing the disruptive behavior and clarifying the consequences.
4. Defining the problem, suggesting alternatives, and determining a plan.
5. Asking the student to leave the room and report to a counselor.
6. Mediating a resolution to the conflict.
7. Referring the problem to a team of school personnel.
8. Assuming responsibility for arranging services for helping severely troubled students.

CLARIFYING THE PROBLEM

The first step in reducing school-related discipline problems is to recognize that there is a problem. Certainly this is a truism, but school personnel commonly do not recognize they have a problem, or give little significance to the discipline problems in their school. More often than not, school personnel engage in the academically interesting but practically useless activity of blame setting.

Blame Setting versus Problem Solving

Blame setting is displacing the problem, particularly the etiology, to a source outside of the school. How often have you heard that "the problem is really in the home"? This statement may be 100 percent true—the origin of a school related problem may indeed be elsewhere, outside of the school. Our position, however, is that even if the origin of the problem is elsewhere, this identification simply does not resolve the problem. We strongly recommend that all school personnel cease blame-setting and become problem solvers.

Blame setting leads to a view of discipline problems that does not help resolve the problems and may in fact hinder attempts to improve the school. First, blame setting is a not-so-subtle way of saying the problems originate elsewhere, not here. So, if the problems are to be resolved, activity must also start elsewhere. Second, blame setting blinds school personnel to the fact that contributing factors may be found within the school system. Third, it relieves school personnel from responsibility. Fourth, it tends to encourage a view of school-related problems as short-term and amenable to simple, immediate remedies. How do we respond?

The problems may have origins elsewhere. Most of the evidence indicates that extreme behaviors of students have been a long time developing and have been influenced by numerous sources including those usually named—family, television, society, and so on. If all of these factors were eliminated tomorrow, which is highly unlikely, there is still little or no evidence to suggest that student behavior in schools would improve the next day or in the near future. As a matter of fact, most psychological evidence indicates it would not improve.

Schools do contribute to discipline problems. This is a factor not usually recognized in the blame-setting process. Ample information exists to suggest that school-specific factors such as size, impersonality, inconsistent rule enforcement, and irrelevant curricula do contribute to disruptive behavior. These factors may be small or they may be large depending on the school, but they probably exist to some degree in more schools than educators would like to admit.

Educators are responsible for what occurs in schools regardless of what has happened or will happen elsewhere. The solutions are complex and contain a network of interrelated factors. It is time we turned our collective efforts to problem solving and away from blame setting.

Information on Problems

If the first step is to cease blame-setting and start problem-solving, the second is to obtain accurate information about the problems. Here the goal is to establish the degree to which there is a discipline problem in the school. The definition of "discipline problem" will vary from school to school. Most schools have some students with problems. Compared to other schools the problems may be less or more significant; but we are not interested in comparisons, we are interested in solutions.

We suggest that information about problems be gathered by school personnel. Too often discussions of discipline problems in a school are dominated by rumor and opinion, the previous conflict, the worst student, or the most severe incident. There is nothing like a little information to help clarify the situation. How many discipline reports are there a day? A week?

A month? How frequent are the problems? How severe are disruptions? What types of problems occur? How much money is spent on vandalism? In order to help answer these questions we have outlined some topics that may form the basis for records. Other additions appropriate to your school may be required. School personnel should add to or modify the forms to meet the unique needs of their school. Information should be collected for at least one month.

SCHOOL CONFLICT DESCRIPTION

The purpose of this section is to provide clarification and understanding of school conflicts. When completing the questions you should keep these guidelines in mind:

1. Describe the conflict in objective, not blaming, terms.
2. Describe the visible effects of the incident on other students, your-self, and the environment.
3. Describe how the conflict was resolved.

In order to be more specific the following questions and checklists may be helpful.

Incident. Describe the actual behaviors and statements of the participants during a conflict incident. This should be an objective factual statement. What did each person say and do?

1. After the incident complete the following:

		Teacher		*Student*
Date _____	Between:	Man ( )		Boy ( )
Grade Level _____		Woman ( )		Girl ( )
School _____Class _____				
	Other (specify) _____			

2. How long did the conflict last?

Less than one minute	( )	7–10 minutes	( )
1–3 minutes	( )	Longer than 10 minutes	( )
4–6 minutes	( )	Indicate how long _____	

3. Indicate the individual student's behaviors in terms of the categories outlined in Table 8–1—Levels of Disruptive Behavior (Refer to Tables 7–1 and 8–1 for discussion of the levels.)

1. Affirmation	( )	Alienation	( )
2. Assertion	( )	Withdrawal	( )
3. Aggression	( )	Depression	( )
4. Violence toward others	( )	Violence toward self	( )

Was this incident part of a recurring or consistent pattern of behavior for the student? Yes ( )   No ( )   Don't know ( )

Context. Describe the setting, circumstances, and origin of the conflict.

4. What was the situation?

COMMENTS

Teacher presentation, e.g., lecturing	( )
Class discussion, e.g., teacher leading	( )
Class presentation, e.g., film	( )
Group work, e.g., laboratory	( )
Individual work, e.g., reading	( )
Student presentation, e.g., discussion of project	( )
Free time in class	( )
Free time in school, e.g., hall, cafeteria	( )
Free time outside of building	( )
Other (specify)	

5. Were there any unusual circumstances that should be noted?
6. What was the rule, policy, or expectation of behavior?
7. Was the rule, policy, or expectation presented or enforced as:

COMMENTS

Prohibitive, e.g., "You should not"	( )
Prescriptive, e.g., "You should"	( )
Benefit to group, e.g., "You must, so we can"	( )
Benefit to individual, e.g., "We must, so you can"	( )
Other (specify)	

8. To your knowledge was the rule, policy, or expectation:

Personal ( )	Stated ( )	Unstated ( )	by either party to the conflict
Classroom ( )	Written ( )	Unwritten ( )	prior to the conflict
School ( )	Known ( )	Unknown ( )	to the accused
Social or Criminal Code ( )	Known ( )	Unknown ( )	to the accused

Comments:

Resolution. Describe how the conflict was ended or resolved.

9. The following are some ways classroom conflicts are resolved. Check the means that best describe those used by each party to resolve or end the conflict you have described. (Check all appropriate categories.)

	Teacher	*Student*	*Comments*
Discussed the issue calmly with the other individual, encouraging alternate behaviors.	( )	( )	
Brought in a third party to settle things.	( )	( )	
Had a group discussion and talked about rules, policies, expectations.	( )	( )	
Turned the situation over to the group for resolution.	( )	( )	
Turned the situation over to a higher authority for resolution.	( )	( )	
Other (mutual resolution); specify:			
Sulked or refused to talk.	( )	( )	
Left the room or situation.	( )	( )	
Insulted, swore at, or verbally demeaned the other.	( )	( )	
Warned the other of negative consequences.	( )	( )	
Promised reward, told of positive consequences.	( )	( )	
Other (coercive resolution); specify:			
Threatened isolation or removal from immediate environment.	( )	( )	
Threatened physical punishment.	( )	( )	
Threatened physical restraint.	( )	( )	
Threatened personal disapproval.	( )	( )	

Threatened peer disapproval   ( )   ( )
Threatened parental disapproval   ( )   ( )
Threatened poor grades, marks,
detention points, etc.   ( )   ( )
Other (threatening resolution); specify:

Removed the individual from
immediate environment   ( )   ( )
Pushed, grabbed, or shoved the
other   ( )   ( )
Slapped or spanked the other   ( )   ( )
Kicked, bit, or hit with fist   ( )   ( )
Hit or tried to hit with something   ( )   ( )
Arranged for physical punishment
by another   ( )   ( )
Other (aggressive resolution); specify:

10. What happened during the short period (3–5 minutes) after the conflict ended or was resolved?

11. How did behaviors change for those directly involved?

12. How did behaviors change for those indirectly involved?

13. Were there any other consequences of the conflict/resolution?

14. Were the parents contacted?

15. Were other methods used to change the student's behavior? Teacher behavior? Environment?

16. Was corporal punishment administered? If so, what was the immediate effect? Long-term (2–3 weeks) effect?

Interpretation. How would you interpret the conflict you have described? What general statements can be made concerning the conflict?

Recommendations. What could be done to avoid further conflicts such as the one you described?

There is also a need to obtain information on vandalism. The form presented below will help in this area.

SCHOOL VANDALISM DESCRIPTION

School _____ Date _____ Time _____
Location _____ Entry _____ Exit _____
Reported to Authorities _____
Description of Damage _____
Estimated Cost _____
Repair/Restitution _____
Suggested Prevention _____

We also recommend the following references on evaluating and improving school climate[1] and on understanding violent behaviors and school related problems.[2-6]

Establishing Priorities

Every teacher and school has priorities. What is the priority of reducing discipline problems and vandalism in your school? Once there is information about the nature and extent of the problem it is easier to make judgments about the amount of time, money, effort, and energy that should be expended in solving this problem.

Share this information with school personnel, the school board, and the community and get their feedback about the situation. It is possible to have a faculty or group meeting to discuss three questions: 1) What is the situation? This could include a presentation of the information collected over the past month or longer period of time. Time also should be allowed for the expression of frustration and feelings of isolation by staff. 2) What can we do to improve the situation? Here is where the discussion must focus on the school and on a cooperative effort among school personnel. 3) How should we proceed? We strongly recommend that short- medium- and long-term programs be adopted. Do something immediately, within the next two weeks. Or better yet, do several things to start resolving the problem. A number of different recommendations are made in the next sections. Many recommendations overlap, reflecting their interrelated nature.

REDUCING ALIENATION

Alienation is the slow and steady disintegration of the bond between an individual and the society within which he exists. Another way of saying this is that the student gradually ceases to value school. A sense of isolation, normlessness, powerlessness, meaninglessness, and self-estrangement may be indicative of the alienated student. We can start the process of reducing alienation by asking, what is it that will contribute to a stronger attraction between students and their school?

Meeting Students' Needs

Abraham Maslow's hierarchy of motivational needs is a good place to start.[7] According to this theory students may be distracted in the classroom or school by their motivations to fulfill needs more basic than the need to learn reading, writing, mathematics, history, or science.

At the most basic level students may need food, sleep, air, or water— the physiological requirements of life. Next in the hierarchy is the need for a safe and secure environment. Knowing that students (and school personnel) have a need for safety provides an even greater incentive to make schools safe places, so education can continue in the best environment possible. Next in the hierarchy are the social-psychological needs of love and belongingness and self-esteem. The need to belong to a group, or the school, is important, and there is certainly a relationship between this need and the feelings of isolation discussed earlier. Self-esteem is likewise related to the problem of self-estrangement and the source of many behaviors that school personnel describe as disruptive.

Finally, there is the weak, but ever-present, need to continue developing. Maslow called this the need for self-actualization. Though some have interpreted this as selfishness or given the concept other negative connotations, it is best thought of as the need for continued personal development.

The implications seem straightforward. School personnel should do their best to meet the needs of students. Teachers, administrators, and counselors cannot meet all student needs all the time. But they can be aware of these needs and particularly their motivational influence. Perceiving school as a place where basic human needs can be fulfilled can certainly help reduce student alienation. We recommend David Johnson's books, *Reaching Out: Interpersonal Effectiveness and Self Actualization*,[8] and *Human Relations and Your Career*.[9]

Being Friendly

One factor contributing to violent schools is the size and impersonality of the school. This factor no doubt contributes to feelings of isolation and estrangement. There may be ways to reduce the impersonal nature of schools through scheduling, e.g., fewer but longer classes, "core" teaching and cohort teaching (one teacher stays with a group of students through the junior and/or senior high years). We certainly encourage these approaches. The bottom line seems to be a more personal relationship between the students and at least one teacher in the school. All teachers do not have to love all the students all the time, but all teachers should care enough for some students some of the time so that collectively all students have a sense that there are individuals who want them in school, who know them by name, speak to them about everyday matters, and show some interest in their lives outside of school.

We would hope that teachers, as professionals, would give a little more effort to helping students move from feelings of isolation to feelings of integration and belonging. Show students you care for them simply because they are persons. Try to establish a friendly rapport around school-related topics and eventually topics outside of school.

Listen to students. Listening communicates your desire to understand. Communicate your perceptions of what the students are saying; we all like to be listened to, heard, and understood. Ask the students questions about school, their interests, activities and so on.

We realize there are students for whom these would be empty gestures, but the number is small. The number could be smaller if we paid more personal attention to those with whom we can communicate.[10, 11]

Being Firm, Fair, and Consistent

There is certainly a need for the time-honored recommendation to all beginning teachers—be firm, friendly, and fair. We addressed the recommendation to be friendly in the last section. The recommendation here is for more systematic enforcement of classroom and school discipline. Make the rules clear and then enforce them fairly and consistently. This recommendation is designed to reduce alienation due to normlessness. Let the students know the behaviors that are expected; let them see that the rules are not arbitrarily enforced and that you expect them to obey the rules. One suggestion is to use the "self-fulfilling prophecy" as a positive force. Instead of expecting students to be unruly because they have problems outside of school, expect them to behave in school; let them know there are established rules and that they are enforced fairly. This is not a recommendation for a harsh and punitive discipline policy.

Enforcement of discipline should be coordinated throughout the school. Teachers, administrators, and other school personnel should work together and support one another in the development and enforcement of rules. The support of the school can then help each individual to be firm in response to misbehavior, fair in regard to the consequences, and consistent with all students.

Making the Curriculum Meaningful

Meaninglessness, a characteristic of alienation, can be remedied through the curriculum. Career and vocational education, work-study programs, contemporary problems classes, law-related education, and many other modifications of the curriculum are possible and recommended. New approaches are not guaranteed to be meaningful, as meaningfulness is in the eye of the beholder. So, some effort should be made to determine simultaneously what is of interest to students and feasible for the school.

Educators have heard much talk about relevancy in the curriculum. Most often relevancy is equated with timeliness, but timely materials may or may not be meaningful to the students. Meaning arises from the physical and psychological closeness of the material to the individual. This is a recommendation, therefore, for a curriculum of activities related to, or presented in the context, of the student's life.

We suggest school personnel review the curriculum with the goal of making revisions or adopting new programs where possible. Teachers can contribute a great deal to makiing the present curriculum meaningful by pointing out connections between concepts and the students' lives. Let the students indicate some topics or projects they wish to study. We are convinced there are numerous ways of creating meaningful curriculum programs. And very importantly, teachers are already aware of these ways and willing to work toward this goal. In order to achieve the goal, however, teachers must be supported by the administration and the school board. We again end with the idea that reducing alienation and ultimately disruptive behavior must be a cooperative effort among school personnel.[12]

Governing the School

The cooperative effort mentioned above carries over to school governance and the aim of reducing powerlessness. This is not to say that students should run the school, but they can contribute to the process. As adults, we do not appreciate being excluded from governmental decision making at local, state, and national levels. And we would certainly become alienated from the democratic process if denied the power to contribute to our system of governance. We do not run the system, but the system does not run without us. This is the parallel we are suggesting for governing the school. Invite students to be on committees, to participate in discussions of curriculum revision and especially to help formulate the discipline policies.

Making Decisions

In many respects junior and senior high schools require students to remain children at a time when they are becoming adults. The structure of schools, personality of teachers, and mandates of administrators require that students be obedient to authorities. As such, students make few decisions concerning their own lives. The controls of their lives are external to them. Yet, educators say they are encouraging self-development or, more importantly for the theme of this book, self-discipline. Excessive external controls on youth, however, are the origins of self-estrangement.

Students' perceptions that they have no control over their fate, that the controls of their destiny are external, can result in attempts to regain and maintain control through disruptive behavior. Several of the earlier discussions relate to this source of alienation. Rules inconsistently enforced and grades given for reasons other than academic achievement tell students that they cannot plan for the future because it is out of their control.

Making personal decisions is an important means of giving individuals a source of control over their lives. Just as we pointed out in the section on governance, students need not be given the power to make major decisions about the classroom and school. But they can be given some freedom to make decisions about their education. Schools or parents contribute to alienation when they deny students access to decision making at the very time students recognize that they are young adults. Placing young adults in this position also contributes to their insistence on making decisions in other areas—such as sex, alcohol, drugs, cars, marriage; or dropping out of school. We think it much more reasonable to allow students some power to make decisions in the context of classrooms and schools. Denying their need to make decisions, or waiting until they make demands that really must be denied, leads to alienated, disruptive, and violent student behavior. There are some sources available on citizen decision making that we recommend.[13]

Some Guides for School Personnel

There are some specific implications that arise from this section on reducing alienation. Though by necessity brief, these statements can suggest directions for your own work.

1. Recognize that students have physiological, physical, and psychological needs that influence their behavior. There are often clear behavioral indicators of the needs; try to be aware of students' needs and fulfill them as best you can within the limits of the school.

2. Indicate your interest in teaching the students and let them know they are wanted and belong in your room. Little things help: address them by name, recognize achievements, visit with them about their ideas and tell them about your out-of-school hobbies.

3. Try to arrange your program so all students can develop a greater sense of esteem. Help students further develop their talents; give constructive criticism and assistance.

4. Have the students contribute to the formation of classroom and school rules. School personnel should then enforce the rules firmly, fairly, and consistently.

6. Allow times for the discussion and clarification of personal values. Class meetings, opportunities to make decisions, and value-clarification exercises all contribute to greater cohesiveness of the student group.

7. Arrange experiences that will allow students to participate in school

governance. Voting on issues, working on committees, planning programs and suggesting ideas for the curriculum are all reasonable activities for students.

8. Provide some opportunities for students to make choices and contribute to their own development and discipline. Students can be allowed freedom within limits.

EDUCATING FOR DEMOCRATIC VALUES

Our earlier theoretical discussions of ethical development lead to practical applications. What do these theories mean for school personnel? What can be done to foster ethical development in schools? These are the questions that we attempt to answer in this section.

Assumptions

Before presenting some of our ideas it is worth reviewing the assumptions underlying the theories of ethical development we have described. Teachers and administrators can then go beyond the ideas we present.

Stage Development Does Not Vary. Individuals progress through the stages in the sequences described by Piaget, Kohlberg, and Tapp. (See Chapter Five.) Requiring individuals to reason and behave at stages higher than their own is not giving recognition to the findings of developmental research. So, for example, students cannot get to Stage 3 in Kohlberg's system without first going through Stages 1 and 2.

Ethical development occurs gradually; it takes time and no small amount of patience. Some serenity can be maintained by not skipping stages or requiring higher levels of moral understanding than are possible for the students. The comforting news is that ethical development does occur and that school personnel can facilitate such development.

Individuals Can Understand Ethical Reasoning at the Stage above Their Own. Stating this assumption in the negative, students cannot comprehend ethical reasoning more than one stage beyond their present level. A student with an orientation toward obeying peers (Stage 3) can understand an orientation toward obeying laws for the good of society (Stage 4), but could not comprehend discussions of social contracts and negotiations (Stage 5).

Students Are Intrigued with the Ethical Reasoning at the Level above Their Own. This assumption is crucial for those facilitating ethical development. There is, to use Piaget's terms, a "moderate novelty" about the arguments at the next stage of development. There are theoretical reasons for this intrigue, but for our discussion it will suffice to say that students sense that the higher level seems to solve problems more adequately. In their minds it seems better and more attractive.

Development Requires Disequilibrium. While students are intrigued with higher-level reasoning they cannot quite understand it. They cannot quite pull all the ideas together. The result is a disequilibrium of cognitive structures. An individual may seem (verbally or nonverbally) to be on the right path, but not understand the reasoning quite yet. During the process of resolving the disequilibrium (i.e., equilibration) it is very important for educators to: 1) help the students understand the higher-level explanation by asking students what they do not understand and supplying information in ways they can comprehend; 2) let them try to use the higher level of reasoning in new situations; and 3) give the students time to restructure their responses.

Ethical Development Results from Interactions between Individuals. Throughout this section we must stress the idea of interaction. In *The Moral Judgment of the Child*[14] Piaget made it very clear that the interaction among children is at least as, if not more, important than the interaction between adults and children with regard to moral development. In schools there are both formal and informal interactions between students and between students and teachers. To the maximum extent possible the interactions should be on a mutual level between adults and youth. This is the foundation for ethical development and educating for democratic values.

The Aim of Development

The interaction between school personnel and students should result in the development of students. Development in its broadest sense includes the physical, cognitive, emotional, social, esthetic, and ethical. We are confining this discussion to ethical development in general and education for democratic values in particular. But we give full recognition to the importance of all other aspects of development.

Ethical development is one goal of education. As educators we are interested in facilitating the continued development of individuals to the higher levels of reasoning and understanding. Our understanding of the developmental process indicates that this is the natural process of growth. It respects the rights of the student and results in students respecting the rights of others.

Awareness of Ethical Levels

One of the first practical implications for school personnel is to be aware of both your own and your students' general level of ethical development. How did you respond to the "teacher assault" dilemma in Chapter Five?

Were you able to identify your level of reasoning within the pro and con statements presented later? Most educators are at the conventional levels of reasoning.[15, 16] Once you are aware of your own developmental level and that of your students, the stage is set for further development through the description of problems and the presentation of higher levels of reasoning.

Group Participation

One approach that has been used successfully in education is group discussions of dilemmas.[16] The dilemmas should have personal meaning to the students; they should not be too abstract or displaced geographically. There are certainly many local problems, or school-related situations, that can form the core of the dilemma. Conflicts can be stimulated by providing alternatives to the dilemma at different stages.

As the discussion ensues the teacher should guide the discussion, making sure the students continue discussing the moral dilemma. The teacher can point out inconsistencies in students' reasoning and direct questions to the students who hint at more adequate ways of resolving the dilemma. Assuming the role of Socratic questioner is a good way of guiding discussions about moral dilemmas.

The approach can be applied to discussions of school rules, violation of rules, and decisions concerning everyday procedures, field trips, and school activities.

Cooperative Work

Students can cooperate on class projects, school activities, problem solving, and games, all within the educational context. With this approach the teacher provides the initial direction and then acts as a guide while students work together, resolving many of the conflicts inherent in the situations. Many of the challenges, questions, and disagreements will occur and be resolved naturally among the students. When teachers intervene they can probe, listen, provide suggestions, and leave the final resolution to the students.[17]

Natural Opportunities

The natural opportunities for ethical development in schools are numerous. Most of these opportunities occur in the process of teaching and generally include the average range of problems teachers and administrators might encounter in a day. We are talking about problems such as talking without raising hands, doodling on a desk, not paying attention, writing notes, chewing gum, running in the halls, and bothering the students on the playground. School personnel deal with these problems as they occur, and they usually end within a minute or so. We think these are ideal opportunities for student-teacher interactions that might facilitate ethical development. In most cases the examples given are violations of a classroom or school rule. Taking a few minutes with the student, attempting to understand the student's explanation and reasoning for the problem, presenting the other (higher) side of the problem, and reaching some resolution result in the student's development and better behavior. This approach to disruptive behavior can result in the mutual resolution of the problem.

Ethical Climate

The last section described opportunities for ethical development that occurred spontaneously. They were short-term occasions and often hard to predict. Our attention in this section is directed toward the long-term climate of the classroom and school. What is the level of ethical development within your classroom or school? Yes, it is possible to think of the institutional ethos. How do students perceive the rules of the school? What are the principles used for the distribution of rewards, punishments, responsibilities, rights, and privileges within the school? You can be certain that students are aware of the answers to these questions. This is why discussion of rules and responses to rule violations is important. School personnel interested in ethical development and values are referred to two excellent sources: *Promoting Moral Growth*[18] and *Value Clarification in the Classroom.*[19]

It may be a useful exercise for teachers and administrators to review the rules they enforce, the level at which they approach rules, and especially the level of interaction between themselves and students. Are the rules prohibitive? prescriptive? principled? How are rules violations resolved—punishment? threats? coercion? mutual decision?

Some Guides for School Personnel

Administrators:

1. Try to understand rule observance and rule violation in terms of the individual's motivations and development.
2. Ask for and listen to the student's explanation of the problem.
3. Avoid placing a judgment such as good/bad or right/wrong on the student's explanation. By understanding the student's reasoning you can direct the student to better behavior, which we assume to be the goal.
4. Explain and justify rules at the student's level of understanding.
5. The consequences and punishments of rule violation should be clearly related to the offense.
6. Students should have opportunities to discuss rules and to participate in designing school rules.

7. Tell students of your expectations for their future behavior. The expectations should be explained at their level and be reasonable as far as their ability to change.
8. Students often say things that we should (and they would later like to) forget. Let the student (and yourself if necessary) calm down before discussing the problem.
9. Provide concrete guidance and examples upon which students can base future behavior. You can appeal to a stage higher than theirs, show how it is better and what behaviors might be expected.

Teachers:

1. Discuss rules with the students and arrive at mutually agreed-upon rules.
2. Punishments should be reasonable and relate to the violation and the effect on other students.
3. Ask students to explain why they behaved as they did. Listen closely to the justification.
4. Avoid confusing academic criticism and conflicts over classroom rules.
5. Give your justification for rules. Be sure it is at the students' level of understanding.

School personnel and students experience each other's ethical positions every day. Applying the ideas presented in this section can contribute to continued education for democratic values.

Curriculum Programs

In most states, schools are mandated to provide instruction in the principles of the Constitution and the United States governmental system—including the legal/judicial branches. This is often referred to as citizenship education. Certainly a goal of such programs is legal literacy. However, educators have not been too successful in developing legal literacy among citizens.

In the last decades, law-related education programs have been developed to counterbalance a waning legal literacy. School programs are designed to involve students in issues they confront daily. Major law-related education projects (see Chapter Five) have a range of goals and approaches. But they all contribute in some ways to an appreciation and respect for the law; use of analytical and critical skills inherent in solving legal problems; an understanding and application of law in our daily lives. As students struggle with concepts such as freedom and justice, due process, and law enforcement, they will no doubt come to understand basic laws that may contribute to a reduction of discipline problems and the facilitation of ethical development.

There are several national programs such as the Institute for Political/ Legal Education (IPLE); Law in Action; Law in American Society; Law, Education and Participation (LEAP); Law in a Free Society (LIFS); and National Street Law Institute. Information on these and many other programs is available from the American Bar Association, Special Committee on Youth Education for Citizenship, 1155 East 60th Street, Chicago, Illinois 60637 and in Chapter Five. We recommend these programs as a direct means of educating for democratic values.

ENCOURAGING APPROPRIATE BEHAVIOR IN SCHOOLS

There are six things schools can do that will reduce the rate and intensity of disruptive behavior.

1. Establish a policy for appropriate behavior.
2. Establish school and classroom rules based on the policy.
3. Establish a method for clearly communicating the rules.
4. Establish an accountability system within the school.
5. Establish methods of conflict resolution in the school.
6. Establish relevant activities for all students in the school.

We are suggesting a social policy model for the prevention and reduction of school-related disruptive behavior. As you would suspect there is more to each of these recommendations than the statement makes clear. The next sections clarify the intentions underlying the recommendations. You may also wish to refer to *School Crime and Disruption: Prevention Models*[20] and *Classroom Discipline* by Laurel Tanner.[21]

A Discipline Policy

The purpose of a school discipline policy is to establish a goal, a principled statement that is valid apart from the school but agreed on by school personnel, students, and the community. In our view a school discipline policy should *not* be a list of rules outlining what is prohibited in the school.

For example, we would *not* recommend the following school policy.

SCHOOL DISCIPLINE POLICY #1

In this high school you are to abide by these rules:
1. No running in halls.
2. No smoking, drinking or use of drugs.
3. No loitering.
4. No unnecessary talking in classrooms.
5. No public displays of affection.

6. No loud and boisterous noise in halls or cafeteria.
7. No long hair for boys or short hair for girls.
8. No unacceptable clothing is to be worn.
9. No late work will be accepted.

Violators will be subject to immediate action by the vice principal in charge of discipline problems.

This policy simply states unacceptable behavior. The apparent intention behind the rules is to prevent various behaviors that have been determined to be detrimental to school operations. There is also the authoritarian tone that results from the straightforward commands and implication that the reason one should follow these rules is to avoid the negative consequences of visiting the vice principal. This is not a good policy for any number of reasons, not the least of which being that the list would have to be much longer in order to incorporate all the adolescent behaviors that might be inappropriate in the eyes of the rule makers.

Let us give a second example that is better but still *not* recommended as a discipline policy.

SCHOOL DISCIPLINE POLICY #2

The purpose of the discipline policy in this school district is to insure the control over those students who cannot control themselves. We have a policy to maintain order in the schools and classrooms and, in addition, to prevent disruptive behavior.

Students' behavior should be such that it complies with the rules of the school and laws of society. These behavior codes are justified on the grounds that they contribute to the welfare of the total school system.

While Policy #2 is better than #1 we think school districts can create a better model for students and the community. Basically Policy #2 states the need for rules, that they are justified for the social good. As such, rules maintain order and should be followed.

Here are some guidelines for school personnel, students, and the community to use while developing a discipline policy.

1. Does the policy suggest that individual behavior can be guided by principles (equality, fairness, or justice)?

2. Does the policy provide a rationale for school rules? In particular, does the policy describe the purposes underlying rules as maximizing the welfare of both the individual and the school community?

3. Does the policy describe the beneficial results of agreed-upon standards?

4. Has the policy been developed in such a manner that it represents standards upon which school personnel, students, and the community agree?

5. Does the policy give recognition to the possibility that a conflict may

arise between the individual and school personnel in which both the individual and school personnel may be right in their actions?

6. Does the policy suggest provisions guarding the rights, dignity, and integrity of individuals in conflict with other individuals, school personnel, and/or school rules?

Asking and answering these questions throughout the process of developing a discipline policy will bring about continued improvement of the statement.

Rules for the School and Classroom

The next step in the process is to develop rules and expectations for appropriate behavior within the school and classrooms. These statements should be more concrete than the discipline policy. But the rules should be logically and clearly related to the discipline policy. In most instances rules for the school community already exist. So, it is a matter of reviewing, clarifying, and coordinating the rules in terms of the stated policy. Again, we strongly suggest this be done by school personnel, students, and the community.

We are not going to list specific rules that are good and others that are bad. There are too many variations in schools, students, and communities to have such an endeavor result in anything constructive. We do recommend that the rules be few in quantity and comprehensive in quality.

Aligned with the statement of rules it is a good idea to outline briefly the process (not consequences) to be used when violations occur. That is, what will happen when rules are broken? This could take the form of what-who-when-where-and-how.

1. What is expected of students in the school/classroom?
2. What will happen when there is a rule violation?
3. Who will be informed about the problem?
4. When will individuals be informed?
5. Where will the process take place?
6. How will personal rights be guarded and sanctions enforced?

Being clear about school and classroom rules will stop some individuals from breaking the rules and it will make rule-breaking behaviors clear. The recommendations in this section are that: 1) rules be clear within a classroom and consistent within the school, and 2) they be arrived at through a participatory process.

Communicating the Rules

There must be ways of communicating the rules to students. Communication is more than handing out copies of the rules or having an assembly and reviewing the rules or announcing them over the school intercommunication system. Though methods such as these are better than no communication, there should be attempts actually to make the rules a part of the educational process.

Throughout this discussion we have maintained the position that the policy and rules should be developed through cooperative participation among school personnel, students, and the community. Following this recommendation initiates the informal communication that is as essential as the formal presentation. The formulation of policies and rules, as well as the final communication of these ideas, could be a part of the education program. For example, homerooms could be used for these discussions. If the school is interested in reducing the rate of inappropriate behaviors, taking some time from other educational objectives should not be difficult. Incorporating the formulation of rules into the educational program has the simultaneous benefits of showing the students they are a part of the system, thus creating a cooperative and purposeful atmosphere, and making them aware of the rules.

Accountability and Sanctions

Motivating changes from inappropriate to appropriate behavior can partially be achieved through meeting the needs of students. In some cases the needs may be physiological, but in most they are psychological. Nurturing, belonging, and caring can encourage behavior aligned with established rules.

Sanctions are means of maintaining appropriate behavior through approval and discouraging inappropriate behavior through coercive measures and penalities. A part of the policy and rule-making process should be the identification of school-related sanctions for rule violations.

As with all the earlier steps, ownership of the sanctions by the school community is central to their effectiveness. Internal sanctions, those that are school-related and owned, are very powerful and effective. We suggest that school personnel consult with students to identify sanctions. There are numerous consequences for rule violations that could act as powerful deterrents and appropriate punishments, and one way to identify them is to ask the students. There are alternatives to suspension[22] and we strongly recommend the elimination of corporal punishment in American education.[23, 24]

Conflict Resolution

Here we are recommending that school personnel and students identify specific and relevant methods of resolving conflicts. (See Chapter Seven.) We know enough about conflict resolution to implement the ideas in school systems, thus providing students, teachers, administrators, and other personnel with methods of preventing serious confrontations, of constructively resolving conflicts that do occur, and of avoiding destructive consequences of conflicts.[25]

A schoolwide program in which individuals are instructed in the techniques of conflict resolution will not stop all conflicts but it could certainly reduce the number of conflicts between students and between students and school personnel. In addition, workshops among school personnel and between teachers and students will nurture closer personal ties. So, as a result of this step in the process, individuals will have the tools to interact with one another, ways and means of dealing with conflicts, and closer personal bonds.

Activities for Students

At first we were going to recommend only curriculum change and program implementation. But it seemed that we were trying to recommend more. There should be some school-specific ways of testing an individual's creativity, intelligence, tenacity, rigor, and so on. Indeed, there are ways: athletics, music, debate, National Honor Society, Future Farmers of America, drama, school newspapers, and student council to mention a few. But, when you consider the students who are behaving inappropriately, they are, by and large, not involved in activities such as those just mentioned. What is it they can talk about as their achievements? Drinking, disrupting class, sex, unlawful activities, and drugs often take the place of other more appropriate means of becoming adults.[26]

Some youth are returning from treatment programs for chemical dependency and bragging about "being on the edge and making it back." The same can be said for many students who have been "sent to the principal's office." Or, to bring up another issue central to discussions of discipline—corporal punishment. Many students who have been paddled in the hopes of changing their behavior have indeed used this as a rite of passage, albeit a negative one.

What do students need to do to feel like they are becoming adults? What school-specific rites of passage can be implemented that will include greater numbers of students, especially those who are not presently involved?

SUMMARY

Violence in schools has made the public aware of the important role of education in our society. Certainly the problems of violence, vandalism, and classroom disruption must be eliminated or substantially reduced in American education if the system is to continue to function. The ever-present question—how?—emerges at this point. Safety devices? School security personnel? These and other means have been implemented success-fully. If there is a need, such devices and personnel should be used. However, approaches that might prevent some problems also should be thoroughly explored. In this book it has been suggested that the issue of school violence has led to a reexamination of our value structure as it ap-plies to education. One of the most important of these values for educators to emerge from this reexamination is that of justice as it applies to the educational setting. Obviously, we must find some way to solve simulta-neously the dilemmas facing education while improving the system. But certainly approaching our educational problems with a greater sense of justice could in no way be interpreted as ignoring the problems or "giving in" and not educating students. It is instead a recognition of the human dignity of all parties and a set of guidelines within which we can work toward a mutual resolution of conflicts.

Justice in American education would include due process as a part of student disciplinary practices, community involvement in the formation and maintenance of school rules and policies, administrative involvement with elimination of the problems, cooperation by colleges and universities in the training of teachers to handle disruptive students, consideration of appropriate safety and security systems, and most importantly, an assur-ance to students of some voice in their own governance. Violent schools have brought the idea of justice in education to our attention, but the principle must apply not only to schools with high crime rates, but to all schools.

The Declaration of Independence and the Constitution adequately pro-vided our ancestors with guides that have continued to serve us well through two centuries. Now an important institution in American society that is being assaulted from many sides is in need of like guidance. In anger, frustration, and with some hope, educators have begun to reeval-uate the educational enterprise and the underlying value structure in order to develop new directions. This crisis in education and the pursuit of viable solutions presents a unique opportunity finally to link the vital value of justice with educational quality.

REFERENCES

1. Phi Delta Kappa, *School Climate Improvement: A Challenge to the Adminis-trator* (Bloomington, Indiana: Phi Delta Kappa, 1975).
2. Irwin Kutash and Samuel Kutsch (Louis Schlesinger & Associates), *Violence: Perspectives on Murder and Aggression* (San Francisco: Jossey-Bass, 1978).
3. Daniel Offer, Richard Marohn, and Eric Ostrov, *The Psychological World of the Juvenile Delinquent* (New York: Basic Books, 1979).

4. Fritz Redl and David Wineman, *Children Who Hate* (New York: The Free Press, 1951).
5. Dan Olweus, *Aggression in the Schools* (New York: Halsted Press, 1978).
6. The National Institute of Education, *Violent Schools—Safe Schools* (Washington, D. C. : U. S. Government Printing Office, 1978).
7. Abraham H. Maslow, *Motivation and Personality* (New York: Harper & Row, 1970).
8. David W. Johnson, *Reaching Out: Interpersonal Effectiveness and Self Actualization* (Englewood Cliffs, N. J.: Prentice-Hall, 1972).
9. David W. Johnson, *Human Relations and Your Career: A Guide to Interpersonal Skills* (Englewood Cliffs, N. J.: Prentice-Hall, 1978).
10. Arthur Combs et al., *Introduction to the Helping Relationship*, Boston: Allyn and Bacon, 1978).
11. Carl R. Rogers, *Freedom to Learn* (Columbus: Charles E. Merrill, 1969).
12. Bruce Joyce and Marsha Weil, *Models of Teaching* (Englewood Cliffs, N. J.: Prentice-Hall, 1972).
13. Roger La Raus and Richard Remy, *Citizenship Decision Making: Skill Activities and Materials (Grades 4–9)*, Reading, Mass.: Addison-Wesley, 1978).
14. Jean Piaget, *The Moral Judgment of the Child* (New York: The Free Press, 1965).
15. Lawrence Kohlberg and Elliot Turiel, "Moral Development and Moral Education," in G. Lesser, ed., *Psychology and Educational Practice* (Chicago: Scott Foresman, 1971).
16. Moshe Blatt and Lawrence Kohlberg, "The Effects of Classroom Discussion on the Development of Moral Judgement," in L. Kohlberg and E. Turiel, eds., *Recent Research in Moral Development* (New York: Holt, Rinehart and Winston, 1971).
17. David Johnson and Roger Johnson, *Learning Together and Alone: Cooperation, Competition and Individualization* (Englewood Cliffs, N. J.: Prentice-Hall, 1975).
18. Richard Hersh, Diana Pritchard Paolitto, and Joseph Reimer, *Promoting Moral Growth* (New York: Longman, 1979).
19. J. Doyl Castul and Robert J. Stahl, *Value Clarification in the Classroom: A Primer* (Santa Monica: Goodyear Publishing Co., 1975).
20. The National Institute of Education, *School Crime and Disruption: Prevention Models* (Washington, D. C.: U. S. Government Printing Office, 1978).
21. Laurel Tanner, *Classroom Discipline* (New York: Holt, Rinehart and Winston, 1978).
22. The National Institute of Education, *In-School Alternatives to Suspension* (Washington, D. C.: U. S. Government Printing Office, 1979).
23. The National Institute of Education, *Proceedings: Conference on Corporal Punishment in the Schools: A National Debate* (Washington, D. C.: U. S. Government Printing Office, 1977).
24. Irwin Hyman and James Wise, eds., *Corporal Punishment in American Education* (Philadelphia: Temple University Press, 1979).
25. Morton Deutsch, *The Resolution of Conflict* (New Haven: Yale University Press, 1973).
26. Maurice Gibbons, "Walkabout: Searching for the Right Passage from Childhood and School," Phi Delta Kappan 56, no. 9 (1974): 596–602.

Index

DATE DUE

6. 15. '83	
7. 12. '84	
7 11 '85	
10. 23. '85	
11. 13. '85	
AUG 0 7 1998	
OCT 2 5 1999	
APR 1 9 2000	
AUG 2 7 2001	
NOV 1 0 2005	
OCT 0 9 2007	
5	5	22